THE TECHNIQUES OF COMMUNISM

THE
TECHNIQUES
OF
COMMUNISM

BY

LOUIS F. BUDENZ

HENRY REGNERY COMPANY
CHICAGO, 1954

AMERICAN BOOK–STRATFORD PRESS, INC., NEW YORK

INTRODUCTION

MOST AMERICANS have not been equipped with the technical understanding necessary to deal with Soviet Communism, the greatest challenge to our time. The skill we applied to science, production, and engineering we have not used in the handling of the Communist problem.

Communism is something to which many thousands of Americans are opposed. But too few know its nature, its methods of operation, and its reflected activities in the community. Most do not yet understand how the Communist actually functions, nor the world of carefully studied directives in which he lives, and its effect on his non-Communist environment. This places a serious handicap on any sustained or successful opposition to Communism in the American community. Instructions from Moscow for the benefit of Soviet aggression are passed through the American Communist Party out into local non-Communist organizations. They are proposed and often adopted as policies in these organizations, frequently without being recognized or challenged by patriotic Americans.

At first blush, this would seem astounding, since all the information for an intelligent appraisal of such situations is readily available. That information is contained in the many Communist documents and directives published by the Communists themselves. These publications are issued for the direction of the Kremlin's followers. A critical study of them as they appear, made with a background knowledge of the Marxist-Leninist classics which always condition or explain them, would give the student of Communism an intimate acquaintance with current Communist objectives.

It is this study of the techniques of Communism on any large scale which has been lacking, although there is no subject more important for the United States. An increasing number of community leaders have become aware of this defect and have sought to remedy it through courses on the techniques of Communism. Certain colleges and universities have introduced such courses into the curriculum. The National Education Association, at its 1952 convention, recommended moves in the same direction by suggesting the study of Communism in the schools. The Senate Sub-Committee on Internal Security, in its July 1953 report on education, strongly recommends the necessity of classes for teachers and students in high schools and colleges, conducted by those effective in combating Communism.

An adequate textbook will make possible a dynamic study of Communism in our schools and in community groups. It will give an impetus to the wider introduction of this subject into colleges and civic organizations which have lacked the material for organizing such courses. The fact that a handbook or textbook of this character was not prepared in the past is one of the chief explanations for the slow progress so far.

The present book, designed to answer this need, is an analytical and critical study of Communism. It deals with Communist ideology, strategy, and "movement" as presented by the Marxist-Leninist classics themselves and by current Communist documents and directives. It examines the relationship of the directives given by the Kremlin to the basic works of Marx, Engels, Lenin, and Stalin. It considers these books and documents as the Communist himself studies and uses them. It analyzes Communist activities as the Communist is instructed to carry them out.

This is the competent manner in which the techniques of Communism can be mastered in order to defeat them.

The study of any subject requires effort, and this one is no exception. There has been the assumption in some quarters that Communism is easily understood and readily dealt with. Nothing could be farther from reality. If we were to ask 1,000 educated Americans, chosen at random, what is the nature of Soviet Communism, not five percent could give the proper answer. If the same group were queried on what is the current line of the Party, an even smaller percentage would be able to reply. The serious successes of the Communist line within the United States, which will be developed in the course of these pages, stands as added and weighty testimony to the complicated character of Communist strategy and tactics, their bewildering effects, and the urgency for mastering them.

The task is by no means impossible, but it demands the same careful reading, examination, and analysis as does any course in economics, sociology, or any of the physical sciences.

Effective consideration of the techniques of Communism requires a devoted adherence to the truth, to the facts as they are disclosed, and therefore to an attitude free of preconceived ideas or narrow partisan bias. There are many individuals who hear of infiltration of the U. S. State Department and immediately close their eyes and ears to what affronts their partisan prejudices. They do not wish to recognize the validity of these charges, although the reports and hearings of the Senate Sub-Committee on Internal Security established beyond doubt that infiltration has occurred on a serious scale. When certain industries are shown to be penetrated by the Communists, there is often a tendency among leading figures in those industries to defend the subversives or explain away their acts rather than to clean house.

It is impossible in any honest analysis of Communist techniques to fall victim to such faulty concepts.

Many valuable publications have appeared during the recent past on various phases of the subject which we have under consideration. Most of these books have been designed to describe personal experiences and to create an abhorrence of Communism. Other works have dealt with the history of the Communist "movement" in general, particularly in its world aspects. Still others have applied themselves solely to the theory of Marxism-Leninism, or to certain features of it. None has been written for the sole purpose of organizing the inquiry into the nature and operations of Communism as a basis for combating it.

The rich library of books exposing Communism itself has aroused that interest which makes essential a systematic study of Communism as related to American life and institutions.

The present book has the advantage of being the result of successful classes in the subject at the Fordham University Graduate School (Institute of Contemporary Russian Studies) where pioneering work has been done in this field. It has had the added benefit of classes I have conducted at Seton Hall University and in the summer school of the University of Dayton. Its outline has been the basis of similar courses for community leader groups, conducted on the college level, in the vicinity of New York City, which are now expanding in number.

It is my hope that the material presented and the organization of the work will be as helpful on a national scale as they have proved to be in this more limited area. That hope is reinforced by the recognition that if Soviet Communism is to be defeated it must be met intelligently here at home and successfully opposed here as well as abroad.

LOUIS FRANCIS BUDENZ

Oct. 13, 1953

CONTENTS

Chapter | Page

Introduction — v

PART ONE. *The Nature and Organization of the "Communist Movement."*

I. The Communist Philosophy — 3
II. The Communist Apparatus — 20
III. Communist Phraseology — 41
IV. Communist Objectives: a Summary — 64

PART TWO. *Communist Methods*

V. Strategy and Tactics — 83
VI. Training the Communists — 102
VII. The Role of the Communist Press — 125

PART THREE. *Communism in Action*

VIII. Affecting Public Opinion — 153
IX. Work in Labor and Industry — 181
X. Invading Education — 208
XI. Use and Abuse of Minority Groups — 250
XII. Infiltration of Government Agencies — 278

PART FOUR. *How to Fight Communism*

XIII. Knowledge and Facts as Weapons — 309

Index — 333

PART ONE

*The Nature and Organization of
the "Communist Movement"*

CHAPTER I

THE COMMUNIST PHILOSOPHY

SOVIET COMMUNISM of its very nature is intent on world conquest. The establishment of the world Soviet dictatorship is bound up inevitably with the Communist world outlook. The very laws which irrevocably govern the course of nature and society, as the Communist understands them, make this goal a necessity. It may be glossed over for tactical reasons from time to time, as it was in World War II in order to deceive the Western world, but it can never be abandoned. It is the guide and measuring rod of all Communist activities. If these activities further that goal, they are desirable; if they retard it, they are "reformist" or "revisionist" and are to be rejected.

It was to keep alive this concept of the world Soviet dictatorship that the representatives of sixty-five Communist Parties, assembled at the Seventh World Congress of the Communist International in 1935, pledged their loyalty to Stalin as "leader, teacher, and friend of the proletariat and the oppressed of the whole world." In like vein, they pledged to him "that the Communists will always and everywhere be faithful to the end to the great and invincible banner of Marx, Engels, Lenin, and Stalin. Under this banner, Communism will triumph throughout the world." (Proceedings of the Seventh World Congress, Communist International, *International Press Correspondence*, Aug. 8, 1935, p. 861.)

It was in the same spirit that the Chinese Communist Party,

in its official greetings to this Seventh World Congress, closed with the announcement of its purpose to "facilitate the preparation for the decisive barricade fights for the Soviet power throughout the world." Their greetings concluded: "Long live the world proletarian revolution! Long live our leader and teacher, Comrade Stalin!" (*Ibid.*, p. 857.)

This objective, too, moved D. Z. Manuilsky, then General Secretary of the Communist International, to explain: "That is why, comrades, the exploited and oppressed in all parts of the world regard our land of victorious Socialism as their fatherland; that is why they regard our Party and our working class as the shock brigade of the world proletariat; that is why they regard our Stalin as the great, wise, and beloved leader of the whole of toiling humanity." (*Ibid.*, Sept. 17, 1935, p. 1173.)

The same theme runs through the Cominform organ, *For a Lasting Peace, for a People's Democracy*, in its special issue celebrating Stalin's seventieth birthday. Its banner headline on the first page reads: "Long Live the Leader of the Working People of the World, Joseph Visarionovich Stalin!" Leaders of the Communist Parties from all countries hailed him as "the light and hope of peoples," "the man who has regenerated the world," "our teacher and father," all expressed in terms of world ambitions. Palmiro Togliatti, General Secretary of the Communist Party of Italy, taking the same global view, declared that "Stalin is in front of us. Our cause is Stalin's cause. The cause of Stalin has never known defeat. It is invincible." He added: "With Stalin's name on our lips, we have always been victorious. With Stalin's name, all victories will be ours."

This interconnection between Stalin and world conquest is explained by D. Zaslavsky, one of the chief theoretical writers of Soviet Russia, who declares that Stalin is "the great innovator of the new epoch, the architect of the new society and the new man." Therefore, "his celebration is a triumph of Communism, because when they say 'Stalin' they mean 'Communism.' " Zaslavsky adds that when people exclaimed with boundless devotion, "Long life to Stalin!" they also meant, "Long live

Socialism throughout the world and may it be victorious." (*For a Lasting Peace, for a People's Democracy*, Dec. 21, 1949.)

With the installation of G. M. Malenkov as Stalin's successor in the Soviet Union and in world Red leadership, the Communist purpose continues. Malenkov is gradually fitting himself into Stalin's place as Stalin did into Lenin's from 1925 to 1928. Just as Stalin was acclaimed as "the best disciple of Lenin," so Malenkov is hailed by William Z. Foster, leader of the American Communists, in the following terms: "Malenkov has been trained in the very best Marxist-Leninist tradition. He long had the tutorship of the greatest teacher of them all—Stalin—and he got his experience in the heart of the world Socialist movement, the Soviet Union." These qualifications and experiences, according to Foster, make Malenkov "a giant compared to the petty politicians currently heading the capitalist states of the world." (William Z. Foster, "Malenkov at the Helm," *Political Affairs*, April 1953, pp. 20, 21.)

Speaking for himself, Malenkov declared to the Supreme Soviet of the USSR on August 8, 1953, that "our cause is invincible." He gave the following as the heart of this "invincibility": "The Communist Party and the Soviet government know whither and how to lead the people, because they are guided by Marxism-Leninism—the scientific theory of social development—the banner of which was raised aloft by Lenin, the genius, our father and teacher, and by the continuer of his cause, the great Stalin." The basis of all Communist views and action is again proclaimed by Malenkov to be "the teaching of Marx-Engels-Lenin-Stalin," and the very core of this teaching is the attainment of the world Soviet dictatorship. This objective was codified in detail in 1928, when Stalin came into full power, in the Resolutions and Theses of the Sixth World Congress of the Communist International, appearing in *International Press Correspondence* for that year. ("Speech by Comrade G. M. Malenkov," at Session of Supreme Soviet of USSR, *For a Lasting Peace, for a People's Democracy*, August 14, 1953, p. 4.)

The world conquest ambitions of Communism were expressed

precisely by Malenkov in his Report to the Nineteenth Congress of the Communist Party of the Soviet Union, October, 1952, when he said: "The teachings of Marx, Engels, Lenin, and Stalin impart to our Party invincible force . . . the Lenin-Stalin ideas shed the bright light of revolutionary theory on the tasks and perspectives of the struggle of the masses *in all lands* against imperialism, for peace, democracy, and Socialism." (Italics mine.) The Socialism which exists in Soviet Russia, "the land of Socialism," is to be extended, by Malenkov's promise, into all lands. (*On the Threshold of Communism*, G. M. Malenkov, New Century Publishers, N.Y., p. 93.)

Thousands of similar declarations with like intent and purpose dot Communist literature and directives. They are to be found as a chief theme of the most fundamental Communist documents, such as the *Program of the Communist International*, which declares its aim to be the setting up of a world system of Communism, with the world dictatorship of the proletariat as the instrument toward that end. (Published in *Blueprint for World Conquest*, Henry Regnery Co.)

We begin, then, with the recognition that in studying Communism we are analyzing a force which seeks world domination, considers world Soviet dictatorship inevitable, and believes that the progress of mankind depends upon its attainment. The embodiment of this necessity for global conquest is Stalin, the continuer of Lenin, hailed as the greatest scientist of our time.

Soviet Objective Arises from Philosophy

When we inquire why Soviet Communism must have this objective, we find that it lies in its philosophy. It is not within the scope of this book to treat exhaustively the philosophy of Communism, but only to examine the essentials necessary to deal with Communist techniques. It is impossible to analyze intelligently the methods and operations of the Communists until these essentials at least have been grasped. For it is Communist philosophy which gives to "the movement" its dynamic, fire the fanaticism of Stalin's followers everywhere, and brings about logically those peculiar modes of operation which are met with in every American community.

What, after all, is Soviet Communism? It is the triumph or climax of the philosophy of materialism, the denial of the existence of God or the world of the spirit. Man is considered exclusively as an animal. In the mass of matter in which the animal man functions, there is at work a dialectical motion, a motion of debate or conflict. Whence this motion comes the Communists cannot say, but they assert that it exists in nature and in society.

Stalin writes in his *History of the Communist Party of the Soviet Union, (Bolsheviks)*, which is the fundamental work for the Communists today:

"Dialectical and historical materialism constitute the theoretical basis of Communism, the theoretical foundation of the Marxist Party, and it is the duty of every active member of our Party to know these principles and hence to study them." (*History of the Communist Party of the Soviet Union, [Bolsheviks]*, Foreign Languages Publishing House, Moscow, 1939, p. 105.)

Dialectical materialism, which operates in nature and is nature's inevitable law, "is the world outlook of the Marxist-Leninist Party." Historical materialism is "the extension of the principles of dialectical materialism to the study of social life," to the development and history of human society.

The motion of debate or conflict at work in nature and society is brought about by the attraction and opposition of opposites. In every natural phenomenon, and in each stage of society, a contradiction exists which brings about a force opposite to that which is dominant. Out of the reaction of these forces upon each other, there arises a new stage of nature and society.

This is the famous *thesis, antithesis, and synthesis*, which forms the trinity of Communist thought and action. The thing that exists, the opposite that grows out of it, and the higher stage that develops from their interaction or conflict, govern all correct thinking and the proper interpretation of life and society.

In our present historical period, the conflict exists between the bourgeoisie and the proletariat, and will inevitably resolve itself after a violent contest in the victory of the proletariat and the inevitable introduction of Socialism.

That which retards Socialism is "reactionary" and is to be destroyed. That which advances Socialism is "progressive" and "liberating" and is to be encouraged and forwarded.

Violence is Agency of Progress

This transition to Socialism can be successfully attained only through violence, in the suppression by force of the bourgeoisie. For the state, from the Communist viewpoint, always represents the interests of the ruling class and is the dictatorship of the ruling class, no matter how "democratic" it may seem to be. But the dictatorship of the proletariat, shattering the existing state machine of all countries by force, will usher in the Socialist era. (Joseph Stalin, *Foundations of Leninism*, International Publishers, N.Y., 1932, pp. 44-57.)

This enunciation by Stalin of dialectical materialism and his stress on force as the agency of progress is a reiteration of what his predecessor "scientists," Karl Marx and Frederick Engels, had declared. More than one hundred years ago, in the Communist Manifesto of 1848, Marx had stated that the proletariat "by means of a revolution" will make itself the ruling class, "and as such sweeps away by force the old conditions of production." In *Capital* he had stressed again: "Force is the midwife of every old society pregnant with the new one." It is force, therefore, that always brings the new society into life. (*Capital*, I, 776, International Publishers Co.)

On the foundation of this necessity of force and violence as a means to progress and the attainment of Socialism, Lenin developed the new dictatorship of the proletariat, particularly as expressed in Soviet power. This has made Marxism-Leninism the fundamental Communist viewpoint, with the theory and tactics of the dictatorship of the proletariat as the center, the guiding principle, and the goal of all Communist thought and action.

Without the establishment of this dictatorship of the proletariat, this organized violence or compulsion, it is impossible to win the Socialist goal which will bring "progress" to mankind. Thus for the Communist, as stressed so clearly by Stalin in his *Foundations of Leninism*, the basic objective of bringing about the proletarian dictatorship must condition and color every tactic adopted and every step taken.

We need consider but for a moment this philosophy or world outlook—with its statement that man is exclusively an animal and that for the animal man the sole agency of progress is violence—to appreciate that it logically brings about the ruthlessness represented by the Soviet dictatorship.

It may be stated at once that both the "proletariat" of Marx and the "proletariat" of Stalin are largely fictitious. According to Marx, this class of factory workers without the ownership of its own tools was to be subjected to progressive disintegration in living standards and income. This has not occurred, specifically not in the United States. With Stalin, the "dictatorship of the proletariat" has become a dictatorship over the proletariat and the masses. It is a dictatorship of the Communist Party, "the vanguard of the masses," which in reality is the dictatorship of the oligarchy in the Kremlin headed now by Stalin's successor Malenkov. A privileged bureaucracy has been created, living on the backs of the people, under the Soviet regime, a bureaucracy which owes its being to the dictatorship and upon which the dictatorship rests. (David Dallin, *The Real Soviet Russia*, Yale University Press, 1947, chaps. vii, viii.)

Both Lenin and Stalin have foretold that this would occur, that the dictatorship of the proletariat is actually the dictatorship of the chosen few over the proletariat. In *Foundations of Leninism*, Stalin cites with approval Lenin's statement in *"Left" Communism* that "the dictatorship of the proletariat is the fiercest, sharpest, and most merciless war" against the bourgeoisie. But he adds, citing Lenin again, that it is just as necessary "to re-educate in a protracted struggle, under the controlling auspices of the dictatorship of the proletariat, the proletarians themselves," who must be rid of their bourgeois habits of thinking. Thus, the proletarians are to be compelled by the forceful compulsion of "their own" dictatorship to think and act as that dictatorship requires.

This concept can lead to only one outcome, the oppressive rule over all the people by a select few, the so-called vanguard, itself dictated to by the all-wise Stalin and his successor Malenkov.

The Classless Society

But every man must have some vision of God or perfection, even though a macabre one, and the Communist philosophy promises such perfection. It promises that out of the Soviet dictatorship, once it is established on a world basis, there will emerge the classless society, which may be described as the earthly paradise of the animal man. Though as yet only vaguely outlined, it is clearly a state of society in which the "new man," the Bolshevik man, will have become so perfect according to the Communist conception that the dictatorship will voluntarily wither away. Since in the Communist view the proletariat can spawn no opposite, and to that extent the dialectical process in society comes to a halt, the state will no longer be necessary. There will be no new ruling class to require such a state. Man will exist in a refined jungle society—without state, laws, compulsions of any kind, money, or family. As Marx wrote it down, long ago, "each will give according to his ability and will receive according to his need." Through the proletarian dictatorship, the foundation will have been laid for an end to neurosis, ill health, and unhappiness. These will not prevail in the classless society.

Forecasting this "paradise," Lenin declared that only in Communist society, "when there are no classes," does "the state cease to exist," and it "becomes possible to speak of freedom."

In other words, freedom is impossible until Communism is reached, where "without compulsion, without subordination, without the special apparatus for compulsion which is called the state," people will act freely and without injury to each other. (Lenin, *State and Revolution, Selected Works*, VII, 81.)

So strongly embedded is this promise of the perfect society in Communist thought and action, that William Z. Foster in his *Twilight of World Capitalism* includes a final chapter on "The Advent of Socialist Man." In those pages he asserts without any proof that many of the beneficial features that will appear in the "classless society" already are evident in large segments of the Soviet population. They are a new type of human being, overcoming ill health and always happy. "Freed from social maladjustments," they are well balanced mentally, far superior to the people of the United States. Foster does not explain how all of this good health, happiness, and freedom from tension has been accompanied by slave labor, the labor passport system, and the widespread Red terror under the secret police. But he must present this "new man" as coming into being because that is the great pledge of Communism.

In like manner, G. M. Malenkov entitles his report to the Nineteenth Congress of the Communist Party of the Soviet Union *On the Threshold of Communism,* that is, on the threshold of the earthly paradise. While in the report itself he is more cautious than the title would indicate, referring to a "gradual transition" from Socialism to Communism, he does conclude the report with these words: "Under the banner of the immortal Lenin, under the wise leadership of the great Stalin, forward to the victory of Communism!" All the leading speakers at this Congress echoed that refrain, as can be read in *Soviet Leaders Speak for Communism and Peace,* New Century Publishers, 1952.

This is the Messianic message or promise of Communism which attracts so many of the intelligentsia and the offspring of the rich to its banner. This Messianic message was recognized and clearly defined by His Holiness Pope Pius XI in his

Encyclical on Atheistic Communism, written in 1937. The Pope
pointed out the fallacy contained in this promise, and the inability of Communism to cure the ills which afflict mankind;
indeed, he stressed that Communism had already been proved
to be thoroughly false and that this made more tragic its progress throughout the world.

As a result of this basic conflict between the Communists'
promises and their inherent inability to perform them, we now
have as the Marxist-Leninist reality the Frankenstein which
is marching across country after country. It is bringing slavery
as it promises "emancipation," and enchaining nations as it
proclaims their "liberation."

The sole road to the classless society, this earthly paradise
for the animal man, this hope of all mankind according to
Communist standards, is through the world-wide proletarian or
Soviet dictatorship. Hence, the absolute necessity for world
domination by Soviet Russia, which must be won at all costs.

While Communism, the other name for the classless society,
may be introduced to a degree in certain regions which have
had Socialism or the Soviet dictatorship for some time, this
state of society cannot be permanently assured until world wide
Socialism has been established. We can then understand why
the *Program of the Communist International* boldly gives
"world wide Communism" as its objective. We can understand,
likewise, why Stalin declared in 1939 that the withering away
of the state, the precondition for the classless society, could not
be entertained as a possibility until the encirclement of socialism by capitalism had been changed to the encirclement of
capitalism by socialism. That is to say, until those conditions
had been established which would assure world wide Soviet
domination. (Joseph Stalin, Report to the Eighteenth Party
Congress, Communist Party of the Soviet Union, March 10,
1939; published in the *Communist International Magazine*,
special no., XIV, 520 ff, 1939.)

For the Communist who works in the American community,
every act he performs must tend to forward this goal of Soviet

world domination, in order to assure the classless society. Every infiltration of a local organization which he carries through, although at first it may seem to be only for immediate objectives, must be related to advancing this end. For him, socialism is inevitable, as the Communist leaders and directives constantly emphasize. But he, as a member of the vanguard, is making that inevitability possible, always with the final Communist society in mind.

Unless we understand this motivation of the Communist, we cannot understand the tactics to which he resorts. Nor will we grasp his use of the Leninist morality, the necessity to lie or perjure or engage in other illegal activities for the advancement of the cause. Communist morality is "entirely subordinated to the class struggle of the proletariat," since that class struggle will destroy the old exploiting society and create a new Communist society. (Lenin, *Collected Works*, XVII, 321-23.)

This Leninist morality, that deceit shall be employed on a large scale for the benefit of Communist aims, flows naturally from basic Communist philosophy. If there be no God or world of the spirit, as Marxism-Leninism claims, then those precepts of morality arising from God's commandments or from any other "ideal" source, as Lenin stressed, do not hold. Any measure, legal or illegal, moral or immoral, may therefore be applied if it tends to win the desired goal. It is the failure to grasp this inherent use of deceit by the Communists, which they regard as the highest mark of moral value, that has led to the successes gained by recurrent Communist lines.

We recognize, then, as a second basic consideration that the aim of Soviet world domination arises inevitably from the Communist philosophy, from the "laws" of nature and society as laid down by Marx, Engels, Lenin, and Stalin. It is not a passing phase. It is not something that can be compromised or abandoned. It is the secret of the dynamics of Communist action and of Communist techniques.

Soviet Russia and those following its leadership will never be content until the world proletarian dictatorship has been achieved, or until Russia has been rocked back on its heels in the attempt. There is no middle ground. From the Communist viewpoint, there is not even an alternative. For the world dictatorship is bound to occur out of the operations of society itself.

Economic Determinism

Man's mind is purely material, according to Marxist theory, there being no spiritual soul or mind. So, also, man's social relationships and institutions are determined by materialistic considerations. It is the mode of production—the means by which men obtain food, clothing, and shelter—which determines the religion, law, and other social institutions and concepts of each period of history. This is economic determinism, and it involves the Communist again in a species of fatalism.

When the fundamental changes in the mode of production are no longer in line with the form of ownership and control of the means of production, class struggles ensue. All history has been a series of class struggles, according to Marx, ending dialectically in a new period or stage of society. The current class struggle, as we have seen, is waged between the bourgeoisie and the proletariat.

A review of Karl Marx's career will show that he adopted the idea of dialectics from Georg Wilhelm Friedrich Hegel, the philosopher of the Prussian State, but "turned it on its head," as he puts it, giving it a materialist instead of an idealist foundation. This materialist conception Marx and Engels obtained from Ludwig Feuerbach, whose *Essence of Christianity* formed the rallying center for materialists in the 1840's. The theory of the class struggle was taken by Marx from Pierre Joseph Proudhon, the early French socialist-anarchist. From this amalgam "scientific socialism" was created, as opposed to the "Utopian Socialism" of Robert Owen, Saint-Simon, and others.

What Marx did, in other words, was to take those ideas

sprouting up in his time and blend them together in an over-simplified and therefore false picture. The process is described in part, of course from a point of view favorable to Marxism, by Friedrich Engels in his *Socialism, Utopian and Scientific*.

It is the declaration that this amalgam is a "science," indeed "the science of society," and therefore above all other science, which gives the Communist once more that assurance and determination to achieve the inevitable—Socialism through the dictatorship and then the classless society.

That this Marxist-Leninist world outlook, while having a certain logic, is based on thoroughly false premises can be extensively demonstrated. Our consideration here is largely to view this philosophy in an introductory manner as a source of the dynamics of Communist techniques. This is not a work on the philosophy of Communism. We shall not seek to refute its false premises in detail, although such refutations can and have been made. (For instance, in the excellent work, *The Philosophy of Communism*, by Charles J. McFadden, OSA, Ph.D., Benziger Bros., N.Y.)

It can be stated here, however, that the Marxist gets himself into a hopeless contradiction with his declaration that there is a dialectical motion in nature and society, expressed through the law of opposites. No matter how he interprets that law, as soon as he speaks of motion, that very motion leads to the existence of a prime mover, Almighty God.

The question raised by St. Thomas Aquinas centuries ago, and answered by him, that the existence of motion requires a First Mover, is evaded by Marxism. Marxism cannot account for the origin of motion or how the material world of motion came into existence. When it declares that life arose out of inert matter through a violent leap, and that man arose out of the animal by another violent leap, it is indulging in fictions arranged to support a preconceived notion. Thus dialectical materialism is no more able to explain the existence of motion or the existence of life than old nineteenth century materialism. Indeed, it is merely that materialism in a new disguise. Even with its law of opposites, it cannot explain what puts these opposites into motion. There must be an outside force, but that force, God, it refuses to recognize. In this it involves itself in a hopeless contradiction from the beginning.

As to economic determinism and the materialistic conception of history, they do not accord with what has happened either in religion or in law. It has been asked, "What great change in the mode of production caused the pagan Roman Empire to change to Christianity?" And again: "How account for the fact that Catholicism has flourished for centuries throughout the world, under methods of production ranging all the way from Roman slavery to American capitalism?"

Marxism cannot account either for retrogression in history. It is based on the concept of continuous historical progress, and the facts of history show that there has been no continuous progress.

The theory that class struggles have always and inevitably been the cause of progress cannot be successfully defended. It is an oversimplification of the undoubted fact that exploitation of classes has existed in various periods of history and that there have been what can be called class struggles. But because this theory has been blindly followed, we have today a condition over a great section of the globe where an absolute State, in the name of the "proletariat," rules ruthlessly over millions of slaves. The working masses under Soviet control find themselves exploited by a small but powerful bureaucracy.

Upon examination, the withering away of the State becomes a great mirage created by Marxism-Leninism to answer man's inherent desire for perfection. For the Communist as a materialist, this perfection must be attained through a Utopia of non-restraint here on earth. But the Communist does have to speak of some "social organization," as Engels puts it, or "society," which after all presupposes in itself some form of State. Man is naturally a social being, and the State did not arise from the exploitation of the subject class by the rulers, but from man's inherent need for society just as for the family. In other words, as St. Thomas Aquinas has said, government was created for the common good. It is only when there is abuse of power that this end is defeated.

In putting forth a false view of the origin of the State, the Communists have inevitably brought about in the name of the final withering away of the State, one of the greatest tyrannies in history.

Stalin: The Teacher and Guide

Since the Marxist-Leninist theory which is bound up with this philosophy is "not a dogma but a guide to action," the question arises who will interpret this theory in this stage of history.

The answer is quite clear: The interpreter and determinant of how the theory is to be applied is Stalin, the continuer of Lenin. And upon Stalin's authority as Malenkov's tutor, the present master of the Kremlin lays down the line for Communists throughout the world.

In his famous *History of the Communist Party of the Soviet Union, Bolsheviks*, Stalin says: "It may be said without fear of exaggeration that since the death of Engels the master theoretician Lenin, and after Lenin, Stalin and the other disciples of Lenin have been the only Marxists who have advanced the Marxist theory and who have enriched it with new experience in the new conditions of the class struggle of the proletariat." (*History of the Communist Party of the Soviet Union, Bolsheviks*, Foreign Languages Publishing House, Moscow, 1939, p. 358.)

The "other disciples of Lenin" to whom Stalin refers, have in one voice proclaimed the Soviet dictator to be their father, teacher, and guide. Every report of the Red leaders in the satellite regimes concludes with such a declaration, as though it were a form of ritual. In the work *Stalin*, prepared by the members of the Moscow Politburo in 1939, on the occasion of Stalin's sixtieth birthday, his position as the determinant of all

Communist policy is affirmed. A. I. Mikoyan sums up this opinion when he states: "In the Party and among the people, unprecedented confidence in Stalin prevails, an unshakable belief in the infallibility of the general line of our Party's policy; for everyone knows that since Stalin is at the helm, there is no cause for disquietude, victory is certain whatever happens." Stalin was then hailed as "the driver of the locomotive of history, the greatest genius of our times, and the world's greatest scientist." Such extravagant phrases were echoed in the Cominform's organ of December 21, 1949, honoring Stalin's seventieth birthday.

Even in the immediate period after his death, Stalin dominated the line of the Communists through his statement to the Nineteenth Party Congress in October, 1952, his report on *Economic Problems of Socialism in the USSR* and Malenkov's report, *On the Threshold of Communism*, prepared with Stalin's approval.

The mastery of Marxism-Leninism, which is urged upon the Communists, has become the ability to respond obediently and quickly to Stalin's decrees and to those of his successor, and to execute them in the most telling manner. By an ironical twist of logic, dialectical materialism in its triumph acknowledges its own bankruptcy. Rejecting God and the world of the spirit, it sets up an infallible guide in the person of Stalin, the god of the Communists, whose will cannot be disobeyed.

The active agency which carries through the Marxist-Leninist theory and applies it to life, the Communist Party, is very much like a chisel in the hands of a sculptor. It is the instrument of the great Stalin, working through his disciple Malenkov, to shape the masses and history according to the Kremlin's plan and purpose.

Communism Admits Its Own Bankruptcy

By this exaltation of Stalin—making him the supreme determinant of what the Communists may think or do—Communism admits its own bankruptcy. It does this in two major ways. In creating this god with feet of clay, it confesses that its materialism cannot explain the world in which we live. Again, in acclaiming Stalin, "the continuer of Lenin," as the fountainhead of Marxist-Leninist correctness in all avenues of thought, it admits that its "science" is unscientific. The development and application of Marxism-Leninism is dependent exclusively upon the will of the Soviet dictator. Experiment, experience, and investigation, so important for true science, can only be registered in Marxism-Leninism if "the driver of the locomotive of history," Stalin, or his successor Malenkov, so decrees.

CHAPTER II

THE COMMUNIST APPARATUS

FOR THE Communist, politics is war and every day is an engagement in the class struggle. There are few phrases more popular in Communist discussion than that of the Prussian General Clausewitz that war is the extension of politics by other means. The converse of this is also held true, that politics is warfare.

It is therefore quite natural that the Communist International apparatus, directing this constant conflict and aiming at world conquest, is organized on super-military lines. Every army at war must have an experienced staff if it is to avoid defeat, Stalin writes in his *Foundations of Leninism*, and the Communist Party, he tells us, is the military staff of the proletariat.

To fulfill this task, the Communist International apparatus is organized around a common center, Moscow, whence instructions flow down to the lowest branch or cell in the most obscure localities. The Communist branch functioning in your neighborhood, and infiltrating your local organizations, is completely in accord with the directives received from the Kremlin.

The agency which formerly was the channel of directives was the Communist International, known popularly as the Comintern. Founded by Lenin in March, 1919, it was for years the guiding hand that ruled the Red invading armies in all countries. In May, 1943, its dissolution was announced, "to advance the fight against Fascism." In actuality, the step was taken by

Stalin to soothe the feelings of the United States and to make easier the granting of huge lend-lease aid to Soviet Russia. The dissolution, it will be noted, took place in the midst of World War II, when the Moscow dictatorship was hard pressed by the Nazi military machine.

As a matter of fact, the Communist Party apparatus continued to function in the same manner as before, all Communist Parties receiving directives from Moscow and following a common line. When the so-called cold war against the United States was initiated by Stalin, the old Communist International appeared again above the surface as the Information Bureau of the Communist and Workers Parties. Commonly known as the Cominform and founded in 1949, it is today the public expression of the centralized world wide control of the Communist Parties in all lands which are in reality invading armies.

Peters on Party Structure

For the structure of the Communist International, which exists in reality today, we can go to the foremost authority of the Communist Party of the United States, the notorious J. Peters, for years the chief Soviet espionage agent in this country.

In consulting his *Manual of Organization*, published in 1936 by the Communist Party, we note that he gives the international Red organization, step by step, as follows:

Unit Bureau
Unit Membership Meeting
Section Bureau
Section Committee
Section Convention
District Bureau
District Committee
District Convention

Political Bureau of the Central Committee

Central Committee

National Convention

Political Secretariat of the Communist International

Presidium of the Communist International

Executive Committee of the Communist International—the ECCI

World Congress of the Communist International

Peters explains that this structure is allegedly built up "in the order of responsibility." We can observe the subservience of the unit to the section, the section to the district, and the district to the Politburo, then known as the Political Bureau of the Central Committee. We can also see from Peters' arrangement the subordination of the Communist Parties in every country to the Communist International under Stalin.

This organization of control is emphasized by Stalin himself, in declaring that the lower organs of the Communist organization must always be subordinated to the higher organs. (*Foundations of Leninism*, p. 110.) It is also emphasized by M. J. Olgin, leading Communist editor in the United States in his work, *Why Communism?* There he states clearly that orders from the higher ranks of the Party must be explicitly obeyed and followed by those below.

This is somewhat ironically known as "democratic centralism." In order to introduce the "democratic" fiction into the organizational set up, Peters has distorted its methods of operation. The Bureaus of each division of the Party—whether unit, section, district, or national—are not the servants of these organs. They are the masters, and they are rigidly directed and controlled by the unit organizer, the section organizer, in each respective case. The leadership principle is pronounced and decisive.

The Real "Democratic Centralism"

In actual life, the Communist structure is as follows:

STALIN—MALENKOV

THE MOSCOW POLITBURO
(Known since October 1952 as "The Presidium.")

THE INTERNATIONAL APPARATUS
(Formerly known as the Communist International, now known as the Cominform)

"C.I. Rep"—C.I. REPRESENTATIVE

THE AMERICAN RED LEADER
(Formerly Earl Browder—now William Z. Foster—but always under the strict direction of the Communist International Representative [C.I. Rep.])

THE AMERICAN POLITBURO
(Known at various times as Political Bureau and National Board)

National Red Publications and Schools   *National Red Agencies of Infiltration into government, education, organs of public opinion, trade unions*

THE RED NATIONAL COMMITTEE
(Formerly known as the Central Committee)

DISTRICT LEADER

DISTRICT BUREAU

District Red Publications and Schools   *District Red Agencies of Infiltration*

DISTRICT COMMITTEE
(Sometimes called State Committee)

SECTION LEADERS

SECTION BUREAU

Section Red Schools and Pub-   Section Agencies of Infiltra-
lications   tion

SECTION COMMITTEE

BRANCH LEADER

BRANCH BUREAU

Branch Red Publications and   Branch Agencies of Infiltra-
Courses   tion

BRANCH COMMITTEE

THE BRANCH MEMBERS
(Now, in the completely underground organization of the
Party to fight the United States, broken down frequently
into units of only five members each)

Some time should be taken to study this chart carefully. It
will be observed that there is a rigid and complete control
from Stalin down to the lowest unit or branch of the Party. This
dependence on Stalin and the Political Bureau of the Communist Party of the Soviet Union has been expressed countless
times by Communist leaders and in Communist resolutions. It
is nowhere stated better than in *Milestones in the History of the
Communist Party*, by Alexander Bittelman, published in 1937.
There Bittelman frankly declares that "the revolutionary vanguard of this country can derive deep satisfaction from the fact

that it unfailingly received brotherly advice and guidance from the Communist International in the struggle for the revolutionization of the American working class." He adds that this world Party has been created "for the victory of the dictatorship of the proletariat, for the establishment of a world Soviet republic."

But in addition to showing the control from Moscow through the Communist International, Bittelman is compelled to deal with the control of the Communist International by the Communist Party of the Soviet Union headed by Stalin. On this he writes:

"The leading role of the Communist Party of the Soviet Union in the Comintern needs neither explanation or apology. A Party that has opened up an epoch of world revolution, and that is successfully building a classless society on one-sixth of the earth, is cheerfully recognized and followed as the leading Party of the World Communist movement. And by the same token, the leaders of that Party—first Lenin and now Stalin—are proudly followed as the leaders of the proletariat of all the oppressed in every country of the world." (*Milestones in the History of the Communist Party*, Workers Library Publishers, N.Y., p. 71.)

Our first observation, from a study of the chart, is then to note the complete autocratic control exercised by Stalin and the Communist Party of the Soviet Union over the entire "movement." This requires constant reiteration, since it is impossible to convey to the reader a full conception of the continuous acknowledgment in Communist publications of directives of the leadership and guidance of Stalin. Later acquaintance in detail with these publications will bring home this fundamental Communist allegiance.

Next we observe the international agency used by Stalin and the Communist Party of the Soviet Union to direct and control the other Parties throughout the world. (Or rather, we should term them the revolutionary armies throughout the world, engaged in political conflict today and armed uprising tomorrow.)

This international agency, formerly the Comintern, now the Cominform, operates in a number of ways to bring its control to bear on the Parties in each country.

Channels of Communication

One of its chief channels of communication is the man who was formerly known as the Communist International Representative or "C.I. Rep." That phrase has become so embedded in Communist Party language that we shall continue to use it. Whoever is acting in this capacity transmits orally to the leadership of the Communist Party in the country in which he is functioning the sharp and brief instructions which are necessary from time to time. Such instructions reach him through the diplomatic mail pouches or codes of the Soviet diplomatic service. They are generally conveyed to him from a Soviet Embassy or Consulate through obscure employees. Among the C.I. Reps in this country were Gerhart Eisler, Boris Williams, and John Pepper (Pogany).

But much more by way of directives is needed than a mere personality, no matter how important he may be. The chief source of these week by week orders is the publications sent into this country, notably the organ of the Cominform, *For a Lasting Peace, For a People's Democracy*, and the *New Times*, published in Moscow. We shall later note the operations and effects of these publications, showing in detail how they are followed in the development of the Communist line or policies. Immediately upon their arrival in this country, they are diligently studied by the leading Communists. The position they indicate and the arguments they advance are echoed in the *Political Affairs*, official theoretical organ of the Communist Party, then in the *Daily Worker*, and thence move out into the non-Communist publications and areas of opinion.

In order to carry through these directives with military precision, within the Communist apparatus proper, there is the constant necessity to strengthen Marxist-Leninist ideology and

Bolshevik discipline over and over again. This necessity is urged in the writings of Lenin and Stalin and in the current issues of the Cominform's organ. The Party, in other ways, is to be constantly instructed and steeled as to its final purpose: the overthrow of the governments under which it is operating and the execution of day to day tasks with that goal ever in mind.

With that is joined the urgency of "broadening the ties with the masses," that is, the most extensive and intensive infiltration of agencies of government, community, and public opinion.

It is precisely the ability of a small group, the vanguard, moving in a strictly disciplined manner and under concealment, into non-Communist organizations, that makes Communist activity so effective.

Orders From Above

When we put the X-ray of careful examination upon the organization of the Communist Party of the United States, we will be struck with its class war basis. The American Red leader, in accordance with Stalin's concept of the Party as the general staff of the proletariat, gives orders like a general to his troops. At least four times a year, the National Committee of the Communist Party meets to learn of any changes or new interpretations in the line as laid down by Moscow. For several hours, the national leader of the Party presents a report in which that line is defined. Thereupon, each member of the National Committee in turn arises and expresses his agreement with the report, explaining how he will proceed to carry out its provisions —what forces he can bring to play in his area and what organizations he can infiltrate.

Immediately after the National Committee meeting, the district organizer (leader in a state or district composed of several states) calls together the State or District committee. To its members, the district leader delivers the same report as that given previously by the national leader, emphasizing the procedure by which it can be carried out in that district.

In the same manner, the report goes into the sections and branches, with the section leader and branch leader respectively leading what is called "the discussion of the report." Expressions of opinion at any level which would be in opposition to the report or critical of it are impermissible. The national leader's statements constitute orders which must be explicitly followed. The discussion is for the purpose merely of determining how his policy recommendations can best be executed, or of learning if any of the comrades are guilty of tendencies harmful to the Party and its line.

This authority of the national leader is based on the understanding that his report is that which Moscow has instructed him to give. It has been formulated with the aid of the C.I. Rep and with the direct instructions received from abroad. The record of the Communist Party of the United States, as registered in its official proceedings, proves that it has never deviated by a hair's breadth from the current policies laid down by the Kremlin. An examination of Communist literature in this country over the past thirty years will reveal a complete adherence to whatever was the dominant view furthered by Moscow and a zealous hour by hour attempt to move the American community to think and act as Moscow wanted it to think and act.

The body which cooperates constantly day by day with the American leader is the American Politburo, composed of from six to twelve members, as the needs of the Party require. In accordance with the Communist custom of changing the names but not the substance or authority of various divisions of the Party, the Politburo has been called the Political Bureau and now is known as the National Board. It is organized on a functional basis, each member of the Politburo being assigned to a special field over which he has control and for which he is responsible. Thus, one member will be in charge of national affairs, directing infiltration into agencies of the government. Another will be in charge of the labor field, a third will supervise cultural and educational activities, and a fourth the organization of the Party itself.

These Politburo members require the assistance of additional personnel and agencies. For that purpose, the Party sets up Commissions, which are not covered by the chart, since they are directly under the supervision of the Politburo members. There is, for instance, the National Trade Union Commission, which meets regularly under the direction of Politburo members entrusted with labor supervision. Within that Commission are laid the plans to penetrate the labor movement and to carry out the concentration policies of the Party, which envisage the capture of the basic industries for Stalinite purposes. There is also the powerful Cultural Commission, which has been headed for years by Alexander Trachtenberg and V. J. Jerome. Its function, as we shall see later, is to direct Communist activities in the entire cultural field—education, the arts and sciences, the theatre, radio, and television.

From time to time, special Commissions are established for a specific undertaking or for a limited period of time. Of this character were the Commissions on infiltration of the publishing industry, radio, and television, and minority or national groups.

The Politburo members make it their business to watch diligently the various directives coming from Moscow, to note the campaigns which the International center calls for, and to advise the district leaders and the Party as a whole what must be done as a consequence. They maintain an hour by hour contact with the *Daily Worker*, instructing its editors on the drives that should be inaugurated and the precise manner in which specific subjects should be handled. Since the *Daily Worker* is not a daily newspaper in the normal sense of the word but a telegraph agency of immediate directives, the Party thus receives its orders uniformly and throughout the country at the same time.

The Communists at all levels, acting under that iron discipline emphasized by Stalin, move immediately into action in response to these instructions. It can easily be understood how a comparatively small group of people, under such procedure,

are able to accomplish a great deal. This effectiveness is multi-
plied by infiltration. Moving into non-Communist organizations and agencies through concealed Communists, they frequently succeed in persuading those organizations to favor the
policies or attitudes advanced by the Party.

In the 1940's, one of their greatest triumphs in this connection was in inducing the American government and much of
our public opinion to aid the Chinese Communists, and thus
bring on the tragedy of Korea. Currently, the Communists have
succeeded in enlisting certain Senators, non-Communist writers
and educators, and even conservative organizations, behind the
campaign to defend the "right" of Communists to subvert the
loyalty and morale of pupils in our schools.

How the Politburo Works

Let us look in on a Politburo meeting in February, 1940, to
illustrate its methods of work. About ten men and women were
gathered on the ninth floor of 50 East 13th Street in New
York, the Communist national headquarters. Several leading
Communists in addition to the Politburo members were in attendance. The chief item on the agenda was the drive against
"the Second Imperialist War." This was at the period of the
Hitler-Stalin alliance and the Communist leaders were well
aware that they were supposed to do all in their power to aid
Hitler. Before them, presented by William Z. Foster, was a directive from Moscow advising that English imperialism was
"the most dangerous incendiary of war" and "the chief enemy
of the international working class." The directive called on the
working classes of all countries to do all in their power to thwart
the plans of English imperialism. In the United States, this
meant prevention of all aid to Great Britain. (See *The Communist International Magazine*, no. 2, 1940.)

The Politburo members showed no hesitancy. They knew
what to do. Strikes were essential to tie up American produc-

tion which might go to Britain, and in order to obtain strikes, agitation for higher wages and shorter hours was essential. Upon that course the Politburo decided, preparing resolutions which called for a fight for "an American standard of living for all" and denounced the war and hunger program of President Roosevelt.

To further this agitation, a meeting of the National Committee was called. On February 17, it unanimously adopted the resolutions which the Politburo had drawn up.

From that time forward, during that period, the Communists sought by every means at their command to instigate discontent and strikes, on the plea that such stoppages were necessary to uphold living conditions. During the entire year 1940, they raised higher and higher this attempt to snowball strikes through the country. The North American Aircraft walkout at Ingleside, California, under Lew Mitchener, was one of the big results. Mitchener was a regional director of the United Automobile Workers but also a Communist, and he followed directions in shutting down aircraft production. Since that episode he has left the Communist Party and was one of the witnesses in the 1950 perjury trial of Harry Bridges.

Still persisting in its campaign to shut down production, the Politburo in the fall of 1940 sent Eugene Dennis, one of its prominent members, to Milwaukee. There he ordered Harold Christoffel, at that time president of the Allis-Chalmers local of the United Automobile Workers, to strike the men in that important war material plant. This act was thoroughly in accord with the injunctions of the Communist theoretical organ of September, 1940, for an all out fight by the workers against "the steady capitalist pressure to whittle away labor's rights and trade union standards."

The reader will note how seriously the decision of the Politburo in February, 1940, affected events in that year and in 1941, and led to a marked reduction in American defense production.

Agencies of Infiltration

The national agencies of infiltration stem from the Politburo and act under its direction. One form of infiltration is the Communist front, an organization created by the Communists themselves.

The Civil Rights Congress is one of the best illustrations that could be presented. In mid-1945, when it was clear to the American Politburo that Stalin had opened a period of warfare against the United States, this group decided to form a new defense organization. They knew that the Communist Party would be committed to a course which would be in violation of the laws of the United States, and which would lead to trials of its leaders. Accordingly, it was decided that the International Labor Defense and the National Federation for Constitutional Liberties should merge into a new organization dedicated "specifically to the defense of individual Communists and the Communist Party." Both of the merging organizations were notorious Communist fronts, the International Labor Defense having been one arm of the Red legal aid organizations set up in every country of the world. Elizabeth Gurley Flynn, the member of the Politburo in charge of Party defense, was assigned to the task of perfecting the new organization. Aiding her were William L. Patterson, long time Communist leader, and George Marshall, a man of wealth attached to many Communist fronts. The result was the formation of the Civil Rights Congress in 1946.

While this organization has run afoul of the government in the mishandling of its bail funds, it has had a powerful influence in confusing American thinking on the Communist issue. William L. Patterson, its executive officer, was permitted by the State Department to go to the December 1951 meeting of the United Nations in Paris. There he presented the charge of "genocide" against the United States, based on abuses against the Negro people. His pamphlet has been published in issues of many thousands for distribution both here and abroad, and has seriously injured the reputation of this nation. Patterson also was invited to speak over television, presenting the pro-Communist view of the Civil Rights Congress. Through its individual members, the C.R.C. has penetrated into other groups with its message of confusion, although it was condemned by the House Committee on Un-American Activities as a subversive organization. (Congressional Committee on Un-American Activities, report no. 1115, Sept. 2, 1947.)

The Civil Rights Congress, which has received a great deal of laudatory mention in the *Daily Worker*, was the agency which furnished the bail for the eleven Communist leaders convicted in 1949. It performed a like function for the sixteen leading Communists who went on trial in New York in 1952. Because four of each group disappeared, the Civil Rights Congress bail fund was carefully scrutinized by the courts and authorities. Two of its trustees, Dashiell Hammett, the detective story writer, and Frederick Vanderbilt Field, the millionaire, went to jail rather than disclose the bail fund records. Despite this notorious record, the Civil Rights Congress continues to wield a considerable influence on American public opinion.

One of the classic examples of a Communist front is the National Council of the Arts, Sciences, and Professions, a descendent of the Independent Citizens Committee of the Arts, Sciences, and Professions. Although I have referred to the formation of this committee in my book, *Men Without Faces*, the matter is of such importance that the account must be briefly repeated. No student of Communist techniques can afford to be uninformed about the way in which this committee came into existence.

As I testified in 1948 before a Senate Sub-Committee, the Independent Citizens Committee of the Arts, Sciences, and Professions was worked out originally from my office when I was managing editor of the *Daily Worker*. It was the product of discussions by the Cultural Commission of that paper. One of the members was Lionel Berman, cultural section organizer of the

Party in New York. It was he whom the Politburo, as a result of a recommendation made by the *Daily Worker* commission, entrusted with the task of forming the Independent Citizens Committee.

So well did Berman perform his assignment that the New York State Convention in August, 1945, praised him for his work.

First forming a nucleus of reliable Communist fronters—such as John Howard Lawson, Ring Lardner, Jr., E. Y. Harburg, and Lillian Hellman—Berman then had the members of this nucleus recruit the Committee on a larger scale. This is standard Communist practice. Thus the hand of the Party is partly concealed in the creation of these fronts, although their turning and twisting with the Communist line is one of the sure signs of their origin.

The Independent Committee did such twisting and turning. Originally its purpose was to support President Roosevelt, but its subsequent history shows that this was merely a means by which the Communists could get greater influence. By August, 1945, the cultural section of the Communist Party could boast at its New York State Convention: "We built the Independent Citizens Committee of the Arts, Sciences, and Professions, and it is a great political weapon."

Eventually, the Independent Citizens Committee of the Arts, Sciences, and Professions was transformed into the National Council of the Arts, Sciences, and Professions. It was this National Council which sponsored the notorious Waldorf-Astoria Conference which opened in the United States Stalin's "peace crusades" as a cover for Soviet aggression. Technically, this conference was known as the Scientific and Cultural Conference for Peace, meeting in March 1949. Its purposes were clearly to promote support for the foreign policies of the Soviet Union, to assail American policy, and to promote a program of opposition to the American government even to the point of civil disobedience.

All Communist fronts are carefully supervised by the Politburo through that member who is concerned with the special field the specific front covers. This member acts through special functionaries of a lower category, who meet constantly with the small group directing the front.

Infiltration goes much further, into every possible non-Communist organization and institution. When an organization has been infiltrated to the point where it has come under Communist control, it becomes a captive organization, being as readily manipulated by the few Communists who have penetrated it as is the Communist front. In addition, the captive organization often has the advantage of being popularly known as non-Communist, and therefore its decisions are of greater weight in molding public opinion.

Transmission Belts

All groups which the Communist Party is seeking to penetrate are termed "mass organizations" in Communist parlance, and by Red penetration and eventual control they are to be made into "transmission belts" for broadening the influence of the Party. In *Foundations of Leninism*, Stalin lays down this use of "transmission belts" by a centralized, disciplined Party as an essential feature of Communist efforts. (*Foundations of Leninism*, Joseph Stalin, Marxist Library, International Publishers, V, 113.)

Stalin follows up this emphasis in *Problems of Leninism*, another standard textbook and guide for Communists throughout the world, by declaring that along with "the vanguard," that is, the Communist Party, it is necessary that there be "belts" or "levers" composed of mass organizations which the vanguard penetrates. It is in this sense that Earl Browder, when General Secretary and leader of the Communist Party in this country, described both the American League Against War and Fascism and its successor, the American League for Peace and Democracy, as "Communist transmission belts." (*Guide to Subversive Organizations and Publications*, House Committee on Un-American Activities, March 3, 1951.)

The same process by which the American Politburo directs
the creation of transmission belts or the infiltration of non-Communist organizations also marks the district bureau and the district leader in their areas. Those mass organizations—whether
labor, educational, or political—which lie within the confines
of the state or district bureau's control are subject to intensive
efforts at penetration.

In the State of Michigan—as a good illustration—much of
the attention and energy of the Communists is devoted to placing
small groups of concealed comrades within the United Automobile, Aircraft, and Agricultural Implement Workers Union,
CIO. For various periods of time, the Reds were in control of
powerful local unions in the Detroit area, not the least being
the large Ford local of the UAW at Dearborn and River Rouge.
With that major task has been associated work within Negro
organizations, women's groups, parent-teachers associations,
and the local school system. The interlocking of these activities,
several functions sometimes being performed by one person, is
shown in the case of William Hood, secretary of the Ford local.
While persuading that organization of 80,000 workers to adopt
pro-Communist resolutions, Hood became a founder and national officer of the National Negro Labor Council, set up by
the Communists in 1951.

This organizational set-up, of an iron bound Party membership operating through transmission belts into the general
community, makes for maximum effectiveness. One trained Communist can be used to work in several mass organizations; as
one witness stated to the California Committee on Un-American
Activities, one Communist can be as one hundred men. But by
moving thousands of non-Communists into action, the concealed
Communist can be still more powerful than that. The majority
of the members of the United Electrical, Radio, and Machine
Workers Union—expelled from the CIO in 1950 for being under
Communist control—are non-Communists. But they are officered
by Communists, and their conventions constantly reflect the current Communist line. Thus, thousands of Americans who are not

sympathetic to Communism carry out the orders given from Moscow and beneficial to the Soviet Union.

Quality Not Quantity

While the Communist Party in this country declares repeatedly that it wishes to become a "mass Party," this is not to be understood in the literal sense that it hopes to embrace millions of members. It becomes a mass Party when it has enough members placed in enough key positions to move the masses as the Kremlin dictates. Georgi M. Malenkov, Stalin's successor, has written in an important article on cadres (which was republished throughout the world) that "in the Party we do not want quantity but quality."

By "quality" from a Communist viewpoint is meant the ability to observe Bolshevik discipline and to execute faithfully orders from above.

In such a "class war" organization as the Communist Party, depending upon the complete obedience of its members, security measures are required. These are entrusted to the all powerful Control Commission, known now as the National Cadre and Review Commission, which does not appear on our chart.

The National Control Commission receives and keeps on file the biographies of all Communist Party functionaries in the greatest detail. It also receives constant reports on the conduct of the comrades under suspicion of being disloyal, and conducts "trials" of those to be expelled from the Party. Aping Soviet police methods, the trial is not called until the person involved has been adjudged guilty, and serves only the purpose of registering a judgment of that alleged guilt. The Control Commission generally endeavors to attach to a charge of political weakness some accusation of personal depravity, in order to destroy the reputation of the expelled comrade, and thereby to impair his credibility in the non-Communist world. The National Control Commission also supervises the work of the District Control Commissions, which function in each district, keeping a close eye on the individual members, their work, and their associates.

In studying the Communist apparatus, we must be aware that there is a frequent change of name for the various organs or bodies of the Party, though their respective functions remain the same. The Politburo has been known over the years as the Political Bureau, the Political Committee, the National Board of the Communist Political Association, and the National Board of the Communist Party. The lowest organ in the Party has been called at various times a cell, unit, branch, and club. A moment's thought will show how this rapid change in name facilitates confusion from a legal and public-scrutiny viewpoint.

In part, these changes in titles are a reflection of the changing lines and tasks of the Party, which require the membership to be on a concealed or open basis to a greater or lesser degree. When the Party goes completely underground because the Soviet Union is attacking the United States full blast, the cell or nucleus of only five members becomes the functioning place of the rank and file. But in the period of World War II, when the Party was putting on patriotic trappings, the club with a comparatively large membership and open headquarters was devised. In this way, the Party put on the appearance of any other political organization.

Operation of the Cell

The permanent name "cell" actually applies to a unit or portion of a unit which is infiltrating a specific organization or institution. In New York, there was a cell in each of the larger social service organizations, although the members of each cell were attached to one branch or unit. There was a cell in the Institute of Pacific Relations, several in Washington in various government departments and in labor organizations appealing to government employees.

In the Parent Teachers Association in any community, a cell

will be set up if the Communists are penetrating such a group. So will it be with a local school system or a local labor union. Needless to say, the cell members go to any length to conceal their Communist affiliations, revealing them only to a few fellow workers or contacts who, they think, will be good material as Communist recruits.

The secrecy surrounding the cell's operations makes it comparatively easy for the Soviet secret police functioning in this country, or for other agencies of the Soviet government, to enlist specific cell members in espionage work.

The approach to the comrades selected is made through one of the superior officers, that is, some functionary whom the comrade recognizes as one from whom he receives orders. Sometimes the individual who is selected for this secret work, as it is called in the Party, may be taken completely out of the cell or branch and divorced from the Party apparatus. Since transfers can be ordered or arranged as in a military group, without any explanation, this is not difficult to do. On a number of occasions, the person carrying on the secret work is permitted to remain in the branch or cell, combining legal and illegal work as Lenin stated the Party should do. Comrade X may therefore be performing espionage work, unknown to his fellow comrades, and at the same time acting with the branch.

This intrusion of those supervising secret work into the apparatus goes on constantly, but in an irregular manner according to circumstances. It is as much an integral part of the labors of the active Communist chosen for the task as any other function. But the variety of ways in which Communists are enlisted for espionage makes it impossible to present this activity intelligibly in an organizational chart. (Instances of how Communist Party members are recruited for espionage can be found in *The Shameful Years*, House Committee on Un-American Activities, 1952, and in the various reports and hearings of the Senate Sub-Committee on Internal Security for 1952 and 1953.)

Each division of the Communist apparatus must be constantly in action, pressed to the performance of its tasks by the authority next higher in the line of leadership. A constant "discussion" of the current Party line and how it is to be applied, accompanied by a continuous examination of how functions are performed, is the regular life of the Communist. Specific comrades are given training in the branch, section, district, or national training schools, so that they may be prepared to advance on the ladder of leadership if necessary. As the chart indicates, these schools are controlled respectively by the Politburo, and the various lower subdivisions of the Party.

When we appreciate this union of discipline and concealment, and understand the constant reiteration throughout the apparatus that the Kremlin is the determining factor in what the Party does, we can begin to grasp what a powerful fifth column agency the Soviet dictatorship has in every country of the world.

CHAPTER III

COMMUNIST PHRASEOLOGY

THROUGHOUT THE international apparatus we have just examined, there is in use a jargon or phraseology peculiar to the Communist world. It grows originally out of the Marxist-Leninist classics, the writings of Marx, Engels, Lenin, and Stalin. It has been developed further for protective purposes in getting over the "revolutionary message" of the conspiracy while remaining legal, and also for purposes of deceit and easier infiltration.

Without a mastery of this Communist phraseology, it is most difficult if not impossible to analyze Communist actions in the nation or community. Unless this peculiar language and the methods of employing it can be understood, there is no key to Communist directives. Without this key it is a Herculean task to fathom the Communist line. And it is precisely the Communist line which is met up with in our various local communities; it is the line with which the Communist confronts the average educated American in numerous organizations, and not through open Communist propaganda at all.

The two basic tasks imposed by Marxism-Leninism upon the Communist organization in bourgeois countries makes this complicated, upside-down language a necessity. In every important pronouncement, which provides the Communists with a guide to thought and action, there must be a strong reminder of their goal—the dictatorship of the proletariat through force and violence. That is constantly embodied in the term, "to strengthen Marxist-Leninist ideology and Bolshevik discipline." Equally, Communists must be instructed in the penetration of mass organizations through which the vanguard will direct the masses along the Communist line in any particular period. That responsibility is conveyed through the dedication, repeated over and over again, "to broaden the ties with the masses." The instructions to the Stalinists, month by month, week by week, and even day by day, must therefore tell them how to deceive the masses with the current line and at the same time not fall victims to their own deceit. The use of roundabout language, therefore, arises from the very obligations placed by Marxism-Leninism on the Communist organization.

No better example of the effectiveness of this method can be furnished than the deception practiced upon the American people to the effect that the Chinese Communists were "agrarian reformers" or "Asia for the Asiatics" people. While concealed Communists and their friends peddled this idea extensively, the Communists could not be permitted to accept this view for themselves. Otherwise, they would be led to believe that the Chinese Communists, who stood out in the international Red apparatus, were guilty of "revisionism." That would have weakened Communist morale everywhere. Therefore, the Communist press in this country, including the *Daily Worker*, praised to the skies those books and authors who subscribed to the "agrarian reformer" viewpoint, but at the same time always reminded the readers of the Red publications that Mao Tse-tung's followers were actually Communists in the full sense of the word.

Aesopian Language

This involved and obscure phraseology, at least obscure to the uninitiated, permeates all Red publications which contain directives. It has come to be known, aptly, as Aesopian language, otherwise called slave language. Why this term has been adopted can be readily seen from its use by V. I. Lenin in the

Preface to the Russian edition of *Imperialism, the Highest Stage of Capitalism*. There Lenin states that he was originally forced "to formulate the few necessary observations on politics with extreme caution, by hints, in that Aesopian language—in that cursed Aesopian language—to which Czarism compelled all revolutionaries to have recourse, whenever they took up their pens to write a 'legal' work." A footnote to the English translation of this Preface explains that Aesopian is taken from the fable writer Aesop; we might add that subsequent Communist explanations have stated that Aesop, a slave, devised this allusive and roundabout style to deride his masters.

Lenin had also recommended "Aesopian language" in his celebrated pamphlet *What Is To Be Done?* In 1938, Stalin had explained its use by the Bolshevik paper, *Pravda*, during the period in Russia after 1912. In his *History of the Communist Party of the Soviet Union, Bolsheviks*, which is the fundamental book today for all Communists, Stalin wrote of *Pravda*: "A legally published newspaper could not call openly for the overthrow of Czardom. It had to resort to hints, which, however, the class conscious workers understood very well and which they explained to the masses. When, for example, *Pravda* wrote of the 'full and uncurtailed demands of the Year Five,' the workers understood that this meant the revolutionary slogans of the Bolsheviks, namely, the overthrow of Czardom, a democratic republic, the confiscation of the land estates, and an eight hour day."

Stalin proceeds to give other examples of the "hints" which fill *Pravda*, and adds: "In this way, the illegal revolutionary activities of the Bolsheviks were combined with legal forms of agitation and organization of the masses of the workers through *Pravda*." (*History of the Communist Party of the Soviet Union, Bolsheviks*, English translation, published by Foreign Languages Publishing House, Moscow, 1939, pp. 150, 151.)

Again in 1934, D. Z. Manuilsky, as General Secretary of the Communist International, commended "the language of Aesop" to the Italian Communists as a means "to observe the rules of conspiracy, to resort to maneuvers in order not to let yourself be seen through at once." Manuilsky criticized the Italian Reds, saying: "They have not mastered the secret of using that language of Aesop which, without diminishing its revolutionary class contact, may stir and capture the imagination of the workers." He specifically emphasized that this was the way to work into mass organizations which might repel open Communist slogans or propaganda. ("The Advance of the Revolutionary Crisis," report by D. Z. Manuilsky, as General Secretary of the Communist International to the Seventeenth Party Congress of the Communist Party of the Soviet Union, *International Press Correspondence*, Feb. 26, 1934, p. 310.)

The term "Aesopian language," and its use, are embedded in Communist history, practice, and phraseology. Current documents of the Communist Party become largely meaningless unless the historic definition of certain peculiar terms and the method of presenting them are understood.

Technical Phrases

There are various special phrases employed in Aesopian or protective methods of expression. The first of these is the technical phrase, known only to Communists or those mastering Communist methodology. Through one word or a series of words which has arisen from the Marxist-Leninist classics and Communist history, a code and at the same time an entire program can be presented.

Most prominent among these technical phrases is "Marxism-Leninism." These words appear in the very first sentence of the Constitution of the Communist Party adopted in July, 1945, at the time when the Party was reconstituted openly as such by orders of Moscow through Jacques Duclos, General Secretary of the French Communist Party. It dots every important document appearing in the Cominform's organ, in *Political Affairs*, and in other fundamental Red documents.

The exact wording of the Communist Constitution reads as follows:

"The Communist Party of the United States is the political party of the American working class, basing itself upon the principles of scientific socialism, Marxism-Leninism."

Now this term—appearing so frequently in Communist documents and in the Constitution of the Communist Party of the United States—must have some meaning. It must have a very important meaning. In the trial of the eleven Communist leaders at Foley Square in 1949, Judge Harold Medina put the matter just that way. The Court put the question to me: "What did you in connection with the other Communists that you were working with there understand that to mean?"

My reply, which is worth recording here, was as follows:

"This sentence, as is historically meant throughout the Communist movement, is that the Communist Party bases itself on so-called scientific Socialism, the theory and practice of so-called scientific Socialism as it appears in the writings of Marx, Engels, Lenin, and Stalin, therefore as interpreted by Lenin and Stalin who have specifically interpreted scientific Socialism to mean that Socialism can only be attained by the violent shattering of the capitalist state, and the setting up of the dictatorship of the proletariat by force and violence in place of that state. In the United States, this would mean that the Communist Party of the United States is basically committed to the overthrow of the government of the United States as set up by the constitution." (Record of the trial, United States of America vs. Eugene Dennis, et al, V, 3638.)

If we turn to the Marxist-Leninist classics, we note how this definition follows the specific statements of Lenin and Stalin. In the Introduction to his *Foundations of Leninism*, Stalin writes: "What, then, is Leninism in its last analysis?"

"Leninism is Marxism in the epoch of imperialism and of the proletarian revolution, or to be more exact, Leninism is the theory and tactics of the proletarian revolution in general, and the theory and tactics of the dictatorship of the proletariat in particular." (*Foundations of Leninism*, Joseph Stalin, Marxist Library, V, 8.)

Since the dictatorship of the proletariat is thus the heart of Leninist teachings (that is, of Marxism-Leninism), Stalin develops throughout this work the path to be followed to the achievement of that dictatorship. The center of his discussion is the emphasis that the dictatorship of the proletariat can come about only through the violent smashing of the governments of the bourgeois states. He cites, as did Lenin in *State and Revolution*, Karl Marx's letter to Kugelman of April 12, 1871, in which Marx declared that the proletarian revolution must not merely "transfer the military-bureaucratic apparatus from one hand to the other, as has been the case hitherto, but *smash* it. . . . This is a condition precedent to any really popular revolution on the continent."

Stalin notes "Marx's qualifying phrase about the continent," to point out that many "opportunists" have taken advantage of this phrase to say that it does not call for force and violence against the governments of England and the United States. In Marx's day, that qualification might have applied, Stalin adds, but today it is no longer applicable—and it is essential that there be a violent smashing of the State machine, that is, government, in both Britain and the United States.

As Lenin wrote in *State and Revolution* on this very subject, so Stalin reiterates:

"Today in 1917, in the epoch of the first great imperialist war, this exception made by Marx is no more valid. Both England and America, the greatest and last representatives of Anglo-Saxon 'liberty' in the sense of the absence of militarism and bureaucracy, have today plunged headlong into the European quagmire of mud and blood, into the bureaucratic-militaristic institutions to which everything is subordinated and which trample everything under foot. Today, both in England and America, the 'preliminary condition of any real people's revolution' is the breakup, the shattering of the 'available ready-made State machinery,' brought in those countries, between 1914 and 1917, to general 'European' imperialist perfection."

Law of Violent Revolution

After quoting these words of Lenin, Stalin adds: "In other words, the law of violent proletarian revolution, the law of destruction of the machinery of the bourgeois State, as a condition precedent of such revolution, is an inevitable law of the revolutionary movement in the imperialist countries of the world." To drive this point home with full force and effect, Stalin continues: "Lenin is therefore right in saying: 'The proletarian revolution is impossible without the violent destruction of the machinery of the bourgeois State and its replacement by new machinery.'" (*Foundations of Leninism,* Marxist Library, V, 51-53; *State and Revolution,* V. I. Lenin, Selected Works, International Publishers, VII, 37.)

From these authoritative declarations, the Communists are constantly aware that the central point of Marxism-Leninism, based on its whole world outlook, is this necessity of shattering by violence the non-Soviet governments under which they operate.

When the student of Communism runs across this term "Marxism-Leninism," he understands that this is a commitment to the conviction that the destruction by force and violence of non-Soviet governments is essential to world progress. When he reads that the American Communists base their views and activities on the principles of Marxism-Leninism, he knows that they are thereby dedicating themselves to the violent overthrow of the government of the United States.

The then General Secretary of the Communist International, D. Z. Manuilsky, could write in January of 1940:

"Marxism-Leninism—the teachings of Marx, Engels, and Lenin, developed and supplemented by Comrade Stalin—is the scientific world outlook of the international working class, the class that has won a historic victory on one-sixth of the globe, the class which, relying on this victory, is destined to overthrow capitalism and build a new, Communist society. Marxism-Leninism is the most revolutionary doctrine that has ever existed in the history of mankind."

To which Manuilsky adds: "Lenin's doctrine of the dictatorship of the proletariat is the backbone of the Lenin-Stalin theory of Socialist revolution. Stalin elaborated this doctrine jointly with Lenin." ("The Great Theoretician of Communism," *The Communist International Magazine*, January 1940, p. 25.)

Dictatorship of "The Vanguard"

This dictatorship of the proletariat has been defined by both Lenin and Stalin as "the fiercest, sharpest, and most merciless war of the new class against its more powerful enemy, the bourgeoisie." (Stalin, *Foundations of Leninism*, p. 47, quoting from Lenin's *"Left" Communism*.)

But this merciless war is to be waged not only against the bourgeoisie; the proletarians themselves must be changed by the dictatorship through force. For it is the duty of the dictatorship, in the name of the proletariat, "to re-educate, in a protracted struggle under the controlling auspices of the dictatorship of the proletariat, the proletarians themselves, for they will not be able to rid themselves of their own petty bourgeois prejudices at the first stroke as if by magic. . . ." (Stalin, *Foundations of Leninism*, p. 48, quoting from Lenin's *Collected Works*.)

"Marxism-Leninism" informs the Communist by these authoritative statements that not only must the dictatorship of the proletariat be brought into being by the violent overthrow of the respective non-Soviet governments. It is, in reality, when established, the dictatorship of the "vanguard," that is, of the Communist Party led by the Kremlin. It is, in a word, the dictatorship of Stalin and Malenkov. For the proletarians, in whose name the dictatorship is being carried out, are themselves to be subjected to force in order to compel their change in attitude and thinking.

These central concepts of Marxism-Leninism are what distinguishes it from the "Marxism" or "revisionism" or "reformism" of the Social Democrats. The Communist split with the Socialists, which was engineered by Lenin, was basically on these points—the necessity of violence both in setting up the dictatorship and in maintaining it. The Social Democratic view that Socialism could be ushered in by peaceful means was rejected as traitorous to the cause of Socialism by Lenin and the Communist International.

There is a number of other phrases peculiar to the Communists which can and should receive scrutiny.

Involved "Scientific" Argumentation

A second and universal application of Aesopian language lies in the involved and so-called scientific treatment of subjects in Communist writings. By this method, slogans and arguments which are to be used for popular consumption in one sense receive another and revolutionary content for the understanding of the Communists.

Through this device, the Communists can be stimulated to present these slogans and arguments in such a way as to deceive the people, in order to persuade non-Communist masses to go along with the Communist line.

An adroit illustration of this involved method of argumentation is presented in an article in the January 1952 issue of *Political Affairs*. Its title is "Lenin's Teaching and the Liberation of Humanity," and its author Alexander Bittelman, Soviet subject and chief theoretician of the Communist Party of the United States.

In that article, Bittelman takes up this very question of Marxism-Leninism, and strives to coin arguments which the Communists can use to persuade the American people that it is not the teaching of violent overthrow at all. Bittelman is pressed to take up this task, which is contrary to his former writings, because of the sharp manner in which the definition of Marxism-Leninism—precisely the planned overthrow by violence of the government of the United States—was brought out in the trials of the Communist leaders at Foley Square.

It will pay us to take some little time in examining this striking and peculiar document. Because he is writing for Communists, Bittelman must open up his argument by insuring that his readers will be loyal to whatever the Kremlin decrees. The fight for Socialism, for Communism is described as "the magnificent historic fight of our epoch . . . whose grandeur overshadows all the previous achievements of mankind." That assertion will place all that follows on the proper Lenin-Stalin basis. And so we note that "this historic fight, we are proud to say, is guided by the teachings of Lenin and his great continuer, Stalin. It is led by Parties of Marxism-Leninism, by Communist and Workers' Parties."

Having assured himself that the comrades will hold fast to Marxism-Leninism, the definition of which each one of them understands fully from study and discussion, Bittelman proceeds to denounce the prosecution of American Communists. "The ideologists and executioners of the growing police state in the United States," he writes, "declare Leninism a criminal conspiracy and put the advocates of Leninism in jail." They do this because the Communists are "determined vanguard fighters for peace, democracy, against Fascism, for the equal rights of the Negro people, and for the defense and protection of the people's living standards."

They carry out this jailing by confusing Communist revolutionary theory with "the police state caricature of Marxism-Leninism as a device for the violent overthrow of the government." It is not such a device, Bittelman intimates; it is not a blueprint for revolution, not a gadget for violence. It is a science, and "science is no blueprint or a frozen set of rules or dogmas." It is something which develops. And Bittelman emphasizes that Lenin developed this science beyond Marx and Engels, and Stalin beyond Lenin.

Aiming at Two Results

By this emphasis on Marxism-Leninism as a science, Bittelman of course aims at two results. First, he gives to the Communists a weapon of propaganda whereby they can cry out that their leaders are being persecuted because they are scientists. Shades of Galileo trials and other like incidents are raised up by that. The other objective in this argument is to convey vaguely the impression that this science is so capable of development that it may some day stand on the idea of a peaceful transition to Socialism. Bittelman never comes to that statement in a forthright way, for he dare not. That would be denying the central point in Marxism-Leninism. But he does seek to convey that impression by stating that "the Marxist-Leninist science means learning to use it in the solution of practical problems of the class struggle under varying and changing conditions."

Having given the Communists this argument about science, which they can use to befuddle the American mind, Bittelman then is compelled to stop short. If he goes further, as we know, and states flatly that there will be a development of Marxism-Leninism into plans for peaceful transition, he destroys Marxism-Leninism itself. Indeed, he sees that danger—and the danger of misleading his readers into "revisionism," that is, into the morass of peaceful and parliamentary action. This he avoids by stressing that the development of Marxism-Leninism must always be in accordance with its "substance."

What this substance of Marxism-Leninism is, which cannot be changed, he does not dare disclose directly. If he did so, he would have to turn to Lenin and Stalin and to their insistence that force and violence are essential. Accordingly, he goes at this indirectly, by showing ways in which the revisionists have sought to change the substance of Marxism-Leninism. Earl Browder is his choice of a revisionist example. Browder tried to revise Marxism-Leninism, Bittelman charges, in at least three fundamentals; a) in its theory of the class struggle, b) in its teachings on the nature of imperialism, and c) in its teachings on the leading role of the vanguard Party of the working class. But these teachings lead at once to the "backbone" of Leninist teachings, the dictatorship of the proletariat with the violence necessary to establish it. It is precisely the combination of the class struggle concept, the analysis of imperialism by Lenin, and the Lenin-Stalin stress on the vanguard Party, that leads to the violent dictatorship.

Double-Talk Instruction

To put the matter simply, what Bittelman does in this article is to instruct the Communists to spread the word that their science is capable of any sort of development, even peaceful, but at the same time he warns them against actually accepting this distortion of Marxism-Leninism themselves, telling them that if they do so they will be guilty of Browderism.

It is typical of Communist methods and phraseology that throughout the article, Bittelman denounces the United States as a "police state." At first blush, this would seem to be an arrogant and futile gesture, coming from an illegal alien who is a subject of the great slave empire of Soviet Russia. But Bittelman and the Communists count on American naivete. They know that *Political Affairs* is read by a comparatively small number of persons, practically all of whom are Communists. It is these Communists, generally concealed as something else, who will peddle this police state libel against our country throughout the nation. It will even appear in certain sections of the responsible press. It will be echoed by people who have no knowledge of Marxism-Leninism but who for personal or other reasons ape any slogan that has a "progressive" connotation.

In like manner, the Communists reiterate endlessly that they are opposed or "persecuted" because they are in the forefront of the battle for social reforms, whereas Stalin has clearly stated in *Foundations of Leninism* that such social reforms are merely "a screen behind which his [the Communist's] illegal activities for the revolutionary preparation of the masses for the overthrow of the bourgeoisie may be intensified." It is always incumbent, therefore, upon a Communist leader who presents in an article of directives this stress on social reforms, to couple it with emphatic references either to the "principles of Marxism-Leninism" or to the necessity of "eliminating capitalism."

A further device which will be encountered on many occasions is the Communist insistence that violent insurrection will not be resorted to until "the majority of the masses" is in sympathy with Red aims. But the decision as to whether "the majority" so agrees lies in the hands of the vanguard, which is armed with the theory of Marxism-Leninism and therefore knows when the situation is ripe for an armed uprising. And that leads again of course to the final decision having been in the hands of Stalin, "the teacher and father" of the Communists, "the leader and teacher and guide of the proletariat and oppressed of the whole world"—and now in the hands of Stalin's successor Malenkov. Such talk of consent by "the majority" is accordingly accompanied in Communist directives with devoted references to Stalin as "the continuer of Lenin," "the greatest scientist of our age," and the guide to all the Communist Parties everywhere. By that very formulation, the Stalinites have brought home to them their dependence upon the Kremlin's decrees as to when they shall act "legally" and when they shall proceed to "illegal" or violent deeds.

Illustrating also in a striking manner this peculiar method of argumentation is the article on "Patriotism" by N. Baltisky, which became well known during the trial of the eleven Communist leaders at Foley Square in 1949. This article of directives was published in the *New Times*, which is issued weekly by Moscow in all major languages to instruct the Communists in every country. Its importance was shown by the fact that it was reprinted in *Political Affairs* of 1945 for the special study of the American Communists.

The Baltisky directives came just as Stalin was unleashing World War III, in that phase which came to be known as the Cold War. Understanding full well that the Communists would be accused of being seditious in many countries, because of their championship of this Cold War policy, the article was designed to give the Communists propaganda ammunition.

Baltisky did this by beginning with the allegation that the Communists were charged in many countries with not being patriotic. At that time, this was pure fiction on Baltisky's part, since all the democratic nations, and specifically the United States, had greeted the Communists during World War II as part of the national unity forces. There was never less criticism of the Communists than at that period, since the huge pro-Soviet propaganda during the war had lulled American leaders and people to sleep. Baltisky made his assertion, however, because he knew that such criticism would soon be forthcoming, as Moscow advanced "the cold war." He asserted: "The patriotism of the advanced workers is called into question on the grounds of their solidarity with the Soviet Union. The disingenuous question, for instance, is asked, 'How can they be called patriots who do not deny that they are loyal friends of a foreign state?' "

Baltisky must bind the Communists everywhere to the Soviet Union, especially at the critical period of 1945. Their service to the Kremlin against their own native countries was vital to Stalinite policy. Therefore, he openly proclaims that they do assert their solidarity with the Soviet Union. And then, in that brand of argumentation with which we are dealing, he declares: " 'But isn't this solidarity in harmony with the noblest aspirations of true patriots in any country?' This is a solidarity and friendship with a Socialist state, a state which by its very nature is free from imperialist appetites, which respects and champions the principles of equality and self-determination of nations, and which is a reliable defender and staunch bulwark of general peace.

"The noble stature and role of the great Soviet state is now appreciated and acknowledged by broad sections of the public in the freedom loving countries. Only the most reactionary pro-Fascist circles continue to vilify the Soviet Union."

And so the argument has brought us around to Baltisky's conclusion, quite evident from these words, that the highest form of patriotism to one's own country is loyalty to Soviet Russia. Anyone who seeks to defend his country from Soviet aggression, under such a formula, is a "pro-Fascist."

The Uses of "Patriotism"

This article, with its tortuous reasoning, has become a foundation for much of the propaganda of the Communists and their friends during the past seven years. Had it been confined to the Communists alone, it would have been bad enough. For under the cover of declaring that devotion to Soviet Russia is the highest form of patriotism to the United States, the Communists could justify any seditious move including espionage and sabotage. But the effects of this argument went much further than the confines of the Communist Party. Concealed Communists and those associated with Communist fronts carried it out into the general community and the representative press. The identification of Communists with loyal Americans thus became the real basis for cries about violations of the Bill of Rights and civil liberties whenever moves were made to check the conspiracy. It also provided the concealed Communists or allies of the Communists with the brazenness to assert before Congressional Committees or other inquiries that they were patriots even when advancing pro-Communist causes. We have seen this method used on a large scale specifically before the McCarran Sub-Committee on Internal Security, in the inquiry into the Institute of Pacific Relations.

Men who had consistently advocated Soviet interests in the Far East to the detriment of American security could arrogantly state to the Sub-Committee that they were moved by patriotism. Experts, who were recommended for the guidance of the State Department and of public opinion, blithely admitted that they had made "mistakes" at every crucial point, when they were cornered with the results of their pro-Soviet advice. But these "mistakes" were the result of patriotism, and of that difference of opinion which is so important to free discussion. Their defense to the same effect was echoed in many sections of the press of this country, even though their consistent acts had led to the establishment of a Red China and hence to the thousands of useless casualties piled up in Korea. The American mind was confused, and largely remains confused.

The Baltisky article, therefore, was not just an exercise in mental gymnastics. In its continual reiteration by the Communists and their friends in various forms, it had a profound effect on the recent history of the United States and on the fate of thousands of Americans.

The contention that the Soviet Union is a Socialist state, has ended "the exploitation of man by man," and can do no wrong, runs through many Communist documents. It is based on an utterly false premise, on that perversion of evidence to fit Communist concepts which is characteristic of this form of argumentation. Exploitation has not ceased in Soviet Russia, it has increased. The careful studies of David Dallin, *The Real Soviet Russia* and *Forced Labor in Soviet Russia,* demonstrate this clearly. Additional proof exists in *Russia's Soviet Economy* by Harry A. Schwartz, and in many other accurate and scholarly studies. The extension of Soviet rule over the satellite states has been marked by the extension of slave labor and the labor passport system under which the worker cannot leave his job without the consent of government bureaucracy. Trade unions have been made organs of the state, devoted exclusively to getting out production and speed-up. (For conditions in the satellite countries see *The Annals of the Academy of Political and Social Science,* Sept. 1950; all issues of *News From Behind the Iron Curtain,* National Committee for a Free Europe, Inc., N. Y.)

But this false contention that Soviet Russia, because of its socialist nature, can do no wrong furnishes the Communist with the glibness of speech to contend that each Soviet measure is for the benefit of mankind. Soviet aggression, from these contentions, can easily be dressed up in the garb of peace.

For the Communist, this perversion of evidence is quite logical, since for him Soviet Russia is bringing about the world Soviet dictatorship from which will come the classless society, hope of the world. But what is amazing is that quite a few non-Communists, who do not accept the Communist premise, agree with the Red conclusions. They do this in whole or in part, arguing that there can be peace with the Soviet dictatorship on the basis of appeasement. We are reminded once more that these involved arguments do not remain the possession of the Communists alone, but in other forms are pushed by Stalin's followers out into the community.

We can never overcome this Soviet psychological warfare within our own country until alert leaders in every important community examine the Communist organs of directives critically and analytically, in order to recognize Communist-created propaganda. At least, these community leaders should be familiar with the sources for such information.

Definitions On Their Heads

A third method of Aesopian language is that of turning definitions on their heads. This is a widespread Communist custom and must be thoroughly understood if what the Communists are aiming at at any particular period is to be grasped.

This inverted content of words can be seen in the use of the term "democracy" to describe the Soviet dictatorship and the Soviet ruled satellites. In numerous Communist documents, including those of the Communist Party of the United States, the Stalinite regime is described as "the highest form of democracy." Hitler crudely acknowledged being a dictator, saying that he ruled by intuition. But the Kremlin will have none of that. Much more shrewdly it takes over the terms of the nations it means to conquer and uses them to describe its own purposes.

The widespread Red terror, the one-party system, the extensive secret police, the far-flung slave labor camps, are all "democracy" in Communist phraseology. The word becomes a convenient means to deceive the people as to Communist purposes. When in the general community the Communists advance the cry of democracy, thousands of people who are influenced by them understand that term in its genuine sense. The Communists on their part, while shouting it out with this intent of deceit, always have in mind the advancement of Soviet rule.

In like manner, the word "peace" becomes on Communist lips a cover for war—the "class war" of the everyday political struggle, the civil war which is to follow it, and the war between Soviet Russia and the United States which for the Communists is inevitable "in the period of imperialism."

A reminder of this turning of definitions on their heads is furnished weekly by the Cominform organ. Under the ironic title *For a Lasting Peace, For a People's Democracy*, it directs the Communists of every land toward aid to Soviet aggression and the advance of the world Soviet dictatorship.

Another term that is turned inside out is "liberation." Since celebrations of the "liberation" of all the satellite nations are staged each year by the International Communist apparatus, we can understand that this term in its actuality means enslavement.

The basis for turning the meaning of this word around is to be found in Baltisky's argument. The Soviet Union as a Socialist state cannot have imperialist designs on any other land. It cannot conquer another country; it can only "liberate" by taking control.

The Big Lie Technique

A fourth method of Aesopian language which follows from the others is the Big Lie. Hitler gave approval to this method, but Marxism-Leninism perfected it. Here, as elsewhere, we observe the close connection in ideology and methodology between Nazism and Communism.

The Big Lie technique is particularly marked in the common

Communist device of accusing opponents or prospective victims of the crimes which the proletarian dictatorship itself commits. Nowhere is this better illustrated than in the Communist accusations against the United States.

A gem in this respect is the article of directives by William Z. Foster in *Political Affairs* of August, 1948, entitled "Specific Features of American Imperialist Expansion." Among other things, it charges that "the United States has built up by far the biggest empire in the history of the world," and that "the combined war conquest of Hitler, Mussolini, and Hirohito did not equal those of Wall Street." In the period to which Foster is referring, Soviet Russia brought 800,000,000 people under its heel. This does not prevent the Communist leader from developing his contention further. "Never before," he adds, "has there been such a wide and rapid imperialist expansion as that of the United States during the last five years."

As a second big point, Foster refers to "American imperialism's boundless objectives." He writes: "German Fascist imperialism did not possess the same seeming advantages for pressing its drive for world domination as does the United States. . . . The central objective of American imperialism is to be the supreme world master, and in order to accomplish this end, it is preparing to deluge the world in the blood of another great war." By turning reality topsy-turvy in this fashion, the world-wide aggression of Soviet Russia, and its set determination to achieve the world Soviet dictatorship, is shunted aside.

Indeed Soviet Russia must be presented, according to the same technique, as "the major fortress of world democracy," and "the biggest obstacle" in the path of America's drive for world domination.

All of these contentions, in which events are turned around, are leading up to Foster's conclusion: that a complete defeat would be inflicted upon the United States in any war with Soviet Russia. The spectre of Soviet "democratic," economic, and military might is conjured up for the use of Communists, to frighten the American people. Needless to say, if such a viewpoint were adopted widely, it would prevent the United States from halting Soviet aggression. And it is significant that this argument did spread out into the American press and into high circles in Washington. It was used as an excuse for not carrying the Korean War forward to victory.

What is significant also is that Foster's article, dated August, 1948, was an echo and elaboration of a previous article written for the Communists of the world by Georgi M. Malenkov, and distributed through the Cominform's organ of December 1, 1947. Malenkov expanded on the idea that the United States had "adopted a new, openly expansionist policy aimed at establishing world supremacy." He dubbed the conquest of the satellite nations as "liberation" and their new dictatorship as "the new democracies." Malenkov stressed the "wise Stalin foreign policy of the Soviet Union" which utilizes the "contradictions existing within the imperialist camp." Over against that policy, he charged that the United States was imitating the Hitlerites, and called upon the Communists of the world to define their attitude to these plans of American imperialism.

Foster's contribution was a response to this demand by Malenkov. It is a very good example of how the Moscow directives, first contained in the Cominform organ, are reiterated and developed by *Political Affairs* for the leading American Communists, and then go out from the Communist organs to the general field of American public opinion.

Changes of the Line

Another exercise in phraseology should be noted. With any change in the line dictated by Moscow, there is a twisting of phrases and arguments, to accord with the change.

As the cold war began to develop, the American Communists referred frequently to "the Roosevelt peace policy" which they interpreted to cover Teheran, Yalta, Potsdam, and other agreements favorable to Soviet Russia. As the war with the West became more pronounced, this phrase was put into the background, and "the wise Stalin peace policy," which had always been stressed, was now used exclusively. During World War II, likewise, the United States was included by Communist propagandists among the "democratic, peace-loving nations," since American lend-lease was so essential to Soviet Russia. But the same United States has now become "Fascist," and in some respects more menacing than Hitler, and has been repeatedly attacked as the center of "imperialist aggression."

Within the Communist camp, certain peculiar expressions grow up out of specific events. Since they are repeated through Communist literature, their origin and definition have to be known as a key to that literature. We can take the term "Browderism" as a good case in point. Up to 1945, Earl Browder was hailed in all Communist documents as "the leading Marxist-Leninist in the Western Hemisphere," and in other extravagant terms of praise. But after 1945, when he was demoted as leader of the American Communists, the term "Browderism" became one of contempt. It stood for "revisionism," which in Communist parlance is "opportunism from the right"—as Trotskyism is "opportunism from the left."

It is this "opportunism," however expressed, which blurs the revolutionary objective of Marxism-Leninism, which tends to obscure the necessity of overthrowing the non-Soviet governments by force and violence. It is therefore the mark of a traitor to Soviet Communism.

Browder's designation as a "revisionist" gives us a new insight into the calculating, unscrupulous methods which Communism develops. For many years, the fallen Red chief had been a complete tool of Moscow, both in the Soviet secret police and as Moscow's representative here. He was always willing to do what the Kremlin decreed. But in 1945, it was necessary to have a scapegoat for the new line of waging war on the United States, and Browder was chosen. He was accused of supporting those very policies which Joseph Stalin had agreed to at Teheran, and which Maurice Thorez of France and other leading Communists had endorsed. That was the line of "generations of peace among the United States, Soviet Union, and Great Britain."

The demotion of Browder from leadership in the Communist Party of the United States for "revisionism" electrified the whole Communist world. His expulsion from the Party let Communists everywhere know in a drastic fashion that the old slogan of "generations of peace"—helpful enough in getting lend-lease and the second front—were now supplanted by war objectives. Proof is the fact that Browder, though expelled from the American Communist Party, was named as a representative of the Soviet Book Trusts here, after conferences with Stalin and Molotov in Moscow.

But the term "Browderism" continued, together with "Kautskyism," the phrase of contempt which Lenin coined to describe the teachings of the Social Democratic leader, Karl Kautsky, accused of relying too much on peaceful and parliamentary methods in the proposed transition to Socialism.

It may be added that "revisionism" arose originally from the effort of Eduard Bernstein, a German Socialist, to revise Marxism. Today the term is applied to any view that might lead Communists to forget their objective, the violent overthrow of non-Soviet governments. (*Marxism and Revisionism, Selections,* Lenin and Stalin, International Publishers, 1946.)

Since the Communists make a great to-do of the reforms which they support, their use of the term "reformism" is of considerable importance. This is the activity of those who actually believe in reforms as a means of remedying certain social evils, and is condemned by Lenin, Stalin, and Communists in general. Reforms, from the Communist viewpoint, are to be used solely to advance revolutionary purposes. If they do not do so, they are to be avoided. "Reformism," as an expression of contempt, is to be distinguished from "revisionism," in that the latter arises largely within the Communist movement from those "renegades" seeking to block its revolutionary aims. "Reformism," on the other hand, arises largely from without the

Communist organization, among Social Democrats, trade unions, and the like.

It must not be thought that these peculiar terms remain within the pages of Marxist-Leninist books or documents. They may not go out into the non-Communist community in their Communist form. But the discussions in which they are used, and which can be understood only if we know their definition, do move the Communist to act, and these acts have definite repercussions far beyond the Communist movement.

It is not suggested here that every active person who is opposing Communism should master the Red phraseology in order to pore over Communist documents. As desirable as that would be, it is often not possible. What is essential is that the active opponent of Communism know the sources of information concerning any current line or any current field of possible infiltration. An ability to read and interpret these documents will give him the equipment to participate actively in community life, to address meetings in which current tactics of Communists are analyzed, and so to make a contribution to his community and country.

CHAPTER IV

COMMUNIST OBJECTIVES: A SUMMARY

THERE IS no better way to grasp Communist concepts than to become familiar with Stalinite documents and the Marxist-Leninist classics, with the view to employing them in a critical manner. There is also nothing which confounds the Communists more than to cite the works of their "scientists" and theoreticians in proof of the nature of Communism and its aims.

In this summary, a selected few quotations from such documents are given, with the most noteworthy phrases underscored for examination and study. It is recommended that these quotations be committed to memory for an easy acquaintance with the peculiar Red idiom.

The Communist Party member acquires a "mastery" of these statements and an understanding of their full meaning by constant reiteration, accompanied by criticism and self-criticism. To the non-Communist such a procedure is impossible. The method adopted here will prove an effective substitute.

The "Program"

The first document to be examined is *The Program of the Communist International*, adopted in 1928 at the Sixth World Congress of that body and reaffirmed at the Seventh World Congress in 1935. While the entire document, a fundamental one, states and re-states the world outlook and objectives of the

Marxist-Leninists as they have been presented here, our examination will be confined largely to one vital paragraph from the introduction. This paragraph summarizes the philosophy and goals of the Communists throughout the world:

"Advocating and propagating the *dialectical Materialism* of Marx and Engels and employing it as the *revolutionary method of conceiving reality,* with the view to the *revolutionary transformation of this reality,* the Communist International wages an active struggle against *all forms of bourgeois philosophy* and against all forms of theoretical and practical *opportunism.* Standing on the ground of consistent *proletarian class struggle* and *subordinating* the temporary, partial, group and national interests of the proletariat to its *lasting, general, international interests,* the Communist International mercilessly exposes all forms of the *doctrine of 'class peace'* that the *reformists* have accepted from the bourgeoisie. Expressing the historical need for an international organization of revolutionary proletarians —*the grave-diggers of the capitalist order*—the Communist International is the only *international force* that has for its program the *dictatorship of the proletariat* and *Communism,* and that openly comes out as the organizer of the *International Proletarian Revolution.*"

(This fundamental document has been published in English translation by the Communist Party of the United States through the Workers Library Publishers and also is recorded in the volume of *International Press Correspondence (Inprecor)* covering the proceedings of the Sixth World Congress. For non-Communists, it has been made available in a collection of Communist documents edited by the noted anti-Communist William Henry Chamberlin, under the title *Blueprint for World Conquest,* published by Henry Regnery Company, Chicago.)

We shall now analyze the phrases in the quotation which we have italicized. Within a comparatively brief paragraph, there are succinctly stated the essentials of the Marxist-Leninist philosophy and its objectives for nature, society, and mankind. "The dialectical materialism of Marx and Engels" is the beginning and the base. From it all other Communist thought and action proceed. In this paragraph it is therefore mentioned first, and in like manner it saturates the Marxist-Leninist classics. Thus, Lenin in 1922 wrote strongly on behalf of "militant materialism." He declared that the Bolsheviks must be committed to "militant atheism," expressed through "untiring atheist propaganda and an untiring atheistic fight." Earlier he had re-quoted Marx in declaring: "Religion is the opium of the people. Religion is a kind of spiritual gin in which the slaves of capital drown their human shape and their claims to any decent human life." He had proceeded further: "Marxism is materialism. As such, it is as relentlessly hostile to religion as was the materialism of the encyclopedists of the eighteenth century or the materialism of Feuerbach. This is beyond doubt. But the dialectical materialism of Marx and Engels goes further than the encyclopedists and Feuerbach by applying the materialist philosophy to the field of history, to the field of the social sciences."

(These quotations can be found in vol. XI, *Selected Works of V. I. Lenin,* issued by the Marx-Engels-Lenin Institute, Moscow, and published in the United States by the Communist Party through International Publishers.)

This dialectical materialism is employed "as a revolutionary method of conceiving reality," under which all reality is declared to be matter—not only nature and society but mental operations and those things which men call spiritual. Within that matter, this alleged reality, violence is "the inexorable law" of progress.

This violence in society, the advancement of the class war, can be carried forward only by Lenin's "professional revolutionaries," the chosen few who constitute that select group known as the Communist Party. This "revolutionary conception of reality," therefore, makes of the Communists (by the very basic laws of the world in which we live) a ruling clique, pre-ordained to lead, guide, and dominate the masses. As Eugene Lyons writes in *Assignment in Utopia:* "Dialectical materialism, whatever else it may be, is the smuggest and most convenient philosophy ever adapted by a ruling caste to its political needs. It finds a bogus consistency in the most startling inconsistencies. There is something monstrous in a dialectical materialism which exploits in order to end exploitation, which flouts elementary human values in the name of humanity, which fortifies new classes to achieve a classless society; which, in brief, presumes to be as heartless as history, instead of opposing its dreams and its hopes to history's heartlessness."

Dictatorship of the Party

The glaring inconsistencies to which Lyons refers will be shown in these pages. They appear in every area of Red activity. Prominent among them is the mental gymnastics which Stalin performs in his noted work, *Problems of Leninism.* There, in order to keep up the fiction that the proletarians have some voice in the dictatorship of the proletariat, Stalin strives to show that the dictatorship of the proletariat is not the dictatorship of the Party. But he actually comes up with the opposite. The "teacher and father" of the Communists agrees with Lenin that the dictatorship of the proletariat is the dictatorship of the Party *in essence.* But he declares that this does not mean that it is *wholly* so. The "essence" is, however, that the Communist Party gives all the directives in the dictatorship of the proletariat, and the "not wholly" part consists in the proletarians following out the directives of the Party!

This form of argument may have some "bogus consistency" for a member of the "vanguard," drilled in the concept that the "vanguard" is the sole agency that can think and act for the masses and that the masses have no hope or existence as such without this direction. To a proletarian or a peasant sent to a slave labor camp in the name of his own dictatorship in Soviet Russia, or to a Bulgarian working man who is told by the Stalinite organ there that the trade unions cannot present the grievances of the workers because they cannot have grievances against their own dictatorship, there is the sour and tragic note of complete inconsistency.

Our consideration is to recognize that these developments, in direct opposition to Marxist-Leninist promises, are the logical outcome of "the revolutionary method of conceiving reality," which creates these cruel fictions in the name of the inevitable laws of nature and society.

The next italicized phrase, "revolutionary transformation of this reality," gets us farther along the road toward reaching the core of Communism. Since "this reality" (matter) comprises the entire world in which we live, including nature, society, and the mind of man, this phrase is a pledge to transform all of these in a revolutionary way. The phrase gives an insight into the fanatical notion which obsesses the Communists, that a perfect world will be established through the classless society. While no blueprint has been presented of this society, the Marxist-Leninist classics are so permeated with it that we cannot fail to know that it is supposed to conquer every weakness in nature as well as in society. The *Program of the Communist International* itself, in its third section, not only predicts that mankind, "freed from the fetters of the capitalist system," will pass from socialism to complete Communism, with world Communism as the ultimate result. It also declares that in this process, mankind will "subjugate the forces of nature" as it "re-educates itself in the spirit of Communism."

Not only will nature be conquered by the classless society, or Communism, so that mankind will have no more troubles from that source, but Lenin tells us it is only there that "it becomes possible to speak of freedom." "Only in Communist society," he writes, will "a really full democracy, a democracy without any exceptions" be possible. "And only then will democracy itself begin to wither away due to the simple fact that, freed from capitalist slavery, from the untold horrors, savagery, absurdities, and infamies of capitalist exploitation, people will gradually become accustomed to the observance of the elementary rules of social life that have been known for centuries and repeated for thousands of years in all school books; they will become accustomed to observing them without force, without compulsion, without subordination, without the special apparatus for compulsion which is called the state." (*State and Revolution*, V. I. Lenin, Marxist Library, International Publishers, p. 73.)

For the Communist, then, true "freedom" can never be realized until the coming of Communism, which follows the establishment, maintenance, and consolidation of the dictatorship of the proletariat, or socialism. It will be readily understood why the Communist is so contemptuous of "reforms," and of the masses who would be the beneficiaries of such "reforms." Those human beings composing the masses are merely the expendables to be manipulated for the winning of the perfected world.

There follows, in due course, the struggle "against all forms of bourgeois philosophy," and specifically against any recognition of the existence of God. It is true that the Marxist-Leninists have proved very coy in refusing to come to grips with the philosophy of St. Thomas Aquinas, but that is largely due to the fact that Aquinian philosophy would put their carefully preconceived world outlook to rout. Aquinas starts from the material world around us, but from that very world proves the existence of a Creator. The Marxist-Leninists prefer to carry on their battle with the extreme "idealists," those who predicate their philosophy upon the premise that the material world is a creation or reflection of our mind, or an idea. While the Communist "scientists" avoid Aquinas, their purpose in carrying on the battle against the philosophies they combat is to assert the triumph of materialism.

The Struggle Against "Opportunism"

The struggle against "opportunism" is emphasized here for two purposes. First, note can be taken of how frequently this term is found in Marxist-Leninist documents and directives. By marking this down in our memory, we become alert to the specific phraseology to which the Communists are constantly resorting. We can drill ourselves in the meaning of these various phrases so that their intent will be obvious to us whenever we meet them. Again, it can be seen here that the Communist leadership deems it essential to emphasize that all views coming from the non-Communist world must be rejected and expelled from the Communist mind, in order not to blur his world outlook or his consciousness of Red objectives. Dedication to the "proletarian class struggle" naturally follows, since Marxism-Leninism makes it essential to the winning of Socialism as a transition to Communism. As early as the Communist Manifesto—to be exact, in November, 1847—Marx and Engels pointed to the "more or less veiled civil war, raging within existing society," which will be concluded with "the violent overthrow of the bourgeoisie," thus laying the foundation "for the sway of the proletariat." In that Manifesto, Marx and Engels go further and declare that the proletariat will use its political supremacy, after the violent revolution, "to centralize all instruments of production in the hands of the State, i.e., *of the proletariat organized as a ruling class.*"

The italics are mine but they are also Lenin's, and in *State and Revolution* he proceeds to use these words as the basis of his assertion that the sole road to socialism leads through the dictatorship of the proletariat to be established by the "violent shattering" of the bourgeois governments. This is the heart of Marxism-Leninism. It is the overall reason for existence of the Communist Parties in every country in the world.

Needless to say, this "dictatorship of the proletariat" is in actuality "the dictatorship of the vanguard" which directs the proletariat. And that, in turn, is the dictatorship of the supreme leader of the vanguard at any time—first, Lenin, then Stalin, and now Malenkov.

In order to preserve the fiction that the Soviet dictatorship is that of the proletariat, Stalin sought in his *Problems of Leninism* to prove that the "dictatorship of the proletariat is not the dictatorship of the Party." But in actuality, of course, he proved the very opposite, as he had to do in order to preserve that authority within the regime which is the very foundation of Soviet rule. Stalin resorted to some very fine hair-splitting. The dictatorship of the proletariat, he tells us, is the dictatorship of the Party *in essence* but *not wholly*. In what way is it "the dictatorship of the Party" in essence? In the sense, as Stalin said, that "not a single important political or organizational question is decided by our Soviet and other mass organizations without directions from the Party." It is the Party, then, that is the Kremlin, that gives all the directives.

In what way, then, is the dictatorship of the proletariat "not wholly" the dictatorship of the Party? In the sense that the other elements in Soviet life, including the mass organizations and the proletariat itself, carry out the directions of the Party! Stalin explained it neatly as follows: "The dictatorship of the proletariat consists of the directions given by the Party plus the carrying out of these directions by the mass organizations of the proletariat, plus their fulfillment by the general population." There could scarcely be a clearer statement showing that the Soviet dictatorship is over the proletariat. They are merely to carry out what the vanguard through its leaders orders them to do. (J. V. Stalin, *The Problems of Leninism*, in *Leninism*, Cooperative Publishing Society of Foreign Workers in the USSR, Moscow-Leningrad, 1934, pp. 278-80.)

From these basic concepts, there naturally flow the other points emphasized by this enlightening paragraph of the *Program of the Communist International*. It is no surprise to learn that the Communists "subordinate the temporary, partial, group and national interests of the proletariat to its lasting, general, international interests." That fact has been well explored in the preceding analysis. It is re-emphasized here in order to point out that it will be found to color and condition Communist activities and tactics in every field of infiltration—whether it be the labor movement, the organizations of the Negro people, education, government, or what not. The "general, international interests" of the proletariat are represented by "proletarian internationalism" which, we have seen, is naturally linked up with adherence to "the Land of Socialism," the Soviet Union, and to the winning of world wide Communism or the classless society. To that goal the Communists are fundamentally committed; they will sacrifice the interests of any group (and as a matter of fact the interests of all groups and people) in the vain effort to reach it.

It is symbolic of this distinction between the ruling caste, the vanguard or the Communist Party, and the workers and other groups they use, that Frederick Vanderbilt Field and other offspring of the rich are members of the "vanguard of the proletariat." In like manner, men so divorced from the mass of the people as Alger Hiss are in this vanguard. Lenin himself sprang from a family in a privileged position for several generations, his father being a prominent government official. The nearest in origin to the proletariat of all the Soviet leaders was Stalin, the son of a cobbler, although he was a student for the priesthood. But the rise of Stalin to power as the dictator of the proletariat is no more unusual than the rise of Hitler the paper-hanger, or of a number of presidents of the United States of humble origin.

The Communists must not only expound and advance their own aims at class war as a prelude to the classless society, but must "mercilessly expose" the doctrines of "class peace." This requires constant warfare against "the reformists," those who, we have seen, would bring benefits to certain groups among "the masses."

The phrase "the gravediggers of the capitalist order" is taken from the Communist Manifesto, and thus harks back to the Marx-Engels origin of the Communist International program itself. These "gravediggers," it is to be noted, are "the revolutionary proletarians," that is, the Communist Party leading an armed insurrection or coup d'état during a period of confusion and Soviet conquest. We have ample evidence now that the mass of the actual proletarians have their own graves dug for them by the Stalinite dictatorship. (See *The Real Soviet Russia*, David J. Dallin, 1947; *Forced Labor in Soviet Russia*, David J. Dallin and Boris I. Nicolaevsky, 1947; also chap. xiii in *Russia's Soviet Economy*, Harry Schwartz, 1950.)

World Communism

The succinct and summary paragraph which we have analyzed properly concludes with the dedication to the dictatorship of the proletariat (socialism) and Communism (the classless society). These developments are to be world-wide, and to attain them there must be "the International Proletarian Revolution." This determination at world conquest is reinforced by section III of the *Program of the Communist International*, which is devoted to an explanation of the fact that "the ultimate aim of the Communist International is World Communism."

It is this Messianic promise that causes Georgi M. Malenkov, new world leader of the Communists, to entitle his report to the Nineteenth Congress of the Communist Party of the Soviet Union (October, 1952), *On the Threshold of Communism*. This report, in pamphlet form, has been distributed by the tens of thousands through Communist channels in the United States. Although a careful reading of Malenkov's words will show that he promises only a gradual transition from Socialism to Communism, he does conclude with these words: "Under the banner of the immortal Lenin, under the wise leadership of the great Stalin, forward to the victory of Communism!" This is the view of the coming paradise that must be held up before Stalinites everywhere, to drive them forward in their subversive moves for a world Soviet dictatorship followed by world Communism. Every move by the United States in the international scene which is based on appeasement, containment, or accommodation of such a force and foe, is therefore futile. Every move within this country against the Soviet fifth column which is not firm as well as intelligently aware of this Red determination to conquer all, will likewise turn out to be worse than useless.

In order to study the *Program of the Communist International* in its proper setting, it is necessary to know that the same Sixth World Congress which adopted it also produced other vital resolutions and theses. Among these were calls to the Communists in non-Soviet countries to undermine their own governments in case of war with Soviet Russia, a program for conquering China and India as the necessary prelude to world conquest, and a resolution based on the designation of the United States ("the Dollar Republic") as the chief leader in the camp opposed to the Soviet dictatorship. The fruits of these resolutions and theses are now being reaped by the Kremlin in its World War III against the United States and the free world.

Milestones

The next document which deserves consideration gives us an echo of Moscow's purposes and leadership as registered within the Communist Party of the United States. It is *Milestones in the History of the Communist Party*, by Alexander Bittelman, and was published in 1937 by Workers Library Publishers, now known as New Century Publishers.

The summary paragraph which brings to a head the devotion of the Communist Party of the United States to the leadership of the Moscow Politburo runs as follows:

"The proletarian vanguard of the United States can justly take pride in the fact that it participated actively in the building of the Communist International, whose fifteenth anniversary falls in March of this year. At the same time, the revolutionary vanguard of this country can derive deep satisfaction from the fact that it unfailingly received brotherly advice and guidance from the Communist International in the struggle for the revolutionization of the American working class. It was from the outset, and continues to be so, a *mutual collaboration* of the revolutionary proletariat of all countries, organized in a world Party, for the victory of the dictatorship of the proletariat, for the establishment of a World Soviet Republic. The leading role of the Communist Party of the Soviet Union in the Comintern needs neither explanation nor apology. A Party that has opened up the epoch of the world revolution, and that is successfully building a classless society on one-sixth of the earth, is cheerfully recognized and followed as the leading Party of the world Communist movement. And by the same token, the leaders of that Party—first Lenin and now Stalin—are proudly followed as the leaders of the proletariat and of all oppressed in every country of the world." (Italics in original.)

This quotation speaks so clearly for itself that its analysis can largely be left to the initiative of the reader. It must be pointed out that the term "proletarian vanguard" is a sample of that reiteration to which the Communists resort and which induces a sort of intellectual hypnosis among the comrades, a willingness to parrot these phrases and accept them unthinkingly. The term also keeps alive that concept of a ruling caste of a chosen few who possess the secret of Marxism-Leninism and are therefore destined to be the leaders. The dependence on the Communist International is also acknowledged, and we note that this is in reality dependence upon the Communist Party of the Soviet Union, which is ruled by the Moscow Politburo.

U.S. Communists' Aim

The aim of the Communists in the United States, thus led by Moscow, is frankly stated to be the establishment of the World Soviet Republic, that is, a world Soviet dictatorship. And the determining factor in all Communist thoughts and actions, the director and dictator of the Communists throughout the world, is proudly proclaimed to be Stalin, the continuer of Lenin. Today that same obedience is due to the leadership of the man upon whom Stalin's mantle has fallen, G. M. Malenkov.

Confronted with documents of this character, Communists make a practice of complaining that these works are a number of years old and were written in a period different from the present. With their usual arrogance bred of their position as "the vanguard," they will fail to add that such documents have never been repudiated. From the record, it can be said that they have been repeated and reaffirmed right up to the present hour. They must be reaffirmed because they flow from the very heart and substance of Marxism-Leninism.

In *Political Affairs* for January, 1952, for instance, there appears another contribution from the pen of Alexander Bittelman. It is entitled "Lenin's Teachings and the Liberation of Humanity." Toward the very beginning of that directive article, Bittelman writes: "Lenin's teachings inspire the actions of the vanguard fighters for peace and democracy. . . . And the magnificent historic fight of our epoch—the fight for Socialism, for Communism—whose grandeur overshadows all of the great previous achievements of mankind, crowning them with the realization of the noblest aspirations and dreams of the human race—this historic fight, we are proud to say, is guided by the teachings of Lenin and of his great continuer Stalin. It is led by parties of Marxism-Leninism, by Communist and Workers Parties."

It takes no great effort to realize how much in tune this statement of 1952 is with what Bittelman wrote in 1937. It contains the same emphasis on the vanguard and on the direction of the Communist Parties of the world by Stalin (now Malenkov) that appears in the 1937 *Milestones*.

Again, in *Political Affairs* for January, 1953, there is published a reprint from the Cominform's organ, entitled "Leninism—Militant Banner of Working People of the World." There the world aims of the Soviet dictatorship are explained by a quotation from Stalin: "Lenin was the leader not only of the Russian proletariat, not only of the European workers, not only of the colonial East, but of all the working people of the globe." This is reinforced by a declaration in the article itself: "Growth of the world Communist movement has become the law of modern development. In the growth of the Communist and Workers' Parties and of their influence among the broad masses of working people, there is widely manifested the all-victorious forces of the ideas of Leninism."

The dedication to the dictatorship of the proletariat through the violent overthrow of all non-Soviet governments is reaffirmed by quoting Stalin's definition of Leninism in the introduction to the *Foundations of Leninism,* which we have used in explaining the term "Marxism-Leninism." At the same time, the dependence on the Communist Party of the Soviet Union as the leader of all other Communist Parties is set forth again as follows: "The great Lenin-Stalin Party is an inexhaustible source of militant experience, a model of revolutionary action for the Communist and Workers' Parties. From its example, Communists in all countries learn how to master revolutionary theory and how to apply it creatively in practice. . . ."

These pages could be flooded with similar quotations from current Communist publications and documents, but these samples will suffice. They bring home to us that Marxism-Leninism, with dictation from Moscow, is unchangeable and unchanging in its substance. And that means that it is consistently dedicated to the violent overthrow of all bourgeois governments and the enslavement of mankind through a world dictatorship.

Analysis by Pius XI

Those who have carefully studied Communism analytically and critically support our analysis of the purposes, program, and practices of the "movement" led by the Lenin-Stalin Party. Notable among critical statements is that of Pope Pius XI in his Encyclical on Atheistic Communism, issued in March, 1937. Even then, the Pope warned of "the peril" which "only grows greater from day to day because of the pressure exerted by clever agitators." He did not hesitate to characterize Soviet Communism as a "Satanic scourge." Going to the heart of the matter, the Encyclical declares: "The Communism of today, more emphatically than similar movements in the past, conceals in itself a false Messianic idea." That is precisely the conclusion we have reached by examining what the Communists state officially for themselves. This Messianic idea is the classless society, but the reality that confronts us is a Frankenstein marching across the globe, with murder and enslavement in its wake.

The world outlook of Communism and what it entails is thus summed up in the Encyclical:

"The doctrine of modern Communism, which is often concealed under the most seductive trappings, is in substance based on the principles of *dialectical and historical materialism previously advocated by Marx, of which the theoreticians of Bolshevism claim to possess the only genuine interpretation.* According to this doctrine, there is in the world only one reality, matter, the blind forces of which evolve into plant, animal, and man. Even human society is nothing but a phenomenon and form of matter, evolving in the same way. By a law of inexorable necessity and through a perpetual conflict of forces, matter moves toward the final synthesis of a classless society. In such a doctrine, it is evident, there is no room for the idea of God; there is no difference between matter and spirit, between soul and body; there is neither survival of the soul after death nor any hope in a future life. Insisting on the dialectical aspect of their materialism, the Communists claim that the conflict which carries the world toward its final synthesis can be accelerated by man. Hence, they endeavor to sharpen the antagonisms which arise between the various classes of society. Thus the class struggle, with its consequent violent hate and destruction, takes on the aspect of a crusade for the progress of humanity. On the other hand, all other forces whatever, as long as they resist such systematic violence, must be annihilated as hostile to the human race."

With this statement, Pius XI puts his finger on the basic Communist premise, its world outlook, dialectical materialism. He shows that it leads to the theory of the class struggle as a prelude to the classless society. It is of the utmost importance that this fundamental world outlook of Communism be thoroughly grasped. So many people (including leaders of opinion) have no acquaintance with it. This lack of knowledge or understanding of what Communism is causes much of our inability to handle it both locally and in the international scene. It is this lack of understanding which is basically the cause of so many defeats of the United States and the West at the hands of the Kremlin and its fifth columns.

As to the earthly paradise, to be obtained through extreme dictatorship, Pius XI gives us this vivid picture:

"When all men have finally acquired the collectivist mentality in this Utopia of a really classless society, the political state, which is now conceived by Communists merely as the instrument by which the proletariat is oppressed by the capitalists, will have lost all reason for its existence, and will 'wither away.' However, until that happy consummation is realized, the state and the powers of the state furnish Communism with the most efficacious and most extensive means for the achievement of its goal."

The Pope proceeds to ask and answer the major question of our times: "How is it possible that such a system, long since rejected scientifically and now proved erroneous by experience, *how is it, We ask, that such a system could spread so rapidly in all parts of the world? The explanation lies in the fact that too few have been able to grasp the nature of Communism.*"

There is indeed the crux of the matter, presented to us sixteen years ago. Had "the nature of Communism" been better understood, there would have been fewer efforts to appease, contain, or accommodate it. Its very nature makes impossible any other attitude on the part of the Communists than that of driving forward to world control in order to obtain their final goal of world Communism. Whether in military conflict or negotiation, whether in the court room or the political arena, each act of theirs must be to defeat their enemies—by force if possible, by deceit or cajolery if necessary.

The Pope also warns of the Communist line when he declares that "the Communist takes advantage of the present world-

wide economic crisis to draw into the sphere of his influence
even those sections of the populace which on principle reject
all forms of materialism and terrorism."

This consideration of outstanding documents, from Communist and non-Communist sources, reinforces what has been
learned up to this point in regard to Communism in itself. The
Stalinite leadership keeps these concepts ever alive by constantly referring to them. In his recent report to the Nineteenth Congress of the Communist Party of the Soviet Union,
G. M. Malenkov stresses "the Marxist-Leninist consciousness of
our cadres," and emphasizes the urgency of strengthening the
ideological work of the Party. He declares that this must be
done on the basis of "the unshakable foundation" of Marxism-
Leninism. And he concludes: "In our epoch, the great teachings
of Marx, Engels, Lenin, and Stalin light for all mankind the
path of development of world civilization. Our Party is strong
because in all its activities it is guided by the theory of Marxism-Leninism."

Thus, the Communists have driven home to them, day in day
out, their materialistic philosophy, their role as the vanguard,
and the goal which they must reach. In order that they will be
sure to do this, the New Century Publishers recommend that
Malenkov's report be read in conjunction with a re-study of
the *History of the Communist Party of the Soviet Union*, which
of course outlines in detail the world outlook of the Communists
and their "inevitable" achievement of the Soviet dictatorship,
followed by the classless society.

Everywhere we turn in Communist literature and directives,
we will find these considerations repeated, underscored, and
pointed up until they completely envelop the thinking and actions of the Stalinites, making them dynamically subservient to
the Kremlin.

PART TWO

Communist Methods

CHAPTER V

STRATEGY AND TACTICS

ANYONE familiar with Communist objectives, whether in a local community or in the international arena, will be aware of the application of military methods to day-to-day maneuvers. It arises from their dedication to "class war," whether it be a small local engagement or a huge clash between the Soviet Union and the capitalist nations.

As early as 1928, the *Program of the Communist International* reinforced this basis for Communist action. Stating that the Communist stand is "on the ground of consistent proletarian class struggle," it asserted that "the Communist International mercilessly exposes all forms of the doctrine of 'class peace' that the reformists have accepted from the bourgeoisie." This applies to every Marxist-Leninist endeavor. Today, in addition, "the class struggle . . . is now being conducted on an enormous and really world scale," since "the working class of the world has now its own state—the one and only fatherland of the international proletariat." (*Program of the Communist International*, in *Blueprint for World Conquest*, Henry Regnery Co., p. 174.)

This conception of military strategy and tactics as the foundation for Red efforts in all fields dominates Communist discussions and decisions. It is evidenced in the constant Communist practice, taken from military science, of a maximum and minimum objective in connection with any Party line or with the infiltration of a local organization.

In a trade union, woman's club, or other local group, the same method is pursued. If full endorsement of the Pact of Peace cannot be obtained, then the comrades seek to put through a resolution committing the organization to endorsement of a meeting between the top level representatives of the same governments included in the Pact of Peace. (This is precisely the directive given to Communists in the trade unions in *Political Affairs* for May, 1952, in the article "Some Problems of Work in Right Led Unions," by John Swift.)

Science of Class War

For a basic consideration of how to carry on their class war strategy and tactics, Communists turn to the discussion of the subject by Joseph Stalin in his *Foundations of Leninism*. The very first topic which Stalin considers under that head is: "Strategy and Tactics as the Science of Leadership in the Class War." Indeed, Stalin emphasizes that there can be no complete strategy and detailed tactics for the proletariat until "the period of proletarian revolution." It was precisely in that period, he asserts, that Lenin dragged into the light of day "the brilliant ideas of Marx and Engels on tactics and strategy that had been immured by the opportunists of the Second International."

Lenin did not rest content, however, with reviving these tactical theses of Marx and Engels. He developed them further, to the point where Stalin could write: "The strategy and tactics of Leninism constitute the science of leadership in the revolutionary struggle of the proletariat."

The grand strategy and tactics necessarily have to do with the final goal—"the world revolution" and world Soviet dictatorship. Since the October revolution in Russia, which brought first Lenin and then Stalin into power, "the period of world revolution commences," according to Stalin.

In this grand strategy, the main force of the revolution is "the dictatorship of the proletariat in one country and the revolutionary movement of the proletariat in all countries." To this has been added, since the conquest of Eastern Europe by the Kremlin, the dictatorship of the proletariat in the so-called people's democracies, the satellite regimes.

On the basis of this main force, what is world Communism to do? Its plan for the disposition of forces, the characteristically military term Stalin uses, is "alliance of the proletarian revolution with the liberation movement of the colonies and the dependent countries." It can readily be seen how closely this plan was followed since the days of 1924, when Stalin wrote these words. While the Western world, including the United States, was cajoled into the belief that the Far East was of small significance and that the Chinese Communists should be permitted to conquer China, Stalin was building up his forces for the conquest of all Asia. That policy has paid off well, and if it carries Soviet arms and infiltration successfully into Southeastern Asia, India, and the Middle East, it will be even more triumphant.

When we consider this grand strategy, we become aware of how deeply the United States permitted itself to be deceived in regard to the value of Eastern Europe ("the dependent countries") and China ("the liberation movement of the colonies"). Because Stalin's grand strategy and tactics were not given serious consideration, the United States has received the most staggering defeats in its history and has permitted 800,000,000 people to be placed under the Stalinite heel.

To Advance the "Line"

We must understand that the technique involved in the grand strategy and tactics is also adopted by the Communists for the battles which must take place within this grand strategy for the advance of the "line." Consultation of Stalin's pages will reveal that he defines strategy under three points. The first is "the determination of the direction of the main blow of the pro-

letariat at a given stage." This refers to the different stages
reached in each country, of the drive to strengthen the Soviet
dictatorship internationally, and the Communist conspiracy
within each nation. Here in the United States, during World
War II, the main blow of the Communists had to be directed
toward the defense of Soviet Russia and therefore against the
Axis powers. The Communists put on the garb of ultra-patriot-
ism and proclaimed the United States one of the great democratic nations, to win for the Kremlin American lend-lease and
the sorely needed second front. The assignment to the American Communists was to inveigle the United States into the war
against both Germany and Japan.

During that period, the conspiracy took advantage of pro-
Soviet propaganda, so unguardedly expressed throughout
America, to infiltrate the government and agencies of public
opinion. This created a favorable position for the next main
blow. The opportunity came with the ending of the war, when
Stalin proceeded on his program by taking over China and
Eastern Europe. The main blow was now against the United
States, but delivered in such a way that this country would
acquiesce in its own defeats. The assignment to the American
Communist Party, in furtherance of this blow, was to work
within America for acceptance of a Red China and a Red Poland. This, too, was successfully accomplished.

As the so-called cold war developed, the main blow became
centered even more on the United States, all the crimes of
Soviet aggression being turned about and hurled at this nation.
Just as the United States had been condemned in 1928 as "the
dollar republic" and the head of the camp of imperialism, so
it was now denounced as "the aggressor" and warmonger.

To make this most recent main blow effective, the Kremlin
initiated its "peace crusades," culminating in the world wide
campaign for "the Pact of Peace." This pact contained conditions that would lead to another complete triumph for the
Kremlin, specifically the recognition of Red China and its
admission to the Security Council of the United Nations. If the

United States accepted these terms, as our Far Eastern experts recommended, then Moscow would win another stunning victory. If the United States rejected the proposal, then the Kremlin's agents everywhere could intensify the cry that American imperialism was intent on war.

There was a way to meet this attack, and that was to turn the blow back on the Soviet dictatorship itself by taking a firm stand. But there were pro-Soviet voices in this country which prevented our taking such a stand with full force and effect, and Stalin counted on that. As late as January 3, 1950, Professor John K. Fairbank of Harvard University strongly approved seating Red China on the Security Council. Writing in the *Reporter* of that date, he declared: "The Chinese veto in the United Nations can have little more nuisance value than the present Russian veto." And he added: "[The Communist regime in China] shows promise on its record thus far of being the best government that modern China has had."

In the *United Nations World* for October, 1950, Owen Lattimore threw his weight on the same side of the scales, stating that the triumph of the Communists in China was a triumph of "Asia for the Asiatics" and not for Moscow.

Recurrent defeats and congressional hearings, fortunately, did to some extent arouse the American people. This prevented acceptance of the Lattimore-Fairbank suggestions, which had previously been successful in assuring Red China itself. The continuance of the "peace partisan" movement indicates, however, that Stalin had gained his minimum objective, the creation of enough hesitancy on the part of the American nation to lay the foundations for further encroachments in the Far East. The "peace crusades" received the open support of many outstanding Americans and people of a like character in other countries. The movement has been instrumental in registering uncertainty and vacillation in the attitudes and policies of the Western nations. It still carries the danger of creating frustration or defeatism within the United States, which is obviously one of its objectives.

Knowledge of Line Essential

We can thus observe that a knowledge of the line of the Communists, as directed by Moscow, is essential to those opposing Communism. They have to be acquainted with the main blow. It is doubly necessary to know the line of the Party, since in most instances the non-Communist will confront Communism in the community in the person of those who are working as "transmission belts" for the Party. The Communist line and its auxiliary proposals will not be put forward as Moscow made. Quite to the contrary, they will be presented as necessary for the American people. The CIO gave an instructive lesson in 1950, when it expelled ten unions for being Communist controlled. The indictment against them was that they faithfully, over many years, had followed the Communist line. In order to make such an indictment, the Communist line must be known.

The second point in Stalin's strategy is "the disposition of forces." Here in the United States, which has many "capitalist-minded" groups, it is obvious that this will require wide infiltration. The trade unions must be penetrated, to keep alive the fiction of a proletarian base for the Party. In addition, the capture of trade unions, or their successful manipulation, can lead to a production stoppage when it serves the Kremlin's interests. That is why the Communist Party of the United States in 1933 adopted its concentration policy, about which we shall hear much more. It means the concentration of all available reserve forces in the areas that contain the basic industries.

For the purpose of propaganda among "the colonial peoples," and to create division within America, the Communists also seek unceasingly to penetrate Negro groups. Nor have the educated and the rich been neglected in America, since they can be such powerful levers of influence on national attitudes and policies. For our country, therefore, and with the transmission-belt technique in mind, we can expect Communist activity in any quarter. It has been the failure to understand this, specifically the disbelief that anyone rich or educated could be Communist-minded, which has caused such havoc in American thinking.

A good view of the use to which the educated are put in Communist propaganda is given in the testimony of Igor Bogolepov, former Counsellor for the Soviet Foreign Office, before the McCarran Sub-Committee. This important witness points out that Soviet propaganda, contained in the *History of the Communist Party of the Soviet Union* [*Bolsheviks*], was taken over bodily by Dr. Frederick Schuman in his work— which is in many university libraries—*Soviet Politics Abroad and at Home.* It is not surprising, then, to find in the reports of the House Committee on Un-American Activities that Schuman has been a member of many Communist fronts.

We learn from the same witness that the much touted two-volume work on Russia by Sidney and Beatrice Webb, *Soviet Communism and New Civilization,* was prepared by the Soviet Foreign Office, and that the chapter on the detention camps was prepared by the Soviet secret police. This book had a marked effect among educators and other intellectuals in the United States and broke ground for much of the infiltration which the Communists have been able to make among these people. Naturally, books were only one method of such infiltration.

Stalin's third point in strategy is that the struggle must carry out the plan decided upon; that is, the line to be followed must be conducted during the whole course of the given period. There has been some jesting in the past at the sudden changes which take place in the Communist line, but this is no laughing matter. In order to make any campaign effective, it must be carried through fully and fanatically, until Moscow decides that a change in the relation of forces makes a new line imperative. The Communists carry forward specific policies with full force and effect even though they may have some thought that the line is about to be shifted. They can thus proceed with the maximum unity directly up to the point that the shift is ordered, and the "zigzag" made, to which Stalin refers. Thus we find the Communists denouncing the late President Roosevelt as "another Hitler" in 1940 and 1941, and a very short time later praising him as "the Commander-in-Chief." These rapid changes have practically always been productive of success. They have, through the skillful use of concealed Communists, swayed thousands of non-Communists back and forth in accordance with the Kremlin's directions.

We must therefore be prepared for quick shifts in line by the Communists—open or concealed—and it is only by being constantly abreast of the transitions ordered by Moscow that we can cope with these lightning-fast transformations.

Changes in the Line

Even within a given period, amendments of some of the auxiliary features of the line are made. Up to 1952, the Pact of Peace included the non-armament of Germany. But during that year the Kremlin, in order to advance the Communist campaign for a "unified" Germany, suddenly came forward with the proposal of an armed but "independent" Germany. Communists throughout the world changed on this issue overnight, making the new proposal one of the conditions of the Pact of Peace.

Familiarity with these amendments to the line is important to an understanding of what the Communists and their sympathizers may bring forward in any community. This is not so difficult as it appears. To anyone who is conversant with Communist phraseology and methods of argumentation, a regular reading of the *Daily Worker* and *Political Affairs* will tell the story.

One of the tasks of strategic leadership, as laid down by Stalin, is to "utilize properly all the reserves" the Party has at its disposal at any given period. Another is to maneuver with the reserves, so as to gain time to "disintegrate the enemy and to accumulate forces in order to assume the offensive later." While Stalin explains these items of strategy in terms of the Bolshevik revolution, we have constant examples of them today in the methods of the Communists here in the United States.

We can note the use of "reserves" today in the peace crusades, which in support of the Kremlin's drive put into motion thousands of non-Communists. It is a constant aim of Communist strategy to draw in as many groups and individuals as is possible to back a stated policy at any given time. During the Hitler-Stalin Pact, pacifists and sympathizers with Hitler were drawn upon to aid the attempt to defeat or delay defense preparations. When the Soviet Union was attacked by Hitler, the Communists proceeded to rally to the Kremlin line all those individuals, groups, and forces which had been bitterly anti-Hitler and favorable to a war against Germany. In an amazingly short time, the Soviet fifth column here had influenced organization after organization to bring pressure for the second front. It was urging that there be no strikes, and that incentive wage schemes be introduced in order "to help the war effort"— in reality to salvage the Soviet dictatorship by American aid. In that aim, too, the fifth column persuaded hundreds of thousands. Both when the Communists were hand in glove with Hitler, and when they were against him, "reserves" were found widely to support them and their line.

As Lenin has said, and Stalin has repeated after him, "With the vanguard alone, victory is impossible." The vanguard, in both its strategy and its tactics, must draw great masses of people into its orbit, and through infiltration of mass organizations press them into doing what the Kremlin wants done at any particular period.

If the concern of strategy is "to win the war as a whole," as Stalin tells us, the aim of tactics is to "win a particular battle." This applies whether the goal is the dictatorship of the proletariat and armed insurrection, or the furtherance of the line helpful to the Kremlin. The object of tactical leadership—and we continue to rely on Stalin for this explanation—is to handle all the forms of struggle and of organization to assure the maximum preparation for strategic success.

First of all, then, it is essential in tactics "to bring to the forefront those forms of struggle and of organization which are best suited to the conditions prevailing during the ebb and flow of the movement." We can understand why the Communists bring forward a variety of Red fronts, changing their names and reorganizing their personnel with such rapidity. By this means, they seek to win the maximum number of individuals, groups, and forces to the line they are advocating under directives from Moscow. Referring to the Communist peace crusades alone—which have forwarded the Kremlin line up to 1953 —there has been a series of organizations designed to win the support of varying groups of unthinking people.

To name but a few of these organizations, we might list the Stockholm Peace Appeal, the Peace Information Center, the American Peace Crusade, the Committee for Peaceful Alternatives to the Atlantic Pact, the Mid-Century Conference for Peace, the National Labor Conference for Peace, the American Women for Peace, and a number of youth groups. These were set going by the notorious Waldorf-Astoria Conference in March, 1949, arranged by the National Council of the Arts, Sciences, and Professions.

An analysis of these Communist fronts indicates that they were brought into existence in order to capture a following of large numbers of people in various fields of activity. Some of them were dissolved when their pro-Communist character became so apparent that they could not carry considerable numbers along with them. They were immediately succeeded by new organizations which could serve the Kremlin purpose to better effect. There is no better example of the reliance upon deceit, Lenin's great formula, than this shift of organizational names to serve in the "disintegration of American public opinion."

With the lightning-fast changes which sometimes take place in the line, those zig-zags of which both Lenin and Stalin wrote, the necessity for new forms of organization and struggle becomes even more obvious. There is the classical illustration of the American League Against War and Fascism. During the period of its negative activities, in opposing Hitler after Stalin first came to fear him, it went by this original name. When a more positive approach was made to the Roosevelt administration, with Communist hopes heightened by the success of infiltration into the government, the name was changed to American League for Peace and Democracy. When Stalin made his alliance with Hitler in 1939, and the Communists were doing all in their power to prevent American defense production, the organization was transformed into the American Peace Mobilization. Its objects were now the very opposite of those which had been put forward by the American League for Peace and Democracy. The White House was picketed. President Roosevelt was scathingly denounced, and everything was done by the newly organized front that would tend to aid the victory of Hitler, Stalin's ally.

The second consideration in tactics is to "locate at any given moment that single link in the chain of events which if seized upon will enable us [the Communists] to control the whole chain." Thus the ground is prepared for strategic success.

A case in point is the current line of the Stalinites. The general strategic line is "the Pact of Peace," which is based upon an understanding that a vulnerable point in the thinking of Western peoples is their intense desire for peace. The Soviet dictatorship raises the "peace" cry in such a way as to make it contingent upon complete Soviet victory in the present period. It does this by a number of demands connected with the Pact, which will shortly be examined.

What is the "chief link" that will make this peace pact serve Soviet purposes? Undoubtedly, it is the recognition of Red China and the seating of Red China on the Security Council. If that can be assured, American security will be constantly endangered. A strong beginning will have been made toward that utilization, to which Lenin referred, of the millions of China, Russia, and India as a guarantee of Soviet world conquest. That is precisely what appears as the first of the conditions of the Pact of Peace: the permanent recognition of Red China.

In local work, whether in an organization or in a community, those opposing Communism will be able to analyze the moves of the Communists and their friends if they are aware of this concept of strategy and tactics. It is employed at every level.

The 1953 Line

To sum up the line of the Communist Party as it stood in 1953, based on Stalinite tactics and strategy, we can say:

The main features of the line were:

(1) The Pact of Peace to be signed by the United States, Soviet Russia, Great Britain, France, and Red China. In this Pact there was involved (a) recognition of Red China; (b) seating of Red China in the United Nations and on the Security Council; (c) non-armament of Japan; (d) an "independent Germany," that is, a Germany which would come under Soviet control; (e) "unification" of Korea, with the same aim for that country.

(2) "The fight against Fascism and McCarthyism," which embraced (a) repeal of the Smith and McCarran Acts; (b) attack on all other measures which curb the Communists; and (c) character assassination against the ex-Communists testifying for the government.

Bearing in mind that within this line there is a minimum and a maximum objective (just as there would be in military engagements), and a plan to "disintegrate the enemy," we can measure its effects more realistically. It has registered in wide areas of the American nation.

In drawing in the "reserves" upon which the Communists count to carry forward their line, special and indeed blatant attention is paid to those demands for reform which would appeal to certain groups. All through the recent trials, the Communists have contended that they are being persecuted because they stand for certain social reforms, among them the rights of the Negro people, the championship of labor's demands, and proposals which appeal to women, youth, and other segments of American society.

It is because of this device that Alexander Bittelman, in his defense of the Communists as "scientists," must conclude by stating the Communist line and then stressing the reforms which the Communists champion.

Bittelman writes: "The Communists, believers in the teachings of Lenin, are the most consistent fighters for creation of people's peace coalitions, for the maintenance of world peace, for the peaceful co-existence of the two systems, for a Five Power Peace Pact." He adds that the Communists are also the most consistent fighters for "the preservation and extension of democratic liberties and civil rights, for the Bill of Rights, for democracy."

This is not only a recitation of the line, but also a directive to the Communists to continue intensive campaigning toward these ends, centered in the Pact of Peace.

The reforms are brought in when Bittelman goes on to declare that the Communists are the most consistent fighters also "for the United Front of the working class, for working class unity, in defense of the living standards of the masses, in defense of the trade unions and other labor organizations."

This assertion could be refuted by the extensive report of the CIO in 1950, that the Communists had entered the labor unions merely and exclusively to advance the interests of Soviet Russia. But we are now interested in Bittelman's stress upon social reforms. He continues: "The Communists, guided by Marx, Engels, Lenin, and Stalin, are the most consistent fighters for the economic, political, and social equality of the Negro people."

There are many persons who take these Communist claims at face value. As a result, we often hear certain individuals stating that while they are opposed to Communism, that does not mean they are against social reform. The Communists have played this tune so well that great sections of the people and of American leadership have been put on the defensive. Defense of the Communists and of their "rights" to carry on their conspiracy is often based on these claims that they are reformers.

Red Use of Reforms as "Screen"

Anyone even vaguely familiar with Red literature knows that "reformism" is condemned in the severest terms. Unless one is aware of Stalin's tactics, this may cause confusion. On the one hand, the Communists shout aloud that they are the greatest champions of social reform; on the other they condemn "reformism."

Stalin is quite pointed on this subject. For the revolution, it is necessary "to utilize the conflict (even though temporary) of interest between one's enemies." It is therefore necessary to temporize and compromise with conditional or vacillating allies. It is essential at times to "go in zigzags."

Now in doing so, the Communist takes up the championship of reforms. But he has no illusions about the matter. They are only the instrument to gather forces, to split possible opponents, and in that way move forward to the real goal—the violent overthrow of the bourgeois government.

"To a reformist," Stalin writes, "reforms are everything while revolutionary work is just something to talk about, a diversion. . . . To a revolutionary, the opposite is the case; the main thing is the revolutionary work and not reforms, for reforms are mere by-products of the revolution." Indeed, reforms are to be used only as instruments to "disintegrate" the prevailing system and to "strengthen the revolution."

Stalin wants this thoroughly understood, and adds: "The revolutionist will accept the reform in order to use it as a means wherewith to link legal work with illegal work, in order to use it as a screen behind which his illegal activities for the revolutionary preparation of the masses for the overthrow of the bourgeoisie may be intensified." (*Foundations of Leninism*, Stalin, Marxist Library edition, p. 101.)

What Stalin has stated on the use of reforms is a repetition of what Lenin had declared before him, and what other leading Communists have said repeatedly from time to time. It is a fundamental Communist view. When the Communists bring forward reforms, they do it in a purely Aesopian way, and not for the benefit of the groups whose cause they allegedly champion.

Championship of the Negro, which is at a new height at the present moment, is brought into prominence when disruption within the United States is the general plan. Solicitude for the Negro marked the Hitler-Stalin Pact period. It was completely submerged during the "national war of liberation," when Hitler's attack on Soviet Russia made it vital to win American support for the Kremlin. In every community, the imprint of Stalin's strategy and tactics will be found in the activities of the Communists, open or concealed, and those allied with them. It will not take too long to discover certain individuals linking up obviously justified demands for reforms, such as better Negro housing, with open or covered suggestions or moves for peace propaganda such as the Communists use. Frequently they will also associate their reform activities with cries for "civil liberties" and "academic freedom" in such a way as to prevent any investigation of any subversive influences.

By this studied method, the Communists have been able over and over again to crush democracy with democratic slogans. In Russia itself, the cry of "Land to the peasants" was the means by which the Bolsheviks came into power and then took land from the peasants through collectivization. The constant reiteration of "civil liberties" is a ready made device to gather the largest support against any effort to curb the conspiracy. On the wave of this demand, into which thousands of non-Communists are drawn, all civil liberties can be destroyed, except for the Communists as they come into power. This has been the repeated story in each of the countries now under satellite regimes.

In non-Communist organizations and in local community work, the same phenomenon occurs on a more restricted scale. Gathering together the maximum number of Communist groups and individuals in support of the line is first of all intended to advance that line itself. But with it there goes the attempted strengthening of the Communist organization within the community for other Communist purposes.

The Party as the Agency

It is the Communist Party which is the agency to carry forward the strategy and tactics laid down by Stalin as an essential part of Marxism-Leninism. In *The Foundations of Leninism,* Stalin analyzed the Party in detail in its role as "the military staff of the proletariat."

The period in history into which we have entered, we are told, is one of "open collisions between the classes, a period of revolutionary direct action by the proletariat, a period of proletarian revolution."

At such a time, there arises the necessity for "a new Party, a militant Party, a revolutionary Party." This is the directing force that will affect the course of history and direct the revolution. To fulfill its task, this force must have three characteristics. It must be bold enough to lead to the struggle for power, ever aware in its understanding of Marxist-Leninist theory exactly where it is going and what it is striving to attain. It must also have experience enough to cope with the complicated problems that arise in the advance toward the setting up of Soviet power. Lastly, it must possess that flexibility which will enable it to maneuver and at the same time to steer clear of any submerged rocks.

These characteristics have been drilled into the consciousness of Communists by constant repetition. They are the mark of Communist activity, to be noted everywhere and on all occasions. The Stalinites can be most flexible indeed, both nationally and in local work, as the dictates of Moscow demand. But through each gyration or maneuver, the Marxist-Leninist purpose to which they are dedicated is kept alive.

Without such a Party, Stalin declares, it is futile to think of "overthrowing imperialism and achieving the dictatorship of the proletariat." This Party is the Party of the *new type,* a phrase which runs constantly through Stalinite literature, the Party of Leninism. (Stalin's study of the Communist Party is contained in section VIII of *The Foundations of Leninism.*)

This creation of Lenin and Stalin cannot be understood in its actual operations unless its character is grasped. Stalin's own analysis is of great help. We learn that the Party of the new type, this Leninist Party, has five specific features which color the acts and thinking of all Communists. First and above all, this Party is the vanguard of the working class. It is the agency which directs the masses in the way they should go, for it is a body of scientists who possess the secret of revolutionary theory. When the Communists speak of what the masses want, as they do so frequently, they are expressing what the vanguard knows the masses should want. When the *Daily Worker,* in articles and editorials, refers to the demands of the people, it has in mind what the chosen ones among the people, the members of the vanguard, demand. It goes even further. An examination of the Communist daily organ will bring out the insistence on many occasions that "the people should raise their voices" or "the American people should let themselves be heard." In each and every case, these phrases constitute instructions to the members of the vanguard to see to it that the people take such steps.

This concept of a chosen few directing the masses toward their historical goal gives to the Communist, in his own opinion, a peculiar importance. It reminds him always of the distinction between the vanguard and the bulk of the masses which both Lenin and Stalin stress. It thus equips him with practices of deceit, teaching him to raise slogans which the people understand in one way, and the vanguard or elite in another.

Discipline is accepted readily under such circumstances, since the very essence of being one of the vanguard is the possession of correct revolutionary theory, and that theory can be determined today only by Stalin and those whom he commissions to give directives. If there is anything that these chosen few must avoid, it is "tailism"—taken from the Russian term which can roughly be translated as hanging on to the coat tails of an individual or group. "Tailism" is, in a word, following the masses or a popular non-Communist mass leader rather than directing the masses. Few greater offenses could be committed than this. The way to avoid it is by the rapid and clear adjustment of each Communist Party to instructions from Moscow, and the proper perception of how to carry out those instructions.

The Party is also the organized detachment of the working class, "the organizing nucleus of the working class." This brings us back to the consideration which Stalin makes quite clear, that the lower bodies of the Party must be subordinated to the higher if the vanguard is to carry out its task. The outcry that this reduces people to mere cogs and pegs is derided by Lenin who stated that it is but an ill-disguised expression of the personal distaste of those who do not like direction from a common center.

Further, the Party is the highest form of class organization of the proletariat, working out (in Stalin's words) a general line and carrying that line into other organizations as "transmission belts." The creation of Communist fronts, and the infiltration of non-Communist organizations, is not an accidental or temporary feature. It is a basic characteristic and obligation of the Party.

All of these considerations lead up to the chief feature of the Party as the weapon of the dictatorship of the proletariat. It must be "an iron Party, steeled in the struggle," capable of keeping track of and influencing the mood of the masses. There can be no misunderstanding on this matter. There must be "iron discipline in our Party," in order that it can carry through the battle for the dictatorship and likewise establish discipline over the masses. As we dig into Stalin's writings, it becomes more and more obvious that the Communists regard the mass of the people as tools, and this puts a stamp on their activities. It is this contempt for the masses which enables the Communist, in community or national affairs, to switch his line of argument and propaganda as the Party orders, and to do so with the maximum drive and effectiveness.

It follows that the Party must be the expression of unity of will and can therefore permit no faction within its ranks. As Stalin says, it cannot afford to be "liberal"—the quotation marks around the word are his. There can be no hedging on this point. Any violation of the Party's decisions—and these are made by Moscow and under Moscow's supervision—will lead to unconditional and immediate expulsion.

If this Party is to carry out the class war strategy and tactics, the final conclusion of Stalin is in order, that the Party is strengthened by purging itself of opportunist elements. Those are his exact words. Any sign of hesitancy within the ranks of the vanguard is apt to ruin everything from the Stalinite viewpoint, and "the retirement of wavering leaders" is looked upon as strengthening the Party rather than weakening it. In the recent past, on the international scene, there has been the liquidation of Rudolf Slansky in Czechoslovakia, who had been Moscow's representative there. There is also the demotion and severe criticism of Anna Pauker, in Rumania, and late in 1952, Mao Tse-tung began a "rectification movement" or great purge in the Chinese Communist Party. Whatever the reasons given for these liquidations, a term dear to the Communist heart, their real purpose was to maintain within the Communist organizations complete subservience to the Kremlin.

The Chinese Communist Party acknowledges this in the Cominform's organ of July 25, 1952, when it explains: "Ever since its establishment, the Communist Party of China has consistently built itself up in accordance with the Lenin-Stalin theory of the Party and on the model of the Communist Party of the Soviet Union."

CHAPTER VI

TRAINING THE COMMUNISTS

EVERY ARMY today is prepared for battle by training in military discipline, in such knowledge of military science as is necessary for specific posts, and in endurance amid the rigors of warfare. The invading armies of the Soviet fifth column, dedicated to continuous warfare on both the political and the physical plane, must have an even more precise and vigorous training.

"Cadres decide everything," is a famous statement made by Stalin in 1935 and echoed through the Communist ranks ever since. The very use of the term "cadre" gives the proper note of the class war. In military language, cadres are the framework of a regiment or other unit, usually the commissioned and noncommissioned officers. The officers of the revolution, of the overthrow of the non-Soviet governments, are the active members of the Communist Party. They are called "Bolshevik cadres" because they are to be drilled and steeled for the day to day battle in which they must engage.

Whenever the Communist leadership discusses the preparation of the comrades for their work, it is under the heading of "the importance of Communist cadres." This consideration cannot be over-stressed, since it is the key to the education of the Communists and to the whole training program of the Communist Party here and abroad.

In January, 1952, Gus Hall, who had acted as General Secretary of the Communist Party in the U.S.A., emphasized this subject in the following words: "Our cadres are our most important capital. We must preserve them, we must expand their number manifoldly. We must mold our cadres in the image of the great Marxist cadres of the world. The work of the Party must be a constant cadre-building process." (*Political Affairs,* Jan. 1952, p. 42.)

In Soviet Russia, where the Stalinists have State power, there is a well established chain of institutions for this training of Party and Soviet cadres. They begin with what might be called a primary course, in a network of Party schools and courses. This is supplemented by a higher Party school with a three-year term of study for the purpose of training Party and Soviet workers for regional posts and institutions. Above that, there exists the Academy of Social Sciences, devoted primarily to the training of higher cadres of Marxist-Leninists for central Party posts and institutions. (Explained by G. M. Malenkov, "Activities of the Central Committee, CPSU," *Political Affairs,* Feb. 1948, pp. 136, 137.)

In every Communist Party, including that of the United States, this gradation in cadre training also exists, although it cannot be on such an ambitious scale. In the United States, this gives rise to the secret and open schools of the Communist Party, in addition to the special courses in the sections and branches for the rank and file members. The secret schools are conducted for those who are full time functionaries of the Party, or are considered to be of the quality to become such. The open schools are dedicated to training those who, for the time being at least, will carry on in branch or mass organization work but who feel the need for special training in Marxism-Leninism in order to operate efficiently.

Before we consider these schools in detail, we must be aware that Communist training goes far beyond these educational procedures. As Lenin wrote in 1900: "We must train men and women who will devote to the revolution, not merely their spare evenings, but the whole of their lives." And J. Peters, in his *Manual of Organization* of the Communist Party of the United

States, explains Lenin's concept of the professional revolutionary as follows: "A professional revolutionist is a highly developed comrade, trained in revolutionary theory and practice, tested in struggles, who gives his whole life to the fight of the interests of his own class. A professional revolutionist is ready to go whenever and wherever the Party sends him . . . If the class struggle demands it, he will leave his family for months, even years. The professional revolutionist cannot be demoralized."

Beyond all that, this Communist, giving all of his life to the "cause," must be prepared for that "voluntary and complete submission" to the line laid down by Moscow, which Stalin underscores in his *Foundations of Leninism*. He must be prepared, in a word, to immolate himself for the vanguard, to blend his will at all times into that of the vanguard—and "the vanguard," in practice, is the will and decision of the "teacher and father," "the man who has regenerated the world," Stalin. That will and decision are now expressed by Stalin's disciple, Malenkov, who speaks as the representative of "Marx-Engels-Lenin-Stalin." (These salutations to Stalin are taken from the Cominform organ of December 21, 1949, but they have been used on many other occasions under varying and even more extravagant forms."

How to Be a Good Communist

The training of the Communist, therefore, is above all the development of a "steeled" personality, one which at the same time is completely subordinated to the interests and decisions of the Party. To make this thoroughly understood throughout the Party ranks in 1953, a special booklet was issued which became required reading for all Communists in the United States: *How to Be a Good Communist*, by Liu Shao-chi, vice-chairman of the People's Republic of China. Constant "self-cultivation" is laid down as the rule for the Communist in order to be the revolutionist in the true sense. This "self-cultivation" is expressed in two major acts: (1) "Strive to become the best pupils of Marx, Engels, Lenin, and Stalin," and (2) "The unconditional subordination of the personal interests of a Party member to the interests of the Party."

The first condition is to be met by studying Marxism-Leninism, but by doing it in such a way as to "have a truly Communist outlook on life, a world outlook," and to "employ the style of Marx, Engels, Lenin, and Stalin." In other words, the Communist is to strive to act in any assignment given him as these "geniuses" would have acted; he is to become a "political figure of the Lenin type," as Stalin declared to be essential.

On the second point, we learn: "A Party member is required to sacrifice his personal interests unconditionally and should not sacrifice the Party's interests to meet his personal interests (no matter under what cloak or pretext)." It is "therefore, only in the struggle for the development, success, and victory of the Party" that a Party member can "hope to develop himself."

Summing up this obligation, the Communist is told: "At all times and on all questions, a Communist Party member should take into account the interests of the Party as a whole and place the Party's interests above his personal problems and interests. It is the highest principle of our Party members that the Party's interests are supreme. Every Party member should firmly build up this conception in his ideology. . . . He should ensure that his personal interests accord with the Party's interests or even merge with them. Thus when his personal interests conflict with the Party's interests he will be able to submit to the Party's interests and sacrifice his personal interests without the slightest hesitation or reluctance. To sacrifice one's personal interests and even one's life without the slightest hesitation and even with the feeling of happiness, for the cause of the Party, for class and national liberation, and for the emancipation of mankind is the highest manifestation of Communist ethics." (*How to Be a Good Communist*, Liu Shao-chi, New Century Publishers, New York, p. 31.)

The Communist must therefore be surrounded by such an atmosphere as will make him this tool in the hands of the Kremlin, as will bring about that submission to the iron Bolshevik discipline which is constantly reiterated as a necessary characteristic of the Stalinite. This is achieved in the first place by the constant practice of criticism and self-criticism, whose power to bring about complete conformity to the line and to the discipline of the Party can never be appreciated fully by the non-Communist. At the Nineteenth Congress of the Communist Party of the Soviet Union, held in October, 1952, rules were adopted which re-emphasized that criticism and self-criticism are duties of Party members, constituting one of the main tasks of all Party organizations.

Criticism and self-criticism are regarded as one and the same process by the Communists. It consists in stating in various conferences, discussions, and inner-Party meetings the weaknesses which have characterized the work of the comrade making the statement or of his colleagues in the Party. Since it is practiced at every possible occasion, it becomes ingrained in the life and thinking of the Communist. It tends to make him think solely in terms of the vanguard, of how better to advance the current line, of how more effectively to further revolutionary work.

Very frequently, this process will be applied to the Communist Party of an entire country, its leading report pointing to errors made, mistakes committed, and weaknesses displayed. It is not an infrequent sight for these reports to appear in the pages of the Cominform organ, prominently displayed and often with editorials calling attention to the weaknesses they announce.

Three purposes at least are served by this indulgence in criticism and self-criticism. First, when a great emergency arises and a sharp change in the line is made, the comrades wallow in self-criticism in order to assure that there is complete submission to the sharp zig-zag that has been ordered from Moscow. Thereby, they obscure by means of a peculiar psychological process the patent fact that the change has been made solely because it complies with the Kremlin's will and wish. By placing upon themselves the blame for weaknesses in the execution of the last line, the one that has been rejected or changed, they seek to prepare a way for an explanation of the new line as having arisen from their own activities. Each Communist, in engaging in these mental gymnastics, is fully aware that the new line to which he is subscribing has been ordered by Moscow and is in accordance with new policies of the Kremlin, and that the switch of his respective Party is being made at the same time as Soviet tactics are being switched.

The Browder Case

Nothing points up this first purpose of self-criticism better than the flood of self-denunciations which accompanied the demotion of Earl Browder as leader of the American Communist Party in June, 1945. The reader can capture some of the atmosphere created in what transpired on that occasion by reading the chapter "Communist Confessions" in my book, *This Is My Story*. Here we have a case in which Jacques Duclos, General Secretary of the French Communist Party, and known as "the voice of Moscow to the West," suddenly indicted Earl Browder for "revisionism." This indictment appeared in the theoretical organ of the French Communist Party, *Cahiers du Communisme* for April, 1945. The National Committee of the American Communist Party hastened to meet in extraordinary session. In June, 1945, at this session, its members proceeded for three days and two nights to denounce Browder as one who had misled them and to blame themselves for having blindly followed him into "revisionism." They who had hailed the falling chief as "the greatest genius of Marxism-Leninism in the Western Hemisphere" now heaped scorn upon his head and criticism upon themselves. This they did although Browder's so-called "revisionist position" was precisely that which he had been obliged to follow in accordance with Stalin's agreement at Teheran with Roosevelt and Churchill that there would be "generations of peace" among the great powers.

To those who had shouted "Teheran" with Browder, it must have been obvious that the former General Secretary of the Communist Party was being made a scapegoat for the new "cold war" policy of Moscow. Through his degradation and demotion as a revisionist, the Communists of the world were to be electrified into waging war against the United States. If it were revisionism to stand for peace between this country and Soviet Russia, as Browder had done in echoing Teheran, then the correct Communist position was to advance war against the United States, after lend-lease was no longer needed by the Soviet dictatorship. And yet, all members of the National Committee joined in berating Browder and in accusing themselves of having been blind to Browder's gross errors. (The account to which reference has been made appears in chap. ix, *This Is My Story*, McGraw-Hill Book Company, N.Y., 1947. It has been republished in large part in the anthology of revolt against Soviet Communism, *Verdict of Three Decades*, edited by Julien Steinberg, Duell, Sloan, and Pearce, 1950.)

Second, another chief purpose of criticism and self-criticism is to establish complete ideological unity within the Communist ranks. By expressing his determination to conform to the line, and by his constant reminder openly stated that he will guard against all weaknesses impairing execution of the line, the Communist conditions himself to the rapid acceptance of any zigzag in policy that may be required of him. This practice, repeated throughout every branch and higher organ of the Party, makes certain that the maximum of submission to the line and to any future line will be attained. As the Chinese Communist leader, Wu Ch'iang, writes in his important treatise "On Problems of Self-Criticism," translated for American Communists in *Political Affairs* of August, 1952: "We must use criticism and self-criticism to overcome and conquer all non-proletarian ideologies which carry out 'surprise raids' and 'insidious infiltration' against us." He adds: "If our revolutionary cadre ignore or tolerate incorrect ideologies, take a non-proletarian line, and indulge in liberalism, then faults will continue to occur, petty errors will become major faults, isolated faults will become general faults, and the cadre themselves, if they persist in these mistaken methods, will be in danger of degeneration."

The Communist, repeating on every possible occasion his complete submission to the Kremlin's line and his determination to carry out that line by overcoming previous weaknesses in revolutionary work, is trained to be an active, effective, and obedient member of the Kremlin's army of psychological warfare.

Third, criticism and self-criticism give that "thrust forward" which enables the Communist machine to put redoubled energy into its efforts and to stimulate added fanaticism and vigor in the individual Communist. Wu Ch'iang declares that "it is a vital daily necessity, which provides us with a stimulus to uninterrupted progress, reinforces and invigorates the revolutionary organization, and increases its strength."

Even the concealed Communist, who does not normally participate in organized discussions or conferences because of the secret tasks assigned him, feels the impact of this practice. Criticism and self-criticism are indulged in by him in meetings with the Communist functionary who is giving him directives. The concealed Communist whom we might meet in any community organization, is not just receiving directions from someone more openly connected with the Party. He is also constantly required to examine his activities and have them subject to examination by others. Even though everyone throughout the Communist organization does not respond in the same manner to criticism and self-criticism, the practice increases the iron discipline, assures complete conformity with the Kremlin's will, and establishes a condition whereby any questioning of the line is looked upon as treason.

Surprise has been expressed from time to time that Communist leaders who have fallen into disrepute with Moscow, such as Rudolf Slansky in Czechoslovakia, make the most extravagant "confessions" of their "guilt." Aside from the human consideration (the desire to protect their families from the subtle

Stalinite method of slow starvation and social ostracism), previous criticism and self-criticism prepares the ground for these bizarre self-accusations. Having been trained for years in the propositions that "socialism is inevitable" and that "Stalin is invincible," and having established these beliefs firmly in their minds by self-criticism, they are easily persuaded in an emergency to make themselves sacrificial victims for Stalinism's advance and to cover up its mistakes.

As Vital as Air and Water

So vital is self-criticism thought to be for the Communists that Stalin has pointed out that they need it just as they need air and water. The Cominform's organ, accordingly, returns to the subject on many occasions. In its issue of November 21, 1952, under the heading "Criticism and Self-Criticism—Powerful Weapon of Communist and Workers' Parties," it calls a roll of the leading Communist Parties and assesses the progress of criticism and self-criticism in their respective organizations. In that connection it declares: "The Lenin-Stalin Party, which for more than half a century has been marching in the front ranks of the revolutionary movement, always devoted and devotes now close attention to developing criticism and self-criticism, regarding them as the basic method of training cadres. . . ."

The practice must always begin and end with expressions of reverence for Stalin and adherence to the Communist Party of the Soviet Union. The directive quoted concludes in like vein. It adjures the Communist Parties of the world to rely "on the inexhaustible experience of the Communist Party of the Soviet Union" in drawing lessons from their own practical activity. That will equip them to fulfill their Communist tasks.

Climaxing self-criticism in times of emergency or crisis is the process known as "the Bolshevization of the Party." This means the steeling and retraining of the comrades, particularly at periods when Soviet Russia is engaged in conflict with the country in which the specific Communist Party functions. It is carried through by binding the individual Communist in adherence to Stalin and the Kremlin, through an insistence upon the re-reading of his works, and specifically those which stress the Marxist-Leninist goal of overthrowing all non-Soviet governments. It is an intensive method of bringing about complete discipline and ideological unanimity within the Party, thus equipping it to stand the shocks which its subversive activities may bring upon it.

An outstanding instance of this process, demonstrating clearly how the steeling of the Communist is accompanied by bringing him closer to Stalin and the Kremlin, is the article of directives by Eugene Dennis, appearing in *The Communist* of May, 1940. The date of this article is important, because it falls into the Hitler-Stalin Pact period. In Communist documents, it is always important to ask: "In what period did this statement occur?" The Hitler-Stalin Pact, which lasted from August, 1939 to June, 1941, was the occasion for Communist preparations to conduct extensive sabotage and subversion against the United States. It was then that Eugene Dennis, the author of this article, secretly went through the country as a representative of the American Politburo, telling the chief functionaries of the Party in the various states to be ready to "turn the imperialist war into civil war." That same reminder appears in this article in print, though in different language, when Dennis emphasizes "the struggle between the two systems, between dying capitalism and rising, liberating Socialism."

In such a period, when the Communists were instigating strikes against American defense production on behalf of Hitler and were preparing for armed insurrection in case the United States went to Britain's aid militarily, the steeling of the Communists became a necessity.

Even at the risk of repetition—and to show the foundation of this "Bolshevization"—I shall quote what Dennis says at the very beginning of the article:

"During the first eight months of the war, the Communist

Party of the United States of America, like the majority of the
sections of the Communist International, has proved more than
ever that it is the revolutionary vanguard of the working class,
that it defends and champions the immediate and the fundamental class interests of the proletariat, that it is loyal to the
cause of proletarian internationalism and Socialism, that it is
guided by the principles of Marxism-Leninism."

This repetition of phrases with which the reader has now
become familiar is essential because it is precisely by such
repetition that Communist leadership maintains a constant conditioning of the comrades to a remembrance of the authority of
the Party and its revolutionary goal. By this repetition of what
has been written in Communist documents thousands of times
before, Dennis reiterates the devotion of American Communists to Stalin and Soviet Russia, through his reference to "the
Communist International" and to "proletarian internationalism."

The "Bolshevization" of the comrades requires more than
that, however; it makes necessary an understanding of the tasks
and goal for that particular period, the steeling of the comrades, and a recognition of errors that may lead them astray.
Dennis declares that the immediate task (in 1940) is "to combat vigorously the war aims of American imperialism and the
Roosevelt administration." This will compel "a tactical re-
orientation," particularly in order to fight effectively against
the Roosevelt administration.

Having set these tasks down definitely as the things that must
be done (and which, of course aided Hitler in his war against
Britain and the West), Dennis takes up the mistakes made by
the American Politburo in its first announcements after the
Hitler-Stalin Pact was published to the world. It is important
to note these mistakes because they give an insight into Communist methods. The author of the article of directives does not
state what these mistakes happen to be, but any reading of these
original declarations of the American Communist Party in the
Daily Worker of October, 1939, will show that readily enough.

The American Politburo, in the beginning, did not realize how closely Stalin was working hand in glove with Hitler, and therefore came out for such slogans as "independence for Poland." No knowledge of Marxism-Leninism could possibly have acquainted the American Communist leaders with the fact that Stalin had entered into a secret understanding with Hitler, whereby a new and tragic division of Poland between Nazi Germany and Soviet Russia was decided. And yet, as we see in Dennis' statement, the reason given for not appreciating that Stalin would do this is a lack of knowledge of Marxism-Leninism.

As soon as the American Politburo understood the true character of the Stalin-Hitler pact in regard to Poland, it called for the destruction of the Polish government and declared that that government "of the Polish colonels" had fallen by its own corruption. Thus, the leadership of the American Communists remedied its original digression from the Kremlin's viewpoint, but Dennis is intent upon making doubly sure that this is understood throughout the Party.

There is a second item of weakness to which Dennis refers in order to "Bolshevize" the American Communists, and that has to do with Soviet Russia directly. He stresses that the Communists have not linked up "the historic role and achievements of the USSR as the world citadel of peace, democracy, and socialism," with the "interests, needs, and problems of the American working class and toiling people." To anyone familiar with Communist phraseology, the concept he is underscoring is quite obvious. To spread the idea that the interests of the American masses are linked up with the land of Socialism, the land where the Stalinite dictatorship rules, is telling these masses in effect to go and do likewise. It is preparing them through Communist propaganda to "turn the imperialist war into civil war." And it is precisely in connection with this directive in regard to Soviet Russia that Dennis emphasizes "the struggle between the two systems, between dying capitalism and rising, liberating Socialism."

Why Did Weaknesses Arise?

Why did the weaknesses arise in the American Communist Party, according to Dennis, to prevent its full "Bolshevization"? It is because "our Party has not sufficiently mastered the theory of Marxism-Leninism." How will the American Communists achieve this mastery? The answer is one which the reader can by now anticipate. First of all, the weaknesses arose because "we did not study deeply and thoroughly enough the *History of the Communist Party of the Soviet Union*," that work of Stalin which the Communists had been reading since 1939 by the midnight oil. But the American Communists, they are told, did not draw enough from "the historical path followed by the Communist Party of the Soviet Union to help master and solve our own problems."

With that admonition, they are also told that they did not study properly Stalin's report of March, 1939, in which he had forewarned of an understanding with Hitler, and that they had not taken to heart A. A. Zhdanov's article in *Pravda* in August, 1939, denouncing "Anglo-French imperialism." Zhdanov was at that time the most powerful political figure in Soviet Russia next to Stalin himself. By this device of emphasizing that Stalin is the fountainhead of Communist strategy and tactics, Dennis emphasizes that Bolshevization consists primarily in devotion to Stalin, his wishes and commands.

Secondly, the American Communists were told that they did not pay enough attention to the "imperialist character" of the democratic nations, as set forth by Soviet leaders. And thirdly, they did not engage sufficiently in Bolshevik self-criticism, which would again bind them to Stalin in complete submission.

Not content with this, Dennis reiterates in great detail the necessity for remedying all weaknesses by reading the *History of the Communist Party of the Soviet Union* and re-studying Stalin's directive on Bolshevization given out in 1925. There are twelve points in this directive, but we can content ourselves with noting two of them. One is the necessity for "mastering the teachings of Marx, Engels, Lenin, and Stalin as a 'guide to action.' " The other is the necessity for the Party to be active among the masses, which underlines the urgency of intensive infiltration. Again we see the twofold objective of the Communists brought out as a chief feature of "Bolshevization."

The conclusion of this important article of directives stresses once again "the devotion of our Party to the teachings of Marx, Engels, Lenin, and Stalin," and the necessity to work with greater determination "to put into practice in the Communist movement Stalin's principles of Bolshevization."

"Bolshevization," therefore, consists in deepening reverence for Stalin and adherence to the Kremlin, the training of the Communists to look to him for all major directives, and the bringing about of that fanatical determination to follow the Soviet dictatorship wherever it may lead.

The processes of "self-criticism" and "Bolshevization" are aided immeasurably by the continual Communist procedure in all discussions which completely excludes parliamentary law and makes the declaration of the leader the decision of the gathering. The fact that no one opposes the line as laid down by the General Secretary (or whoever represents the Party in a particular discussion) brings about an atmosphere in which self-criticism and "Bolshevization" become part and parcel of the discussion, particularly in a crisis. The additional fact that these sessions of the Communists are used solely to state how the line can be carried out, and to detect deviations, intensifies the spirit of obedience to Stalinite instructions.

In this background of intensive training for Party members as a whole, the secret schools were designed to drill the functionaries who would act full time within the Party apparatus. They were the men and women who supervise the rank and file, make certain that orders are executed, and even sometimes regulate the actions of important men and women in mass organizations. This category includes the section organizers, district organizers, and other participants in national leadership, or those who are considered to be "good material" for induction into these offices.

National Training School

Climaxing the whole series of secret section and district schools in the country is the national training school, which formerly was held generally at Camp Nitgedaiget (later known as Camp Beacon) near Kingston, New York. Extraordinary measures of secrecy and discipline were thrown around its six-weeks sessions. Husbands and wives were normally forbidden to be at the school at the same time. Those attending were compelled to leave their families and to have no connection with them during the course. They were known to each other only by first names, and were not permitted to leave the school except in an emergency, when they had to be accompanied by one of the school's directors. Under such instructors as Jacob "Pop" Mindel and George Siskind (the latter has recently been deported to Poland), the functionaries were drilled in strictest discipline, and made into different personalities. Many of these men and women had entered the Communist movement because they were "militants," that is, engaged in individual protest against real or fancied abuses in our social system. In the secret training school, they were remolded in the sense that they were made to channelize this sense of protest into complete obedience to Stalin and the Kremlin and to the American Politburo as Moscow's representative. Through vivid examples taken from "the class struggle," they were indoctrinated in the Leninist morality that any means can be adopted to advance the cause. They were trained in the techniques of deception and concealment, and in how to impart this method of procedure to others so that it could be used in the courtroom, in the penetration of trade unions, and in the infiltration of other mass organizations. They were given intensive drill in how to produce riots, stimulate strikes when necessary to aid Moscow, and engage in "illegal" work for the Party.

The core of all this careful secret training was instruction in the doctrines of Marxism-Leninism. These were presented in the raw. We have at our disposal evidence in the various Communist trials and Congressional hearings which shows that George Siskind, for instance, explained in detail at these secret sessions the program for armed insurrection and the seizure of power by violence. Parliamentary law was sometimes included in the secret curriculum, but solely for the purpose of its use by the Communists in mass organizations. Thus, this select corps of functionaries was drilled in the methods by which incessant delays could be obtained in mass organization discussions, meetings could be snarled up in hopeless parliamentary tangles, and confusion or control could be attained. Parliamentary law was forbidden within the Party itself, since Communist discussions do not follow democratic procedure but consist in the report of the leading comrade, the acquiescence of all others, and the summary (decision) by the leader. A study of English for class struggle purposes, such as the writing of leaflets, preparation of material for Communist and "progressive" publications, and the organizing of speeches, was also included. A marked stamp of uniformity characterizes all Communist writings and documents as the result of this training. Functionaries are trained to follow the language of the directives which emanate from Moscow, so that there will be no change in the meaning or the interpretation of those directives.

It must be noted that the concealed Communist operating in the mass organization, though directed privately by these functionaries, is expected to "translate" this peculiar Communist method of expression into popular terminology.

Above all, those attending the secret training schools are drilled in slavish adherence to Stalin's teachings. The degree to which this disciplined adherence is carried cannot be fully grasped by a non-Communist. Stalin's works are studied meticulously and commented upon as the guiding rule for the functionary. His role in history and particularly as "the leader and teacher of the toilers of the world" is presented in the most extravagant terms. The functionary is reminded that on all fundamental issues he should refer to what Stalin has said and to what Stalin has done. Now Malenkov becomes Stalin's heir as the authority on "Marx-Engels-Lenin-Stalin."

The Open Schools

The open schools of the Party were formerly known as Workers' Schools, and were generally located in Communist headquarters in the various centers. In 1944, in a maneuver designed to impress public opinion with the fiction that the Soviet fifth column was essentially "American," these schools were re-organized under various patriotic or popular names. In Chicago, Boston, New Rochelle, and San Francisco, they were transformed into the Abraham Lincoln, Sam Adams, Tom Paine, and Tom Mooney Schools respectively. In Harlem, the open Communist School was named after George Washington Carver, the noted Negro scientist. The largest of all these Communist creations and the one which deserves special study and consideration is the Jefferson School of Social Science in New York City.

The Jefferson School was formed by a fusion of the New York Workers' School, which had been located for many years in the Communist Party building on East 13th Street, and the School for Democracy. The latter was ostensibly a product of the Teachers' Union, completely dominated by the Communist Party, but was actually established through Party impetus and direction.

The character of the Jefferson School, which is that of all the others, can be measured by "the committee of eminent educators, trade union, and community leaders" who joined in establishing it, according to the *Daily Worker* of February 1, 1944. These founding fathers of the "people's university" include Professor Lyman K. Bradley, who went to prison for the Communist cause, Frederick V. Field, now notorious as a Red leader through the exposure of the Institute of Pacific Relations, and

A. A. Heller, long an active Communist and a member of the Party's radio and television committee. To these were added Lewis Merrill, Communist head of the United Office and Professional Workers at that time, Professor Walter Rautenstrauch of Columbia University, who was a member of fifty Communist fronts up to the time of his recent death, and Harry Sacher, the lawyer who was sentenced to jail for contempt in connection with the Communist trial at Foley Square in 1949. (The records of these people are given so frequently in the hearings and reports of the Committee on Un-American Activities that they cannot all be given here, though reference to that committee itself would confirm these statements. For instance, Dr. Rautenstrauch's membership in fifty Communist fronts appears on page 107, *The Communist "Peace" Offensive*, April 1, 1951.)

These "leaders" were joined by Professor Margaret Schlauch of New York University, who has now gone to Red Poland to advance Stalin's cause, Professor Dirk J. Struik of the Massachusetts Institute of Technology, recently indicted in that State, and, as leader of them all, Alexander Trachtenberg, Soviet representative on culture in this country and a veteran Red leader.

In order to attract a large enrollment, the Jefferson School offered a wide range of subjects. These included special classes for children, including instruction in puppetry, and embraced politics, writing, political economy, history, music—and above all, Marxism-Leninism. Dr. Harry F. Ward, professor emeritus in Christian ethics at Union Theological Seminary, presented in 1945 a series of lectures on Religion and Society, which was in keeping with his record as a member of more than sixty Communist fronts. The content of the music courses offered can be judged from some of the titles: "Music of Protest," "Music of the Class Struggle." All subjects were thus permeated with the Marxist-Leninist ideology.

In 1953, the Jefferson School is still functioning on a big scale. The *Daily Worker* of December 19, 1952, announced that the Jefferson School had launched a campaign for 4,000 registrations in the winter term classes beginning January 12,

1953. "The school's winter term catalog," the *Daily Worker*
states, "announces 78 ten-session courses, providing for the
study of Marxist-Leninist theory and practice in the fields of
economics, politics, history, philosophy, science, and the arts."
Three grades of seminar program, in a special Institute of
Marxism connected with the school, are also mentioned. The
reader will note that it is the Marxist-Leninist interpretation of
these varying subjects which is stressed.

The director of the Jefferson School is Dr. Howard Selsam,
whom the *Daily Worker* has played up (specifically in its
issue of February 9, 1944) as having a Ph.D. degree from
Columbia University and having taught at Brooklyn College
for ten years. His choice as director was necessarily prompted
by his complete adherence to the principles of Marxism-Leninism. Nothing illustrates this better than the testimony of
Frank Meyer, ex-Communist and former instructor at the Jefferson School, in the 1949 trial at Foley Square. According to this
evidence, the entire teaching staff of the Jefferson School, including Dr. Selsam specifically, were arbitrarily ordered by
Jack Stachel, leading member of the American Politburo, to
work for the destruction of "Browder revisionism." These directives were given to Dr. Selsam and his staff when Stachel
appeared before them at a special meeting in the fall of 1945.

Of the Jefferson School's director, the Senate Sub-Committee
on Internal Security says: "Howard Selsam has been identified
by numerous witnesses in sworn testimony as a member of the
Communist Party. He was suspended from the New York City
school system in 1942," and the committee points out that "a
full account of Selsam's Communist record" appears as early
as the report of the Rapp-Coudert Legislative Committee of New
York State in that year. The Sub-Committee adds: His books
have been published by International Publishers, the official
publishers of the Communist Party. When he was subpoenaed,
he was asked about all this evidence, and he invoked his Constitutional privilege rather than deny it. In doing so, Selsam issued
a statement "completely at variance with the printed testi-

mony," and of this statement the Sub-Committee declares: "The biased and inaccurate strictures of Mr. Selsam, whom the Sub-Committee considered a recognized Communist spokesman and educator, have for reasons difficult for the Sub-Committee to understand, been reflected with remarkable similarity in the comments of certain educators, editors, and well known public figures." It is apparent then that the influence of the Jefferson School goes far afield indeed. (Report of Sub-Committee on Internal Security, *Subversive Influence in the Educational Process*, July 17, 1953, pp. 26, 27.)

Since the Senate Sub-Committee makes such a point of Selsam's example in pleading the fifth amendment to the Constitution when asked about his Communist affiliations and activities, it can be stated that the first example of all was set by J. Peters, the notorious espionage agent and representative of the Communist International. Peters set the pattern for pleas under the first and fifth amendments when subpoenaed by the House Committee on Un-American Activities in the Alger Hiss case. Subsequently the evidence against Peters was so great that he "voluntarily" left this country when he was about to be deported as an illegal alien and Communist agent. The pace set by the Communist International espionage agent is followed by Selsam of the Jefferson School and then aped by others. This simple set of circumstances around the pleas under the first and fifth amendments before Congressional committees is symbolic of the control of the Jefferson School by the Communist leaders and the influence, direct or indirect, which it then exercises upon others. (*Hearings Regarding Communist Espionage in the United States Government*, House Committee on Un-American Activities, 80th Congress, second session, pp. 1267-1271.)

Through the years since its establishment, down to this writing, the Jefferson School has relied for its enrollment upon the orders sent out through the Communist Party to make certain of a large registration, and through favorable notices and advertisements in the *Daily Worker*.

Because of its special emphasis upon enrolling Communists

who are not engaged in full-time professional work for the Party, this school proves an effective agency for training those who are to infiltrate mass organizations. To protect them in this infiltration, the school recently ruled that the full name of students would not be kept on any permanent rolls. By this measure, a mantle of strict secrecy was thrown over the identity of the individuals in attendance, both to evade the FBI and to make it possible for these concealed Communists to enter government posts and other key positions. The Jefferson School can be described, accordingly, as the training and drilling ground for the infiltrators for the Kremlin into the various avenues of American life. It is no wonder that it receives frequent mention in the reports of the House Committee on Un-American Activities and is prominently listed as subversive in the *Guide* published by that Committee on March 3, 1951.

The entire training of the Communist is in preparation to carry through that combination of "legal" and "illegal" work which Lenin so specifically stresses. There are two aspects to this form of combined activity. The first of these is the general "legal" and "illegal" work of the Party as a whole, which leads it openly to advocate reforms and other "popular" measures on the one hand, and to forward its "revolutionary" goal on the other. The second aspect is the individual Communist's legal and illegal work, the latter of which may go over into espionage. There are scores of Party members who are not called upon to engage in illegal work in this sense. A chosen few, selected because of their aptitude or position, are designated for underground activities. Some of these may be ordered to devote their full time to such underground work, especially when it embraces espionage, and to cut themselves off completely from any organic connection with the Party. Their sole Red contacts become the Soviet secret police agents who direct their work, in addition to those very few concealed Communists or fellow travelers engaged in the same "ring."

It is the custom, arising from conspiracy as a whole, for the Soviet espionage representative to organize secret agents in separate "rings." In that way, should one of these groups be discovered by American security agencies, the others will continue to function. Sometimes, this causes momentary difficulties, as when a member of one ring seeks to recruit a member of another. We note the clash between Hede Massing, former wife of Gerhart Eisler, and Alger Hiss over which espionage group Noel Field was to function for in the State Department. It is recorded in Mrs. Massing's testimony. There is also my own experience in attempting to place Communists in the Office of Strategic Services for Jacob Golos, Soviet espionage agent, and the discovery that some of these people were already penetrating the OSS under the direction of Eugene Dennis. (Hede Massing's testimony on this point appears in *Hearings of Senate Sub-Committee on Internal Security*, Institute of Pacific Relations, Part I, pp. 233-34.)

To carry on such work with the minimum of friction and the maximum results requires an exercise of obedience, discipline, and readiness to accept orders which flows from careful training. In the main, the Communist has had this training in advance of his secret work, by the methods of drilling and conditioning used for the Party as a whole. Extra cautions and directives, often given arbitrarily by the Soviet agents, round out this original education. In some instances, however, the Party has conducted for a short period of time special classes for those who were to engage in infiltration and who could be used, if necessary, in more serious secret work.

There are also quite a few of the comrades who are called upon from time to time to mingle their open activities for the Party with secret and even espionage work. A noticeable case in point is that of Steve Nelson, who represented the Party in various capacities as section and district organizer, but was also engaged in obtaining information from atomic laboratories for the Soviet embassy. Those who have read my affidavit in *The Shameless Years*, a report on Soviet espionage on the House Committee on Un-American Activities, will get a good glimpse of the combination of open and secret Party work.

The summation of Communist education is contained in the constant exhortations to the comrades to study and re-study the "great treasury of revolutionary theory and revolutionary experience," Stalin's *History of the Communist Party of the Soviet Union*, and his other works. In the September 26, 1952 issue of the Cominform organ, as one illustration, there appears a lengthy recitation of the necessity to study this *History*. It is declared to be "the great treasure house of revolutionary theory and revolutionary experience, a genuine encyclopedia of basic knowledge of Marxism-Leninism." To which is added this thought: "Comrade Stalin, leader and teacher of the working people of the world, placed in the hands of the Communist and Workers Parties a powerful and ideological weapon which has equipped and is equipping the cadres of the Party with knowledge of the laws of social development and of political struggle, with an understanding of the motive forces of revolution." The work is hailed as "Marxism-Leninism in action."

In the same issue, it is stated that during the fourteen years since "this brilliant work by Comrade J. V. Stalin" was published, it has been sold in 41,000,000 copies in Soviet Russia. In Hungary, since the Communists seized power, the sales amounted to 664,000. In Bulgaria, after the Communists came into control, the total sold was 355,000. In Rumania, since Communist control, the editions have reached 1,000,000. In short, it is compulsory in Soviet Russia and under the satellite regimes to buy this book. In non-Soviet countries, there has been a more limited distribution, but the Communists have sought to spread it widely in their own ranks and among sympathizers.

Through this work, the experiences of the Communist Party of the Soviet Union are made the guide for Communists throughout the world—teaching them complete discipline, devotion to Stalin, to his successor Malenkov, and to Soviet world conquest. Through this device, and the other teachers of Communist training, non-gangsters are developed into acceptance of a gangster philosophy and blind acceptance of any decree handed down in the name of "the leader and teacher."

CHAPTER VII

THE ROLE OF THE COMMUNIST PRESS

THE COMMUNIST press is distinctly different from all other forms of journalism. It is the telegraph agency sending directives from Moscow throughout the world, and passing them on and making them understandable to the comrades in each country. It is the means of transmitting the Communist line, so that it will be carried forward with maximum effectiveness in every part of the globe, and applied specifically to each non-Soviet country.

Every attempt to analyze official Communist publications is futile unless this distinctive characteristic, its very essence, is fully appreciated. That characteristic arises from the conspiratorial nature of Soviet communism. If the Kremlin were to cable every week to its fifth columns throughout the world: "Work up a synthetic campaign for peace in order to aid Soviet aggression," it would soon be clear what Moscow had in mind and was seeking to persuade American public opinion to believe. Or if Malenkov were to cable William Z. Foster, at present head of the Soviet fifth column here: "Work for recognition of Red China, so that we may be able permanently to endanger American security and make China the base for world conquest," there would be no doubt of the repercussions. And if in the United States, in turn, Foster were to wire Communist district leaders throughout the country to the same effect, public indignation against these conspirators would be thoroughly aroused.

A much more cunning scheme has been devised, the conveying of precisely these instructions—and many more to the same subversive effect—through articles and editorials in the official Red press which often have the appearance of "scientifically" discussing current world problems. The Communist conspiracy thereby has the huge advantage of being able freely to convey instructions which lead to the defeat of non-Soviet countries, and have led to the defeat of the United States at Yalta, Potsdam, and in Korea, while hiding their conspiratorial messages under the guise of "freedom of the press." Once again we observe "democratic processes" used for the destruction of democracy. Many non-Communist newspapers have defended the right of the *Daily Worker* to publish its subversive directives, which are the immediate occasion for subversive acts, when these same newspapers might oppose the direct cable and telegraph instructions to which I have referred. They would consider them "an overt act"—but the Soviet fifth column carries on overt acts every day through the medium of the Red press which blinded non-Communist editors and publishers defend.

The official Communist publications are a chief item in Soviet psychological warfare within each non-Soviet country. This has too often been overlooked by American leadership, and brought the United States to the serious pass in which it finds itself today. A number of tendencies in American life facilitate these operations. The widespread dissemination of the philosophy of pragmatism is one of these. Pragmatism, while not a Communist philosophy, is a groundbreaker for Communism. But the stimulus, the initiation of campaigns to obtain acceptance of the Communist line, stems from the fifth column and its press.

From Moscow Into American Life

Before proceeding to an analysis of the Red press, we can refer to a case which lights up the whole subject. In October, 1952, in his address to the Nineteenth Party Congress of the Com-

munist Party of the Soviet Union, Joseph V. Stalin called upon
the Communists "in the imperialist countries" (that is, the
United States among others) to raise higher "the banner of
bourgeois civil liberties." This was the height of arrogance on
the part of the dictator who had sent hundreds of thousands of
men and women to death and millions more to slave labor
camps. By "bourgeois civil liberties," we learn from Stalin's
discussion of "social reforms," the Communists mean merely
defense of their conspiracy with the outcry that if it is ham-
pered, the liberties of all the others will be in jeopardy. The
contention is thoroughly false, since the Communists are the
chief enemies of civil liberties in the democratic world, but
it has frequently proved successful in blunting any genuine
efforts to curb the conspiracy.

Stalin's words were published for his followers throughout
the world in the Cominform organ, *For a Lasting Peace, For a
People's Democracy*. They were re-published in *Political Affairs*, the official theoretical organ of the Communist Party in
the United States, and burst forth in the pages of the *Daily
Worker*, the daily telegraph agency to the conspirators in this
country.

The Communists here had to translate these instructions into
concrete American terms, so that the "transmission belts" would
carry them out into American life. A barrage against every attempt to deal with the conspiracy, reached its high point in
Political Affairs in February 1953. An official statement of the
National Committee, appearing in its pages in draft form, declared "McCarthyism" to be the main menace. Immediately, the
Daily Worker filled its pages with editorials and articles against
"McCarthyism." In one edition, no less than eleven articles
in the eight pages were devoted to that subject.

Now an article is as much a directive to a Communist as an
editorial; the Red functionary or member never reads a Communist article merely to get information. He always looks for
the order that is given by it. During the spring and early summer of 1953, the concealed Communists accordingly got busy,

influencing some leading political figures and a number of organizations to condemn "McCarthyism." As time went on, in order to stimulate this practice, the Red organ ran a column every day entitled: "Americans versus McCarthyism," which recorded expressions by community figures, politicians, and newspapers in echo of the *Daily Worker*. As has frequently occurred, former Attorney General Francis Biddle opened the assault early, to be followed very quickly by Americans for Democratic Action, of which he is a leading member. Into the charge also rushed Senator Herbert H. Lehman of New York, the state where the Communist-controlled American Labor Party has had so much effect on the thinking of many political leaders. The hysteria against "McCarthyism" extended far beyond the Communist Party periphery, reaching even into conservative circles.

By June 1, the *Daily Worker* could state exultingly that it was the "initiator" of the crusade against "McCarthyism," calling the roll of those who had followed the Communist line in this respect. In an editorial entitled "Our Crusade Hits Home," it went on to demand that everyone seeking to curb the conspiracy be driven from public life. For according to the Communist interpretation, "McCarthyism" is every move to halt subversion, from the Federal Bureau of Investigation, through the Department of Justice, to the Federal Courts.

Although the chief butt of all this agitation were the Congressional inquiries into subversion, headed respectively by Senators William Jenner and Joseph R. McCarthy and by Representative Harold H. Velde, the larger plan also met with success. On July 17, 1953, a careful observer, David Lawrence, could state in the *United States News and World Report* that the government in the six preceding months had pursued a "soft" policy toward the Communists in the United States. This was in contrast to the demands of the people at the polls, Mr. Lawrence contended, who had voted for a "one-hundred percent" attitude against Communist infiltration. The Washington commentator could also state that the last six months had seen the government "fumbling the anti-Communist problem," yielding to the clamor about alleged "book burning," and entering into a truce in Korea which does not recognize the perfidy of the Reds in Asia.

While all of these results are not exclusively the outcome of Communist agitation, but arose also from appeasement tendencies in certain leading American circles, they were given their impetus by the unceasing work of the concealed Reds. Thus, it was Stalin, although dead by the middle of 1953, who through unloosing Communist activities by "transmission belts," had shaped once again American policies and a considerable segment of public opinion.

The reader must not forget that, while this subversive agitation was going forward so well in our own country, the Communist press in other lands was stirring up anti-American sentiment. This, again, was in accordance with Stalin's directive in his famous report of October, 1952, to create "contradictions" among the Western Powers, and with Malenkov's report at the same time that the United States was the chief menace to world peace.

Transmission of the Line

The foundations for the Communist line, and therefore for the directives which appear in the Communist press, are laid down by the official statements of the masters of the Kremlin. For the current line of 1953, the basic documents are Stalin's speech to the Nineteenth Congress; Stalin's report on *Economic Problems of Socialism* in the USSR, published in October, 1952; and G. M. Malenkov's leading report to the Nineteenth Congress, *On the Threshold of Communism.*

These official declarations are published and republished in the Communist press, quoted in that press on numerous occasions, and made the broad basis for Communist activity during any given period. They are reiterated in a hundred forms, to keep them before the Party membership. In June, 1953, in order to stress the importance of Stalin's report as guiding the line of that time, *Political Affairs* issued a 31-page supplement in the form of a reader's guide for the study of the report. (*Economic Problems of Socialism in the USSR*, Joseph Stalin, International Publishers, New York, 1952; *On the Threshold of Communism*, G. M. Malenkov, New Century Publishers, New York, 1952.)

If a larger number of leaders in American thought and government had examined these reports carefully, they would have been informed as to the weaknesses of Soviet rule, of which we should take advantage. They would also have learned of the irrevocable determination of the Soviet dictatorship to utilize any move—and specifically the Korean "truce"—to expand the Kremlin's aggression. The Communists know all this, for they have been busily engaged in studying these reports.

Since Stalin had to speak to the people of the Soviet Union as well as to the Communists of the world, his report (however cautiously) had to reflect some of the difficulties within the Soviet regime which later on burst into public notice with the liquidation of Lavrenti P. Beria, former head of the Soviet secret police. By stating that "man-made laws cannot do away with the laws of science," Stalin is frankly answering the impatience of those who expect the Soviet dictatorship to fulfill its pledges. By his declaration that "mental labor will always be different from manual labor," of which he makes much, he is strengthening the hand of the Soviet bureaucracy which is so essential to the dictatorship and which lies so heavily on the people of Soviet Russia. His new condition for attaining "the classless society," which in effect postpones the coming of that society, is also designed to bolster up the dictatorship.

But Stalin also told the Communists how they can win in the current world struggle. It is through penetration of Western thought and the development of "contradictions" among the Western nations, which may bring them into friction with each other but which may also lead those nations which stand most for appeasement to influence the policies of the United States in that direction. That is precisely what was emphasized during the months which followed Stalin's report, and we can not fail to recognize that his dead hand has been leading the Communists to victory over the West. This need not have been the case had the United States (carefully studying Stalin's words before they were carried into action) adopted a firm policy that would have made the nations associated with us take to a different path.

In Malenkov's report, four tasks are set down for the Communists "in the sphere of foreign policy." The first of these is to continue "solidarity with peace supporters all over the world," which expresses itself in encouragement of the "peace partisans," those men and women who join Communist peace fronts and aid to undermine the morale of the United States and other non-Soviet nations. The second is to forward East-West trade, which has already shown its ugly features in the exposes of the Senate Committee under the chairmanship of Senator Joseph R. McCarthy. While the South Koreans were losing 45,000 men, the United States 25,000, Great Britain 600, and all other nations on the UN side 1900 by death on the battlefield, Great Britain and several other of these nations were engaged in trade with the enemy, Red China. East-West trade will never be an honest arrangement on the part of the Kremlin, because of its controlled economy. Soviet Russia and its satellite regimes will buy what they need for building up their military machines, and will sell to the West only what Moscow wants sold.

The third task outlined in Malenkov's report is "to strengthen and develop inviolable relations of friendship" between Soviet Russia and the satellite-controlled nations. In Soviet parlance, that merely means consolidating the Kremlin's iron rule over these countries.

The fourth task, which should not be passed over lightly, is "tirelessly to strengthen the defense might of the State" in order "to give any aggressor a crushing blow." The "aggressor," from Malenkov's view is, of course, quite obvious. It is the United

States of America, described at great length in his pages as the "aggressor" in Korea and as also the source of all possible future aggression.

When these reports are summed up, they indicate clearly that Soviet Russia will observe no "truce" or peace arrangement. The Kremlin is consolidating its control over the subject peoples, for the purpose of having a larger base to proceed toward world conquest. In the same manner, Stalin forecast, in the *Foundations of Leninism,* that the establishment of "socialism in one country" would be the base or fulcrum for the overthrow of all non-Soviet countries, a forecast which, unfortunately, almost no one but the Communists heeded seriously.

The Communist press is the vehicle throughout the world which has conveyed this general line for the 1953 period that has been so profitable for Soviet purposes. As events develop, that press forwards important portions of this line. It brings it "into life," in other words, drives it home to the concealed Communists, and moves them to persuade non-Communists to take up the cudgels for this or that portion of the Communist line. In this way—and this has been a specific feature of the first six months of 1953—what Moscow wants done is retailed in various forms in certain American newspapers from San Francisco to New York.

The Cominform's Organ

Of the transmission agencies for conveying the Communist line to the leaders of the Soviet fifth columns, the first to be noted is the organ of the Cominform, *For a Lasting Peace, For a People's Democracy.* It is published each week in Bucharest, in the world's major languages, and comes into the United States regularly in its English translation. Its columns are filled with lengthy and often complicated articles and reports from various countries, which do not readily invite constant reading. The Communist leaders in every land, however, study them avidly to find the directives they contain, and to learn how the alleged facts in these articles and reports can be used in their own publications to influence the country in which each of them is operating. In addition, each issue contains a leading editorial on the front page which the Communists of each country are required to translate into propaganda and action with all speed.

Second in importance in the line of transmission is the *New Times,* also published weekly as a supposed supplement to the magazine *Trud* in Moscow. *New Times* appears in Russian, English, French, German, Spanish, Polish, Czech, Rumanian, and Swedish editions. It also reaches the United States regularly and with considerable speed. It is devoted to less lengthy articles than the Cominform organ, rarely runs any official report, but tends to concentrate on journalistic contributions which can aid the Reds throughout the world in developing the line. Generally it also contains a leading editorial which stresses the important ideas to be spread or the important work among "mass organizations" to be stressed during a specific time.

The line as developed by the Soviet leaders, and as broken down into specific tasks by the Cominform organ and *New Times,* is then transmitted for the enlightenment and action of the Communists in the American scene through *Political Affairs,* the official theoretical organ of the Communist Party in the United States. (Prior to 1944, this publication was known as *The Communist.* Every Red organization in every country has its own theoretical organ. That of the French Party is *Cahiers du Communisme,* in which Jacques Duclos wrote his famous article in 1945 which brought about the deposition of Earl Browder as leader of the Communists in America. For the "mother Party," the Communist Party of the Soviet Union, this organ was known as *The Bolshevik* until October, 1952, when its name was officially changed to *The Communist.* It was in the last edition of *The Bolshevik* that Stalin published his *Economic Problems of Socialism in the USSR,* which now dominates the Communist line throughout the world.)

Through *Political Affairs*—written specifically for the Party functionaries, though it has to pose as a magazine of general circulation—notice is given in advance of how the line is to be developed and intensified for application in the United States. Certain articles also deal with the handling of specific American organizations or problems which arise within this country, all dealt with, however, against the general background of the international Communist line.

A Sample of "Political Affairs"

A summary of the June, 1953 issue of *Political Affairs* shows that the first article is by William Z. Foster on "Fighting War with Peace and Democracy." It is an application to the United States of the orders given by Stalin in October, with instructions to the Communists here how they must carry out this order in the AFL and CIO, among other organizations, and in the newspapers. Foster specifically gives the basis of his instructions: "What is happening now to the Soviet peace campaign is the concretization of these basic policies of Stalin, the great Marxist-Leninist theoretician and leader. The present peace offensive, stemming from the Nineteenth Congress, is the fruition of the historic peace policy of the USSR."

A second article, "The Anatomy of McCarthyism," records some of the non-Communist sources which have echoed the Red attack, and then emphasizes that "the fight against McCarthyism" is the fight against any attempt to curb the Communist conspiracy. This article echoes Stalin's order of October 1952, to raise the banner of "bourgeois civil liberties."

Next we have two contributions that deal with problems within this country, "Lessons of the Struggle Against Opportunism in District 65" and "Labor and the Democratic Party." The latter piece unfolds still further the program for infiltrating the Democratic and Republican parties laid down by the National Committee of the Communist Party, first in February and reiterated in the July issue of *Political Affairs*. Such infiltration, which is in accord with the amended Trojan Horse policy of the conspiracy in 1953, is to be made more effective by the Communists' reacquainting themselves "with the real situation in the local and State Democratic parties (and in many areas the Republican party)." This is all for the purpose of defeating "McCarthyism" fully, and for the added purpose of forwarding the "peace policy" of the Soviet Union. That this new Trojan Horse tactic must not result in any concessions by the Communists or any softening of their intention to destroy the United States, is stressed by the article "against opportunism in District 65," which outlines "the path of renegacy" which the Red trade union leaders in that labor organization have followed in their attempt to ally themselves with "the old political parties" and the CIO.

There is also, in that June issue, an important directive article on "Zionism and Bourgeois Nationalism," designed to arm the comrades with arguments against the charge that Soviet Russia is anti-Semitic. At the same time, by denouncing Zionism as "reactionary" but stating that the whole problem must be viewed "in the context of the struggle for peace," it keeps the door open either to assail the Jews again or to put on a more hypocritical face in their regard, according to the progress which Soviet Russia makes in coming to terms with the State of Israel and the international Zionist movement.

The entire June issue is climaxed by the Reader's Guide to Stalin's report, which makes this foundation of the present line a required study in every Communist unit. It makes it also imperative that there be frequent references to this report in the Communist press, so that the comrades will be constantly reminded to go back to it.

Functions of the "Daily Worker"

The *Daily Worker* has the obligation to drive every day for those things that comrades must do from day to day to make the line register in this country. On some occasions, certain sections of our press, grossly misinformed about Communism, have reported the imminent collapse of this Red organ. They

have jested at its small circulation and have tended to dismiss
it as unworthy of consideration. These jests are completely out
of order. The *Daily Worker* is the most powerful publication in
the United States today and has been for a number of years.
In 1945, it demanded the removal of official after official from
the State Department, all of these gentlemen being opponents
of Soviet policy; its demands were acceded to by the then Secretary of State Stettinius and "the head of the pro-Soviet bloc
in the State Department," Dean Acheson. The latter soon succeeded to the post of Secretary of State, to the great satisfaction
of the *Daily Worker*. (Consult my *The Cry Is Peace*, chap. II,
"The Kremlin in the State Department." The designation given
Mr. Acheson is that of Adolf A. Berle, former Assistant Secretary of State.)

In the first six months of 1953, the *Daily Worker* conducted
a frantic campaign for a Korean truce on the basis of the Red
Chinese and Red Korean proposals—and that was the truce that
was finally established, as the *New Times* of June 23 trium-
phantly declared. Again, there were the feverish drives against
"McCarthyism" and "book burning," which were echoed
through concealed Communists in many organizations and newspapers in this country, and which ended in a Communist victory
for the retention of a number of books by subversive authors
in our libraries. By shouting that "freedom of religion" was
being endangered by any inquiry into subversive affiliations of
the members of religious groups, the Red organ succeeded in
distorting the issue completely. More than that, by its directive
editorial of July 17, it threw the mantle of "freedom of religion" around all its own atheistic and subversive ventures,
preparing for a like outcry whenever anyone of its fronts is
exposed or becomes subject to government prosecution.

The power of the *Daily Worker* cannot be measured by its
subscription lists. I must repeat that it is not a normal newspaper but a telegraph agency for the conspiracy. It will continue to be published even if its circulation were to fall to
8,000, as it was on one occasion, or below. Every morning the

Communist leader in each part of the country picks up his *Daily Worker* to learn from its editorials and articles what he should order to be done immediately. Thereupon, he calls in the functionaries of the District bureau, who are in charge of the various areas to be penetrated, and gives them instructions. These instructions are based on the *Daily Worker*, plus such mail drop secret directives as he receives from time to time. He has already a forewarning of the application of the line from *Political Affairs* and the Red organs that come from abroad. But from the *Daily Worker* he gets his instructions on what should be done that day to make the line move forward in the community.

The functionaries of the District bureau then get in touch with the representatives of the cells planted in newspapers, religious groups, cultural organizations, and labor unions—transmitting to them the orders which have come from above. Many of these persons also read the *Daily Worker*, and are prepared for the orders they receive. Some of them have kept closely in touch with the Cominform organ *New Times*, and with *Political Affairs* (especially with the latter), and not only have a perception of how they should develop the line but also know some of the arguments they can use on the unwary or gullible.

From the Red Press "Into Life"

In this fashion the Communist official publications provide a chain of conspiratorial directives which become effective weapons in penetrating the thought of non-Soviet countries. If any attempt is made to interfere with their transmission, they can always appeal to "freedom of the press." During the Hitler-Stalin Pact period, when the Communists suspected that they would come into a physical clash with the United States on behalf of Hitler, the *Daily Worker* openly prepared this defense by naming the "corporation" by which it is allegedly controlled, the "Freedom of the Press Company, Inc."

The reader will keep in mind that the concealed Communist

in his agency, community organization, or neighborhood is following the line set down in the Red official press, in accordance with his own readings and the directives he gets from the functionary in charge of his work. A Communist who is a newspaperman in charge of educational coverage for a large daily paper will proceed according to such directives. Recently, the Soviet fifth column has shouted "academic freedom" whenever the question of subversion in the schools is raised. The Communist newspaper man, or the newspaper man under Communist influence, will proceed to dig out every bit of "evidence" that he can to support the fifth column's contentions. He will put the Communist issue in the background and play up the "grave danger" to academic freedom. Interviews will be arranged with those presidents of colleges who have been known to protect Communists on their faculties, in order that they will repeat the Communist chant "academic freedom is in peril." Alleged surveys will be made of educational institutions aimed at showing that "fear" has been created among faculty members in general. It matters little to the Communist newspaper man that this is a false and distorted presentation—and that real intimidation has been practiced by the concealed Reds for years through smears, whispering, and charges of "fascism" and now "McCarthyism." Through this one person, placed in a strategic position on a newspaper, the Communist line can be insinuated into the thinking of thousands of non-Communists.

So, also, with the concealed Communists or their allies, who have means of working upon the petty political bias or personal weaknesses of men in high public office. When the Red official organs give the word, and the Party functionaries order it to be carried out, these concealed followers of the Kremlin can readily persuade such a public figure to assail "McCarthyism" and to attack the ex-Communists who testify for the government. It has been done and it is still being done, and thereby the whole fabric of American thinking is endangered.

But this method of the conspiracy gives a certain advantage to patriotic and thoughtful Americans, if they will give serious time and attention to it. They can be forewarned in advance of what Moscow wants Americans to think. They can oppose the "line" in their communities, in local organizations, through letters to the newspapers and their representatives in Congress, because they are intelligently informed as to what this "line" is.

So far the "line" has not been opposed often enough, nor early enough, and has been eminently successful. From the record, it can soberly be said that the Kremlin has too frequently persuaded non-Soviet countries, including the United States, to do what it wanted done.

Case History: East-West Trade

A few case histories of the triumph of the Communist line, even though briefly reviewed, will be in order. An important component of that line in recent years, second only to "the pact of peace," has been the demand for "East-West trade." There could be no honesty in this demand, for with the Soviet-controlled economy that trade will be manipulated solely to satisfy the military needs of Soviet power. Soviet Russia and its satellite regimes will accept only such goods as build up their military might and dispose of such goods as they wish to get rid of. And yet, in the midst of the opening guns of World War III, in Korea, significant advances were made by the Soviet-controlled countries in this field.

It began as a small cloud on the horizon, as is usually the case, and developed into a huge thunder-cloud. The Soviet government began it all by calling the "International Economic Conference" in Moscow beginning April 3, 1952. Correspondents for the general press told us that it was not well attended by Western business men, and intimated that it was a failure. This was highly inaccurate, as so many predictions by the general American press prove to be when Moscow is involved. The *New Times* of April 9 and 16 served notice on the Communists throughout the world that "East-West trade" must be made a success. The Cominform organ took it up through 1952 and

1953, recording the number of municipal councils and other organizations in Europe which voted in favor of such trade.

We pause here to observe that this method of recording certain events favorable to the "line" is the common device for intensifying the instructions to carry out that line in all countries and communities. When a Communist reads that a certain organization in France has taken a stand which fits in with Moscow's current instructions, or when he notes that this has been done by a group in New York, he does not regard this merely as information. It is also, and specifically, an order for him to go out and do likewise. The Communist press has to be read in that sense.

"East-West trade" was taken up by *Political Affairs* and the *Daily Worker*, their great argument being that anyone opposing the building up of Soviet strength in this matter was "bringing on a depression." The argument was thoroughly unsound, for the reason that Soviet Russia will purchase only what it needs in comparatively small quantities, will copy as much as it can of the machines and other material bought, and will clamp down on any trade when such an act will do most damage to the Western world. When the Senate committee headed by Senator Joseph McCarthy publicized the billion-dollar-trade which Great Britain and others of our "allies" had carried on with Red China, thus aiding Mao Tse-tung to slaughter the UN forces in Korea, the *Daily Worker* hurled its "depression" charge. In its leading editorial of July 21, 1953, "McCarthy Wants Depression," the Red daily organ wrote: "Senator McCarthy's committee achieved a big publicity splash over the week-end with its 'exposé' of the growing east-west trade, especially with People's China . . . it appears that McCarthy would rather have a depression America in which pro-fascist demagogs could bid for power than increased trade with the world and new stimulants for the wheels of industry."

Against this Red charge—which, incidentally in varying forms was repeated in some non-Communist circles—the harsh facts stand out: the large proportion of South Korean and American dead among the UN forces in Korea. We have to repeat that while this gruesome monument was being built, Great Britain (with very small forces in Korea) and some of our other "allies" were engaging in this trade that directly or indirectly aided the slaughter and helped the enemy.

By July 24, 1953, East-West trade had developed so far that the Cominform organ could state in its issue of that date: "The growing capacity of the world democratic market (that is, the Soviet-controlled market) opens wide perspectives for developing trade relations with all countries. World public opinion has welcomed with satisfaction the recent news of the signing of a trade and payments agreement between the USSR and France, of the signing of the Soviet-Danish protocol for extending mutual deliveries, of the development of the Soviet-Finnish trade relations, and also the news of trade transactions between Britain and China, between France and China, etc."

The Red international organ compliments "business circles in those capitalist countries" which have taken this new turn, and denounces the United States as the villain who is seeking to prevent "peaceful trade relations." Just how "peaceful" this trade has been, and will prove to be, has been revealed by the figures released by Senator McCarthy's committee. It is little wonder that the Moscow directive organ, *New Times* of July 15, 1953, warmly praised Great Britain almost as though that country were a Soviet ally. In following the course of the Communist line on "East-West trade" from Moscow and the Cominform into American life, two conclusions stand out: first, that the same line is being advanced in other countries simultaneously, and that we must offset it there with *deeds*, a firm American policy; and second, that the triumph of the line in this respect up to the present time is largely due to the basic failure of the American policy of "containment" and to the vacillations to which that policy gives rise. This policy, as opposed to firmness and liberation of the subject peoples, presupposes that we must buy allies by giving them billions of dollars, and must hold them by yielding to every weakness they display.

"The Pact of Peace"

A study of the transmission of the "pact of peace" idea would prove to be a good project for readers who wish to familiarize themselves thoroughly with the operations of the Communist press in forwarding Moscow's desires and purposes. The "pact of peace," we know, is the central point in the Communist line since 1951, when Soviet Russia suggested a meeting of the Big Four Powers which would include eventually Communist China as a fifth. The entire scheme was definitely for the purpose of bringing about recognition of Red China and its seating on the Security Council of the United Nations, as both the Cominform organ and *New Times* emphasized. Throughout 1952, the front page of the latter publication was emblazoned with "the crusade for the pact of peace," to be advanced through "the world front of peace partisans." There seemed to be little chance at that time, particularly with the Chinese Communists taking up aggression in Korea, that any such scheme as this could possibly succeed. Only a few warning voices, of individuals who knew thoroughly the operations of the Communists, could be heard telling of its dangers.

From Moscow and the Cominform, the cry was taken up in all countries, here in the United States by *Political Affairs* and the *Daily Worker*. Article after article dealt with "Soviet peace policy" and reiterated the demand for the "pact of peace." From within the United States and throughout the world, Communist organs published the names of organizations and outstanding individuals who came out for "the pact," and for recognition of Red China. The accumulated effect of this campaign, carried on in repetitive fashion by the Communist press, and echoed beyond Communist circles, finally burst into view in 1953. It was then that Great Britain came out for recognition of Red China. Within our own country, certain newspapers, notably the *Louisville Courier-Journal*, joined the chorus. By August 2, 1953, the *New York Herald Tribune* could say that it was only a question of time how long the United States could hold out against recognition of Red China, that is, against the pressure of its "allies" in that direction.

It is now clear that had American leadership on the whole been aware of the implications of this feature of the line from the beginning, as it should have been, an entirely different story would have been told in 1953. The United States would have insisted that Great Britain withdraw recognition of the Chinese Communist government if it is actually an ally of the United States.

By its frantic shouts for "peace," "peaceful coexistence between the Soviet Union and the United States," and its companion charges of "McCarthyism" and "fascism," the Communist press has succeeded in getting the concealed Communists to penetrate non-Communist groups with these same slogans. And out of the turmoil, the Soviet fifth column (manipulating the thinking of these non-Communist groups) has been able to bring enough pressure on Washington to make government action partially ineffective in the international arena.

The Korean "Truce" Campaign

With the Korean "truce" proposals, the same phenomenon is to be observed. Moscow let it be known, particularly through *New Times* of June 10, 1953, that the terms agreed to at Panmunjon were those which it wanted and which favored future Soviet aggressions. The leading editorial of that date declared that the "truce" marked "the successful conclusions of the negotiations," and also that the terms had been settled "on the basis of the Chinese-Korean proposals," that is, the Red aggressors' proposals. But *New Times* made it clear that this was only the beginning of the struggle. One of the issues requiring settlement in the earliest future, it declared, "is undoubtedly the question of restoring the legitimate rights of the Chinese and Korean peoples in the United Nations."

That statement, letting the Soviet cat out of the bag, referred to the coming ultimatum to the United States that Red China must be recognized. But it also said quite clearly that Moscow intended to have a Red Korea, since Syngman Rhee and his government had been denounced as "fascist," as "war criminals," and as "no legitimate government" at all.

The *Daily Worker* responded at once. It conducted a frenzied campaign to compel the United States government to accept the terms based on what pleased Moscow. Instructions were given in its pages on the need to get resolutions through organizations, to flood Washington with letters, and in other ways to stimulate "American expressions" in favor of the terms that the Kremlin wanted.

Taking the cue from Moscow about the plans for a Red Korea, the *Daily Worker* sought to channelize American concern at the battle casualties from opposition to the Communists in Asia to hatred of Syngman Rhee and the South Koreans. Almost immediately, this animus against President Rhee found expression in news scripts on radio and television and in certain newspaper commentaries. By July 5, 1953, the week-end edition of the *Daily Worker* could give a huge front page display to recording the success of its drive within America against Rhee and South Korea. Its account contained quotations from newspapers and magazines which had responded to the Communist line as laid down by the *Daily Worker* in mid-June.

By July 28, in furtherance of this plan for a completely Red Korea, the *Daily Worker* sent out to the faithful Stalinites an alarm about "the plot against the peace." This was the title of a leading editorial, which opened with these words: "Dulles is going to Korea to see his gangster-stooge, Syngman Rhee. He is taking with him 'the Senator from Formosa,' Knowland of California. So here we have three men meeting in secret before the Korea peace conference, every one of which hates the truce, hates peace, and hopes for more war as soon as possible." Here we have one of the thousands of examples of how the Communists, granted concessions of a serious character, press on for more. Placing all blame for any breach of the peace on the vacillating United States government, which has shown every sign of seeking to conciliate Moscow, the Red organ continues: "What is Dulles going to promise Rhee, now, with the China lobby agent Knowland sitting right next to him to make sure that peace does not come in Asia?"

Examine those terms "China lobby agent" and "Senator from Formosa" and you will be made familiar again with the manner in which the Communists coin phrases against their opponents, get them echoed in the American world, and then re-use them more effectively. The term "Senator from Formosa" first appeared in the pages of the alter ego of the *Daily Worker*, the *Peoples World* of California. "The China lobby" is an invention of the *Daily Worker* itself. Both terms broke into the general press in a big way. Lattimore borrowed them from the Communist press, and from his lips they were taken up and repeated by scores of concealed Communists and non-Communist commentators. In July, 1953, they were brought forward again by the *Daily Worker* in the expectation that they would be even more readily spread around the country than before. This is a striking illustration of the manner in which the Communist press manipulates the thinking of a considerable section of commentators and opinion makers in the American scene.

The concluding paragraph in the July 28, 1953, editorial is worth noting: "The greatest pressure by the people on the White House is needed now to make sure that Dulles does not steal the truce and start new killings, or prepare the way for new killings as Rhee criminally shouts for." By "the people"— and this should be remembered—the Red organ means its own Stalinite readers. They were to go out, either directly or indirectly, into the mass organizations ("the people") and under the guise of being non-Communists to persuade them to this course of action. The Marxist-Leninist ruling caste concept was at work here again.

By directing their fire at the Secretary of State, John Foster Dulles, and getting out the impression that he and Rhee were plotting war, they expected to raise such a hue and cry from self-appointed organizations which they penetrate as to weaken still further an American stand in the Far East. The way was paved for forcing American agreement to a Red Korea and a permanent Red China. The orders in the *New Times* to this effect were thus made a part of American thinking.

The Accumulation of Articles

There is one practice of the Communist press which must be known if we are properly to appraise what it is up to. It is the accumulation of a series of articles around a given subject. It is used at times in order to cover up the Communist designs in vague phraseology, these being clarified and made definite by articles which follow up on the same topic. The Communist functionary has this constantly in mind, and of course reads all Communist material as a whole. It is only by doing as he does that the full content of certain official directives can be intelligently studied.

When in 1936, the American Politburo decided to support Franklin D. Roosevelt for president, the announcement was not made bluntly, and most of the country did not know that this was the Communist policy. The official Red declarations accomplished the purpose by saying a few words critical of Roosevelt and then assaulting his opponents—the Liberty League and the "Hearst-McCormick-Patterson axis"—as "Fascists" and enemies of American liberties. In accompanying articles, both in *The Communist* and in the *Daily Worker*, rising to higher tones of stridency as the campaign went on, the denunciations became centered entirely on the president's opponents. In this wise, concealed Communists in all sorts of organizations did everything in their power for the election of Mr. Roosevelt, swaying hundreds of thousands to favor him. The sole cause for this attitude was that Moscow had divined that Mr. Roosevelt would be more favorable than his opponents to saving Soviet Russia from the Hitlerite regime which the Communists had helped to create. But, as is always the Communist custom and as the CIO committees state in their findings against the Red-ruled unions, this real object of the fifth column was hidden in a welter of charges against Roosevelt's opposition on domestic issues.

And so in 1953, the "Resolution on the Situation Growing Out of Presidential Elections," issued by the National Committee in February and July, 1953, would be almost unintelligible were it not for the articles in *Political Affairs* accompanying the resolution. Without those articles, it could be seen that the Communists (taking advantage of the new Trojan Horse policy of Moscow) plan to penetrate anew the Democratic and Republican parties. This could be understood from the conclusion that the two-party system is still strongly entrenched in the United States and that the Communists must recognize this reality. It could be gleaned from the statements indicating that "McCarthyism" is the main menace and that "pressure" must be exercised on certain politicians to combat this danger to the conspiracy. It could be caught sight of in the declaration that "the masses" still cling to the Democratic Party, and that the Communists must not remain aloof from "the masses." But the official resolution becomes more sharply understandable in reading two concurrent articles, "Labor and the Democratic Party" and "The Anatomy of McCarthyism." From the former I must repeat what I have quoted earlier in this chapter: "The left today in any event needs urgently to reacquaint itself with the real situation in the local and state Democratic parties (and in many areas the Republican party)." There is also the instruction for "the left forces in the CIO and AF of L (as well as in independent unions) to explore new possibilities for united labor action in the legislative and electoral field." All of this is for the purpose of advancing in a "pro-peace direction" (that is, in the "peace direction" which Moscow desires) and to compel large sections of the Democratic party to speak out "for an all-out struggle against McCarthy and his crowd."

From the second contribution, we learn definitely: "The immediate and broadest rallying ground in the struggle for democratic liberties is the fight against McCarthyism. This means the fight against Joe McCarthy the individual, against each and every McCarthyite—the Jenners, Veldes, and McCarrans—and against all manifestations of McCarthyism." This fight is to take place everywhere, but particularly "in the political field." (For an intelligent examination of this matter, consult *Political Affairs* for June and July, 1953.)

From these directives, it is plain that the Soviet fifth column in mid-1953 planned to penetrate the Democratic party (especially its "liberal" wing, to which definite reference is made) and also areas of the Republican party. The objective of this penetration was to halt all effective action against the conspiracy, which is labeled "McCarthyism," and even to punish anyone who would dare oppose the conspiracy. How far the Communists plan to go is exemplified by an editorial in the *Daily Worker* of July 30, 1953, entitled: "Expel the Stool Pigeons." This declaration demands nothing less than the discharge from his position of any person daring to testify at Congressional inquiries or elsewhere against the Soviet fifth column. This bears out the contention that many of those who cry out about "academic freedom" and "civil liberties" in defense of the Communists, in the majority of cases have no interest in these topics. They are bound by their Communist viewpoint that the civil liberties of all non-Communists must be destroyed. They are bound immediately by the *Daily Worker* directives that all those acting against the conspiracy must be deprived of a livelihood.

In addition to the official publications mentioned, the Communists have built up auxiliary magazines and newspapers in the United States, as they do in all other countries. One of the best known of these in the U.S.A. is *Masses and Mainstream*, published for the intellectuals at the same address at which *Political Affairs* is published. Another pro-Stalinite voice, with considerable influence, is *Science and Society*, a quarterly devoted to the Marxist interpretation of higher intellectual subjects. A number of foreign language dailies and weeklies, issued in almost every immigrant tongue, reach out into the "language communities," and follow the line laid down by the *Daily Worker*. On the West coast is issued the *Peoples World*, a localized edition of the Red daily organ published in New York. The *Daily Freiheit*, issued in the Yiddish language, is the second largest Red organ in circulation, after the *Daily Worker*, and is edited and printed in the same building with that paper.

Through these many channels, the Communist Party is able to transmit Moscow's orders in the most diversified and speediest fashion. By the uniformity of line which is established, and the readiness with which this line goes out of the Communist press into other journals, the publications under Moscow's control are among the most powerful in this country. They have not yet had the effect they had hoped for among "the backward masses," for the man in the street in this country has shown an instinctive abhorrence for the Communist cause and its line which many others, far better educated, might well have imitated. The strength of the Red press, it must be repeated, lies in moving concealed Communists and their allies to prevail upon non-Communist organizations to speak out for the Kremlin's position at any given time.

These methods can be defeated, as can all other Communist techniques. What is required is a number of people in each community throughout the country alert to the recommendations of the Communist press and zealous enough to expose them.

PART THREE

Communism in Action

CHAPTER VIII

AFFECTING PUBLIC OPINION

DURING THE past several years, "psychological warfare" has come to the fore in American discussions. A great deal has been said and written about it, and it is now acknowledged as one of the important phases of the current world conflict. From the very beginning of their existence, the Communists were aware of the power of this weapon as an outstanding means to advance the "class war."

To the followers of Lenin and Stalin, this procedure did not consist so much in hurling propaganda across national boundary lines, although they did not hesitate to carry on along this line also. Their great asset was infiltration of the institutions and organizations of the country they plan to undermine, following Lenin's instructions to employ perjury and deceit and Stalin's directive to make transmission belts of those organizations for the Communist line. One member of the vanguard could thereby become as a thousand men, moving hundreds of thousands of people unwittingly into action according to the Kremlin's wishes. By entering a "mass organization," as a cell, a small group of Communists could often influence and direct the entire course of that organization. By getting into a key position, such as secretary or head of a technical staff, the Communist could move an entire group along the path desired by Moscow. Even when such key positions were not immediately obtained, the representative of the conspiracy working under orders from the Party could frequently influence the policies of those in administrative posts, playing upon their prejudices, predispositions, and gullibility.

With this topic, then, we get into the heart of our subject and begin the examination of the real secret of Soviet success. Within the United States, the Communists have been able to win triumph after triumph in the field of public opinion through penetration under the guise of non-Communists.

Every act of the Communist is for the purpose of affecting public opinion, of making others think or act as Moscow desires, or at least of making them so uncertain that they are paralyzed in any effective opposition to the Stalinite dictatorship and its line. Infiltration, therefore, is deserving of our major consideration. In many ways, it is more powerfully effective for the Communists and more dangerous to American security than espionage, which is merely an extension of the same process.

In most instances, the infiltrator can easily be turned into an espionage agent, if that serves the purposes of the Soviet secret police. He is already equipped with a facility at secrecy, lying, and obedience to orders, requisites for the successful spy. The search light of exposure, thrown upon an espionage agent, reveals what is obviously an act against the security of our government and nation. But infiltration is much more subtle, and when exposed frequently leads to a cloud of dust in the form of controversy which befogs its menace.

Infiltration goes beyond espionage, and serves to protect and even justify, in certain segments of public opinion or leadership, the results of the espionage agents' work. Poland and China were taken over by Soviet Russia by a combination of espionage and infiltration, including in large measure infiltration of the American State Department. But it was the power of infiltration alone which persuaded the United States to acquiesce so completely in the permanency of a Red China and a Red Poland after these countries had been overcome by the Kremlin. This prevented our leadership from taking those moves that would have regained these countries to the free world. The Red argument that we should agree to peace at any price led to the crushing of the Four Freedoms which we had heard about so extensively during World War II.

Guide for Penetration

A guide for the comrades in penetrating trade unions, which is always the general model for working secretly in all organizations, was re-stated concretely by John Williamson, a member of the American Politburo, in the November, 1950, issue of *Political Affairs*. What he set down there has always been the procedure of the Communists, but he was compelled to present it again in definite terms because of the number of new functionaries who were being brought up as reserves in the Party.

From Williamson's directives, we learn that the individual Communist who is engaged in infiltration, and the Red cell with which he works, must look around for "immediate needs" upon which he can base agitation. He must seek out those grievances or arguments which will appeal to those around him as non-Communist in character; that is the meaning of "immediate needs." As soon as he has gained a foothold by this type of discussion and agitation, he is obliged to link up these "immediate needs" with the line of the Party, with those things the Kremlin wants done in America.

Next, he is to give to this whole operation a larger organizational form by establishing "close contact with those who are more inclined to progressive thought through belonging to progressive organizations in the communities or reading progressive papers." For "progressive" read "near-Communist" and the idea becomes clear. The aim is to bring forward constantly "new militant workers" behind whom and through whom the Communists can work. This will assure that the Red infiltrator is properly protected, a caution which is given not once but twice to underline its importance. Special precaution must be taken, says Williamson, against throwing the comrades into the kind of activity which will lead to their dismissal. That would cause them to be completely shut out from their field of operation.

We may pause for a moment on this particular instruction because it is so generally misunderstood. Many people in leading positions in government and in other agencies talk loosely about penalizing or unearthing "known Communists." A distinguished Senator even stated, in early 1953, that Communists should be permitted to teach in our educational system provided they did not expound Communism in the classroom. Normally, as Williamson's instruction shows, this is the last thing that they would do openly. They would get over the Communist line by reference to the works of concealed Communists or alleged non-Communists. They would pervade the classroom with Marxism-Leninism without anyone being able to state definitely that they had advocated Communism. But when they find a student susceptible to Communist ideas, they would encourage him privately in that direction; so also with colleagues on the teaching staff whom they may find to be inclined toward pro-Communism. That is not the end of their activities, for they cooperate secretly with Communists in parent-teachers groups, sometimes join Communist fronts and also extend Red propaganda in disguise in non-Communist organizations.

One reading of Williamson's directive shows us that such is the case. Not only does he caution the infiltrating Red against exposure, which might cause him to lose his influence or to be dismissed from his job; the Politburo member goes farther and also gives instructions as to how to make Marxists secretly. This is to be done by having systematic discussions with individual workers, winning them to the Party, or by small gatherings where Marxist literature is discussed. In other words, the Red infiltrator keeps his Communist affiliations hidden, save from those few who seem to be likely recruits to the conspiracy. Even they are to be approached carefully and only on an individual basis unless circumstances make small study groups in Marxism possible. ("Trade Union Tasks and Perspectives," John Williamson, *Political Affairs,* Nov. 1950, pp. 53, 54.)

Many times in years past, this concealment of the infiltrator's identity with the Communist Party went to the point where he would say to some fellow worker or colleague who was a non-Communist: "Why don't we both join the Communist Party?" Some time after this had been done, the infiltrator would let the new Communist know that he had been a member for a number of years. By that time, the deception would be looked upon as a comradely jest and the recruit was ready to practice it on somebody else.

That is the way in which Communists are made, in secrecy and not by open appeal for enrollment. Of course, Williamson also recommends the distribution of Red literature, but this literature is frequently so involved in its contents (except certain popular leaflets and certain issues of the *Daily Worker*) that it does not win adherents. The general Party literature is for the training and disciplining of the comrade after his affiliation.

There are two roads of Red infiltration into "mass organizations," from the top and from the bottom. The former is very frequently used, and it is more generally ignored by the non-Communist. How far Red penetration has been carried forward by getting into top posts in various groups has not been generally grasped. A moment's consideration will show that the ruling-caste-attitude of the Communists toward "the masses" makes infiltration from the top desirable. It is a quick and easy way to get control of the education of thousands of people.

In not a few cases, the working of Communists into top posts is arranged by a secret Red fraction or caucus, which meets regularly with a Party functionary assigned to direct them. Deciding upon each move that the respective infiltrators will make and the alliances they will arrange, this Red group has the advantage of concealment and yet of working together. Their aim often is first to get a comrade into the post of secretary, where he can have control of the membership lists, can get to know the members, and can also sneak in Communists for "colonizing" purposes if necessary. Should the organization have an educational department or educational director, the Communists will strive to get control of that post or posts. In that way, it is possible to put over thinly disguised Red ideas and pervade the membership with a pro-Communist attitude. The Communist destined for such a position is given the task of being particularly active on behalf of the "immediate needs" of the members, winning friends and influencing people, while a carefully organized claque sings his praises.

In penetrating from the top, the Soviet fifth column considers very carefully where the actual power in the specific group or organization lies. In the case of organizations in which busy industrialists, lawyers, and university presidents are interested, the Communists seek control of the executive staff, knowing it to be decisive. The Institute of Pacific Relations is a case in point. The facade of distinguished citizens constituting its national officers and trustees was even an asset to the Communists, as they worked diligently to take control of the secretaryship and other technical positions which really took care of the day by day operations of the IPR. Even though the national officers and trustees formulated the policies of the Institute, the execution of those policies was in the hands of the executive and technical staff. The policies in themselves were ambiguous enough for the staff to use them for Communist ends. (Report by Senate Sub-Committee on Internal Security, Institute of Pacific Relations, July 2, 1952, pp. 223-25.)

In order to solidify themselves in positions won at the top, or also when necessary to carry on penetration from the bottom, the Communists organize a so-called "progressive" group. In many instances, particularly in the early forties, such Red-controlled groupings to further or initiate penetration were termed "rank and file committees." While the members of these groupings may not all be Communists, they are all sympathetic to the Red cause, and their course of action is strictly supervised by the conspiracy. This supervision is generally carried out by some Party functionary who remains in the background but meets secretly with at least the most important and reliable Red members of the group.

From Williamson's directive of November, 1950, a good idea can be gained of infiltration from the bottom. The Communists seize upon slogans and grievances which they believe will be popular, and many of which are so "immediate" that they have no relation to the Red objectives and indeed will be scrapped by the Communists once they come into power. One of these slogans is "the rights of the trade unions." Another is "academic freedom." Both of these cries are used by the Reds to advance their prestige and to protect their infiltration of labor and education; both are crushed underfoot wherever Soviet power is established. But this method of gaining influence goes beyond general slogans or campaigns. It also seeks out ways and means to make higher demands than non-Communist leadership can justifiably make, or to raise issues which are distorted or false.

When working from the bottom, the Red cell frequently brings forward its purposes through resolutions presented from time to time. Some of these resolutions have nothing to do with the Communist line, but are merely to gain influence. Always, however, they will eventually be linked up with the line, in advocacy of which a whole series of resolutions may finally be presented. It is by checking on those who consistently support the measures which are definitely of a Communist line character that the infiltrators frequently become aware of those whom they should approach to become members of the conspiracy. By the same token, a knowledge of the current line as set forth by Moscow and its echo, the American Politburo, will enable anyone opposing Communism to detect Communist influences at work.

"The United Front"

Another devastating tactic of the Communists, whether working from the top or the bottom, is that of the "united front."

It consists in an arrangement whereby non-Communists and Communists work together to control an organization, agency, or government. In the last-named case, this "united front" is expressed by what has come to be known as "coalition government."

Since the days of Lenin, this tactic has been a favorite one with the Communists, in coalescing or uniting with those whom they cannot destroy except by allegedly working together with them. The tactic has been most valuable to the Stalinites in destroying all opposition and finally taking over full control. The path of success for the Communists in capturing organizations and governments has been strewn with the wreckage of "united fronts," initiated by the Kremlin's followers and then sabotaged by them.

Anyone who studies carefully the proceedings of the Seventh World Congress of the Communist International, the "united front" Congress, will be made aware of the results of this tactic. George Dimitrov, who was brought forward by Stalin to voice the "united front" proposals, quite frankly told the delegates from the sixty-five Communist Parties at that Congress what was the real goal of offering to join with non-Communists. The method was aptly described by Dimitrov as a "Trojan horse" tactic, devised to enter the camp of the enemy in order to destroy him. When laying down in detail the conditions under which Communists may enter the united front, Dimitrov gave the Red objectives—defeat of non-Soviet governments in "imperialist" wars, overthrow of those governments by violence, the eventual setting up of the dictatorship of the proletariat in all countries—as the aims to be advanced by the Stalinites through this device. It was made quite clear that the Communists enter upon such arrangements merely for the purpose of establishing their own complete control. (Third section of Report by George Dimitrov, *International Press Correspondence*, XV, no. 37, 976.)

An outstanding event on the international scene, tragic for the United States, was the Red maneuver on China. It persuaded our State Department to insist upon Chiang Kai-shek's entering into a coalition government with Mao Tse-tung. Although the matter was not actually consummated, due to the refusal by the Chinese Nationalist leaders to accept the impossible conditions of the Chinese Reds, our State Department's insistence decisively aided the Nationalist defeat. Under the false impression that the coalition government would end civil war in China, and advised by Stalinite infiltrators, the State Department demanded those truces, and laid down other conditions, which delivered China into Stalin's hands. In Poland, too, the enforced coalition government imposed by American policies on Stanislaw Mikolajczyk, the real leader of that unhappy country, was used by the Kremlin to crush all anti-Stalinists and make Poland what it is today.

Within this country, the device has been used so frequently and successfully that the full record cannot be given here. The International Fur and Leather Workers Union, which was expelled from the CIO in 1950 because of Communist control, came under such control through a united front agreement made in 1936. The United Electrical, Radio, and Machine Workers Union is now completely under Red domination because its first president, James B. Carey, permitted the Communists to come into positions of leadership in 1937. By 1941, the Communists had made such new alliances that they could push Carey out of the presidency and assume one-hundred percent control. The American Labor Party of New York, founded originally by the social-democrats, was entered by the Communists under the banner of "unity" and was soon their pawn. So much did this become the case that the original founders of the ALP felt compelled to withdraw and to form what they called the Liberal Party.

"The Open Letter"

There have been three major periods of Communist infiltration into leading agencies of American life. The first was in 1933, with the issuance by the American Politburo of *The Open Letter to the Party*. Of course, Red penetration into various agencies had gone on before that, following the precepts of Lenin in *Left Wing Communism*, and of Stalin in *The Foundations of Leninism*. (This latter work had not yet been translated into English, but it was known to the Communist leaders through its Russian editions.) It was in 1933, however, that the infiltration became organized, systematized, and extensive. The directives for this concentration on entering and influencing American agencies and organizations came directly from Moscow. It was contained in the report of Sergei Ivanovitch Gussev to the Twelfth Plenum of the Executive Committee of the Communist International (the ECCI). Under the name of P. Green, Gussev had served as Comintern representative and Stalin's personal agent in the United States. In 1932, he returned to Moscow to make his famous report on "The Main Tasks of the Anglo-American Sections of the Communist International," ordering a "turn" in the Party's practices in the United States. Gussev commanded the Communists in the United States to take up four tasks: defense of the Soviet Union, furtherance of Red conquest of China, social insurance, and self-determination in the Black Belt.

It will be noted how justified reforms, such as social insurance, were to be mingled by the Communists with those goals set for them directly by Moscow in pursuance of its world-conquest plans. Self-determination in the Black Belt, at the same time, was devised to create dissension within this country for Stalin, and to be a distinct disservice to the Negro people. Both domestic issues were to be raised primarily to gain influence for the Communists among special groups and those sympathetic with those groups, so that the Reds might more effectively advance Soviet Russia and Chinese Communist ambitions.

The heart of Gussev's instruction, however, was "to go to the masses," which in Communist parlance means wide infiltration. This flows from Communist methodology as set down by Stalin;

if the vanguard is to make transmission belts of "mass organizations," it can do so only through concealment and infiltration.

"As *Political Affairs* so proudly reported on the Thirtieth Anniversary of the Party in 1949, the Gussev order also opened the way for the subsequent infiltration of the CIO in the steel, automobile, and similar industries. But it did more than that. For a number of years, it also made possible Communist control of the American Newspaper Guild, whose national office is, however, out of Red hands. It gave the Party an entering wedge into lawyers', artists', writers', and other professional groups of many kinds. The number of these people, indeed, reached such a considerable size by 1937 that the Party began to take more open and official cognizance of them as Party members. In a now famous article, William Z. Foster instructed them that it was their duty to be conscious of their Communist membership and Marxist responsibility at all times." (*Men Without Faces*, Budenz, Harper and Brothers, 1950, p. 52.)

The Communist Party of the United States had gone about obeying Gussev's order in a thorough manner. The Party leaders had called an extraordinary conference in 1933, out of which came the *Open Letter*. A special new representative of the Communist International, then known as E. Edwards but later notorious under his correct name of Gerhart Eisler, was secretly sent into the United States by Moscow to make sure that the *Open Letter* was carried out.

It was in that year, 1933, that practically the entire Washington cell, including Alger Hiss, Lee Pressman, John Abt, and others, entered the Department of Agriculture, then under the direction of Henry Agard Wallace. From that vantage point, these men later spread out into other agencies. It was also in 1933 that the old course of Red infiltration received a tremendous push forward in the official recognition of Soviet Russia by the United States.

The second big infiltration drive dates from 1936, when the Communists first indirectly and then directly supported the Roosevelt administration. Conditions now became even more favorable for easy penetration, as open Communists began to hob-nob with leading political figures and the whole situation was softened up for wider entry into the newspapers, radio, and eventually television and all other fields of opinion making. These favorable conditions were to be halted in part, but only temporarily, during the Hitler-Stalin Pact period of late 1939 to the summer of 1941.

The third large period of infiltration begins with the opening of World War II for the United States, that is, after Pearl Harbor. It was during this time that the Communists made their greatest headway in getting into every decisive avenue of American life, so that the job of dislodging them has become a colossal one. The many unguarded statements of a large number of American leaders in praise of the Soviet dictatorship gave the fifth column here a golden opportunity of which it quickly availed itself. Communists planted themselves everywhere—in the publicity services of the armed forces, the Office of War Information, the Office of Strategic Services, the Board of Economic Warfare, and strengthened their channels into the State Department. The repercussions of this large-scale Communist colonization into governmental posts were felt in other American fields of endeavor. (For a full account of the background for this third and largest infiltration, read *The Cry Is Peace*, by Budenz, Henry Regnery Company, 1952.)

The Communist Front

In affecting public opinion, and in expanding Red penetration into wide areas of opinion-making, the Communists rely very definitely on two types of organization: the Communist front, and what we can call the captive group or institution. The building and strengthening of these two types of Red control are the constant subject of discussion in the American Politburo and National Committee meetings.

The Communist front is never referred to by that name in Red circles. In writing, any specific front is mentioned as "a leading progressive organization," and sometimes with the addition of the phrase "in which the Communists have influence." It is only rarely that a Red leader will come out as openly as Earl Browder did on one or two occasions in stating that certain specific front groups were "transmission belts for the Party." For instance, The Committee on Un-American Activities states: "Earl Browder, testifying before the House Committee on Un-American Activities on September 6, 1939, in his capacity as general secretary of the Communist Party, admitted that the National Lawyers Guild was a Communist transmission belt." (Report on National Lawyers Guild, Sept. 17, 1950, p. 2.) In oral discussions, within such organs of the Party as the Politburo, the National Committee, or a District Bureau, the front in some specific case may be more definitely pointed out as being "created and controlled by the Party."

In Chapter II, we have dealt briefly with the standard practice in forming Communist fronts, and have presented some selected examples of fronts as agencies of infiltration. The reader should review that procedure, in order to be fully aware of the creation and supervision of every front by the Politburo. The best way here to bring out the widespread effect of these fronts is by examining the records of two or three typical Communist fronters.

The Communist front is not merely a collection of names on a letterhead or a list of "distinguished people" in the pages of the *Daily Worker*. As such, it is true, the front has large influence. The names of a number of educators, scientists, clergymen, and other professional people attached to pro-Communist literature cannot fail to make an impression on the unwary. The lists in the *Daily Worker* are referred to frequently by concealed Communists as showing that a viewpoint parallel to the Communist line is backed up by good authority. It is not uncommon for an obscure pro-Red professor to declare: "If scientists like Harlow Shapley and Kirtley Mather, with such high positions at Harvard University, stand for the peace crusades, there must be something good about them." This argument is not confined to such higher levels, but goes down to various communities. The pro-Communist position of some "leading writer" or "outstanding business man" in the community involved is often cited in order to advance Communist ideas locally.

This is only the beginning of the damage done by the Communist fronter to American morale by the aid he gives to Stalin's "psychological warfare." He is more than a name; he is also active, both in his own field where he plays a part in affecting the thoughts of his colleagues, and often in other fields where he gives aid to the Communist cause. Through personal relationships, he is interlocked with others who are spreading the message of the line as directed by Moscow.

A few case histories of Communist fronters will make this apparent. It must be borne in mind that what these conspicuous cooperators with Communist causes do on a national scale is duplicated by concealed Communists on a local basis. The average "rank and file" concealed Communist who is a teacher or professional person of some other sort is expected to penetrate at least five local groupings, if this will not lead to exposure.

A Case History: Dr. Stern

Our first case is that of Dr. Bernhard J. Stern, lecturer in Sociology at Columbia University. On April 1, 1951, the report of the House Committee on Un-American Activities on the "Communist Peace Crusades" cited Stern as an affiliate of from 31 to 40 Communist fronts. On September 24, 1952, he appeared before the Senate Internal Security Sub-Committee investigating infiltration in education, and refused to state whether he had been a member of the Communist Party in the past. His grounds were those which Communists have used repeatedly during the past several years, that it would tend to incriminate him. This refusal to answer was repeated on March 27, 1953, before the Senate Investigating Sub-Committee inquiring into the "Voice of America." Some of Stern's books were among those volumes by Communist and pro-Communist authors which had been placed in United States overseas libraries for use by citizens of various countries "in the fight against Communism." Nothing was more illustrative of the power of Red infiltration than the ironical fact that works by champions of Communism were used by the International Information Administration of the State Department in what was alleged to be an educational campaign against Communism.

On the witness stand, Stern went beyond refusing to answer on past Communist affiliations, and defended Soviet Russia and the Communist fronts. By adopting this attitude, he gave courage to the others who have done the same, and it is of the highest importance to the Communist conspiracy that it create a chain reaction of unity and discipline on any method or measure decided upon as a tactic. There have been those who thought that the Communists made a mistake in ordering those who might have been members of branches at some time in their career not to answer the question as to their affiliation. But the conspiracy understands that in this way questions are dodged which could require a witness under subpoena to reveal acts and associations that would show the amazing extent of Red infiltration. The refusal to answer gets very little news notice, and the subversive acts which the conspiracy is attempting to conceal are legion. Stern's contribution to the chain reaction desired by the Stalinites is therefore notable.

In the many fronts which Stern joined, his name is generally accompanied by his title as a sociologist at Columbia University. This is an old device designed to give the impression that institutions like Columbia support the purposes to which the respective fronts are dedicated. It is given added weight in the public mind by the long silence of so many institutions, including Columbia, who do not protest effectively against the use of their name.

All through the country, down in the grass roots, the concealed Reds and their allies press this point home. "If such a well-known sociologist as Dr. Stern of Columbia University, our leading educational institution, sponsors the Civil Rights Congress or the Jefferson School of Social Science, or the Veterans of the Abraham Lincoln Brigade, these must be causes which every American can aid," the argument runs.

But Professor Stern, busily backing every conceivable type of front for the past two decades, did not confine himself to the halls of Columbia University. He is also a lecturer on sociology at the New School for Social Research, which enrolls many students who have no idea that there are Communists or pro-Communists on its faculty. Thus his area of influence grew.

Meanwhile, under the name of Bennett Stevens, Stern was doing yeoman work for the Communist Party proper. Under that name, he wrote books that have been published by International Publishers, Moscow's official publishing firm in this country. In addition, he has also written for the Communist magazine *New Masses* (now known as *Masses and Mainstream*) and for *Soviet Russia Today*, Red duplicate here of similar magazines spreading Soviet propaganda in almost every country of the world. In 1953, he was chief editor of *Science and Society*, Stalinite quarterly organ of Marxian dialectics. His co-editors include Professor Dirk Struik of the Massachusetts Institute of Technology, who has been a member of at least thirty Communist fronts and is a co-founder of the Communist Jefferson School of Social Science, and Edwin Barry Burgum, professor at New York University, who was suspended in late 1952 after he refused to tell the Senate Internal Security Sub-Committee whether he was a Communist Party member. Burgum has been a member of from 41 to 50 Communist fronts, according to the April 1, 1951 report of the House Committee on Un-American Activities. Thus we see how Communist fronters interlace in their activities and building up such important aids to the Red cause as *Science and Society* (which will appear later in these pages as a powerful factor in infiltration of the educational process).

Stern's relationships go still further. His wife, Charlotte

Todes Stern, a veteran Communist, was an official for some time of a Communist-directed local of the Hotel and Restaurant Workers Union, AFL. She was no small factor in making the Communists such a power in the New York Joint Council of that organization, which has in turn obliged the national president of that union to take a stand in defense of the Communists. As a board member of the Joint Anti-Fascist Refugee Committee, organized to bring leading Reds to this Continent, Charlotte Todes Stern went to jail for contempt in 1950. She and the other officials of that Committee refused point blank to give Congress that front's record, whose disclosure would have greatly aided American security. For this group was a cover for bringing into the United States a number of those assigned to aid Red espionage.

Stern himself was prominent in the Federation of Architects, Engineers, Chemists, and Technicians, which has been charged by Congress with cooperating in the Kremlin's atomic espionage activities against the United States. All the while this was going on, and even after it had been exposed, Stern continued to teach at Columbia. Following the Communist pattern, he sought out those students and fellow faculty members who seemed to be susceptible and moved them in a pro-Communist direction.

It is important to note, as a sample of Communist tactics, that Stern swore he was not a member of the Communist Party in 1952 or a year before, but refused to answer as to whether he was a member in 1947 or before. This makes plain one of the chief purposes of the refusal to answer on the ground that it would tend to incriminate the witness. In 1947 and before, Stern knew very well, a number of persons had met with him in cell or branch meetings who had later left the Communists and could testify against him. But after 1947, the situation was different, either because those with whom he had been associated in Communist work had not left or because all vestige of membership had been removed from him by the Party. We are aware that since 1949, at least, no Communist has had any vestige of membership, and even the rank and file members are only associated in units of five or six members. For many years, those in key and delicate positions were obliged under Party discipline not to attend branch meetings and no cards were issued to them. In Stern's refusal to tell whether or not he was a Communist in 1947, we get a key to the tactic whereby some persons who are asked the question refuse to answer and some others with a long pro-Communist record answer in the negative. The former group includes those who attended branches and had cards when they were in an obscure position; the latter group has among it those who were in key or delicate positions when they became Communists. These latter people can easily swear that they are not affiliated, since charges of perjury cannot successfully be placed against them. It is the *records* of pro-Communists in education, government, or other agencies which should be primarily considered, therefore, and not whether technically they can be proved to be Communists. If those records reveal a consistent aid to Soviet Russia, its fifth column here, and its fronts, then these individuals are enemies of the United States and should be recognized as such.

One Fronter's Record

This is underscored by the record of front affiliations piled up by Stern since 1947, during the period when he swears he was not a Communist. Some of the fronts, all of them deeply injurious to American security, which he has sponsored and supported (with dates for those joined since 1947) are:

African Aid Committee, 1949–50; American Committee for Democracy and Intellectual Freedom; American Committee for the Protection of the Foreign Born, 1948–51; American Labor Party (now N.Y. section of Progressive Party); American League for Peace and Democracy; American Russian Institute; American Slav Congress; Bill of Rights Congress (in defense of the CP's Politburo), 1949; Book Union, Inc.; Citizens Committee of the Upper West Side; Civil Rights Congress, 1949; Committee for a Democratic Far Eastern Policy, 1946–48;

Cultural and Scientific (Waldorf) Conference for World Peace, 1949; Jefferson School of Social Science; League of American Writers; National Committee to Aid Victims of German Fascism; National Committee for the Defense of Political Prisoners; National Committee for Peoples Rights; National Conference on American Policy in China and the Far East, 1948; National Council of Arts, Sciences, and Professions, 1951; National Federation for Constitutional Liberties; National Non-Partisan Committee to Defend the 12 Communist Leaders, 1949; National Committee to Win the Peace; Progressive Citizens of America; Schappes Defense Committee; School for Democracy; School of Jewish Studies, 1948; Veterans of the Abraham Lincoln Brigade; Voice of Freedom Committee, 1949.

This list includes not only every type of front initiated by the Soviet fifth column during the period under study; it also comprises the most vital fronts to the Red cause that were operating during that time. While Stern was "not a Communist Party member," according to his sworn testimony for those years, he was doing everything that the Red leadership here would want him to do as a Communist. His continued and extensive sponsorship of these causes, in addition, is the logical record of a man who as far back as twenty years ago was a backer of the American Committee for Struggle Against War, which has been cited as Communist by three investigating bodies. It is also a follow-up to the activities of the man who taught at the Workers School, open Communist Party institution, under the name of Stevens. Only one versed in Marxism-Leninism would be permitted to engage in teaching of this character.

Only the most gullible or those who wish to pose as gullible will fail to see that Stern's alleged "disassociation" from the Communist Party, which he says took place in 1947, is a purely technical arrangement to protect him from perjury while he can go on serving the Kremlin as fully as before. This device for defeating American legal processes and suppressing the presentation of the whole picture on Red infiltration has been so successful that it deserves continuous study. (See *Counter-attack*, April 3, 1953, for an excellent review of Stern's record. This publication is required reading for every student of the techniques of Communism.)

Second Case History: Schuman

Another case history that stands out is that of Frederick L. Schuman, professor of government at Williams College in Massachusetts, and before that on the faculty of the University of Chicago. Schuman, like Stern, appears as an active sponsor of Communist causes in Eugene Lyons' *Red Decade*, even before the big infiltration of 1933 began. The year before, the League of Professional Groups for Foster and Ford, supporting the Communist candidates for president and vice-president of the United States at that time, announced that Schuman was one of the prominent backers of the Red ticket. In that same year, 1932, Schuman was a leading member of the National Commit-tee arranging the Student Congress Against War at the Univer-sity of Chicago, which was initiated by the Communist National Student League. In 1933, Schuman visited Soviet Russia and returned to lecture in favor of the Soviet dictatorship through-out the following year. These lectures were under the auspices of the Friends of the Soviet Union, the predecessor to the well-known Communist front, the National Council for American-Soviet Friendship. In November, 1937, he went even farther and was one of the chief speakers at a gala meeting in Carnegie Hall, which turned over a "Golden Book of American Friend-ship with the Soviet Union" to representatives of the dictator-ship. The significance of this act can be gleaned from Lyons' comment: "Several hundred thousand signatures were gathered for that book. In view of the fact that the Kremlin was then in the midst of bloody purges which will continue to horrify man-kind for generations, the size of the Book indicates once more how extensive the Stalinist penetration of American life had become." (*The Red Decade*, Eugene Lyons, 1941, p. 259.)

Two years later, in the *Daily Worker* of August 14, 1939, Schuman's name appears among those who joined in the notorious Open Letter for Closer Cooperation with Soviet Russia, which defended the Stalinite dictatorship against being classified as "a totalitarian regime." This Open Letter, organized by the American Politburo, was got up for a specific purpose: to delude the American public into the belief that a pact or agreement between Hitler and Stalin was impossible. It denied the "fantastic falsehood" that Stalin could have anything in common with Hitlerite Germany, although nine days later Moscow entered into its alliance with the Nazis. By 1940, Schuman had performed valiant service on behalf of Soviet "psychological warfare," in confusing public opinion as to the bloody purges in Russia and as to the true affinity between Stalinism and Hitlerism. In subsequent years, and specifically in World War II, the United States was to suffer ignominious defeats at the hands of Soviet Russia as the result of the misconception planted years before by these skilled Communist fronters.

But Schuman's work on behalf of the Soviet fifth column was not yet done. In 1946, when Gerhart Eisler was exposed as the Communist International representative in this country and put on trial the following year, Schuman was one of those who rushed publicly to his defense. He also signed the Party-line brief to the United States Supreme Court on behalf of the so-called Hollywood Ten, those leading Communists in the motion picture industry who defied Congress and were punished for contempt. He lent his support to Communist bookshops and protested the listing of Red schools as subversive by the Department of Justice.

Conscious of the power of books in the molding of American thinking, Schuman has written a number of his own, an outstanding contribution being *American Politics at Home and Abroad*. We now know from the testimony of Igor Bogolepov, former counselor to the Soviet Foreign Office, before the Senate Internal Security Sub-Committee, that Schuman prepared this book in close collaboration with the Soviet authorities. Another production of his, *American Policy Toward Russia Since 1917*, was published by International Publishers, Moscow's own publishing house in the United States. In 1953, a third book of his appeared, *The Commonwealth of Man*, prepared with the help of a grant from the Foundation for World Government, headed by Stringfellow Barr, now another Communist fronter. On January 17, 1951, Barr joined certain Communists and other veteran Communist fronters in an ad in the *New York Times* attacking government efforts to curb the conspiracy; in December, 1953, he initiated an appeal for release of the Communist leaders; and in January, 1953, sponsored the Emergency Civil Liberties Conference, a Communist front. (See *Counterattack*, Jan. 26, 1951, Dec. 19, 1952, Jan. 23, Feb. 6, Feb. 20, 1953.)

Schuman's book is predicated on the premise that America is insane, that it should not arm its allies for defense against Soviet aggression, and that Congressional investigations of Communism are a sign of "the American madness." Specifically, he assails ex-Communists who testify for the government, particularly attacking Whittaker Chambers, Louis Budenz, and Elizabeth Bentley. These ex-Communists are also under the special fire of the Communist conspiracy, and Schuman gives aid and comfort to that conspiracy by his entire attitude.

It is obvious from this partial record of the Communist fronter Schuman that people of his type do not remain static. The appearance of their name on Red-created fronts is merely a signal that they are engaging in many other widespread activities helpful to the Stalinite fifth column. Schuman has made many contacts beyond the campus of Williams College and, working with other Communist fronters, is a force in the poisoning of the wells of public opinion.

The influences of these fronters is not divorced from local communities. The name of a man like Schuman, his position as professor, the books he writes, can all be used to advance the pro-Soviet and anti-American attitudes which he supports. The average educated American will be unaware of his whole history and will often be persuaded that what he says is merely the expression of another authoritative American voice, one that has not expressed itself so frequently and over so many years on behalf of the Kremlin and its line.

Schuman is mentioned as a member of from 21 to 30 Communist fronts, in the Report of the House Committee on Un-American Activities for April 1, 1951. Since that time, he has been identified with others. A partial list of his front record from the early Thirties up to 1953, presented by *Counterattack*, runs as follows:

American Committee for Anti-Nazi Literature; American League Against War and Fascism; American League for Peace and Democracy; American Committee for Protection of the Foreign Born; American Council on Soviet Relations; American Slav Congress; African Aid Committee; Bill of Rights Conference; Committee for a Boycott Against Japanese Aggression; Civil Rights Congress; Cultural and Scientific Conference for World Peace; Golden Book of American Friendship with the Soviet Union; Interprofessional Association for Social Insurance; Jefferson School of Social Science; Joint Anti-Fascist Refugee Committee; Lawyers Committee on American Relations with Spain; Legislative Assembly and Rally to End Segregation and Discrimination; National Wallace for President Committee; National Council of the Arts, Sciences and Professions, vice-chairman; National Council of American-Soviet Friendship; National Committee to Defeat the Mundt Bill; National Conference on American Policy in China and the Far East; National Committee to Win the Peace; National Committee for the Student Congress Against War; Progressive Party, platform committee member; Soviet Russia Today (Communist magazine), contributor for many years; World Congress for Peace (Paris, 1949).

Again, we have included in our list all the leading and most effective fronts serving Stalinite purposes. It reveals Professor Schuman as one who has done tremendous damage to the United States, for these fronts have a large share in the responsibility for the hesitation and lack of initiative marking American international policy.

Third Case: Justice Wolfe

A third Communist fronter case is that of James H. Wolfe, former Justice and now Chief Justice of Utah's Supreme Court. Wolfe began his pro-Soviet activities by supporting the Communist fronts having to do with the Spanish Civil War. Among these were the Coordinating Committee to Lift the Embargo and the Lawyers' Committee on American Relations with Spain. During the Hitler-Stalin Pact period, Chief Justice Wolfe faithfully followed the Communist Party line, denouncing the "war hysteria" of President Roosevelt. He also rushed to the defense of the Veterans of the Abraham Lincoln Brigade, one of the favorite Red fronts for developing strong-arm men and forces for creating disorder in an emergency. In 1942, he made a special appeal to President Roosevelt to release Earl Browder, then in prison at Atlanta for a passport fraud.

Wolfe has sponsored the subversive Waldorf-Astoria Peace Conference of 1949 and the Stalinite Stockholm "Peace" Appeal. The sinister extent of Communist influences in this country can be noted when a Chief Justice of a State Supreme Court, pledged to uphold the Constitution, lends his name to a conference such as took place at the Waldorf-Astoria, which denounced the United States, praised Soviet Russia, and heard calls for civil disobedience against our government.

Wolfe became an initial sponsor of the American Peace Crusade, the Communist Party's chief peace front, and also backed that organization's peace pilgrimage to Washington in 1951.

Among the other front affiliations and pro-Soviet activities of Utah's Chief Justice are the following:

Sponsor of: Civil Rights Congress, the National Council of American-Soviet Friendship, the National Council of Arts, Sciences, and Professions, the National Conference on American Policy in China and the Far East.

He signed the statement denouncing prosecution of eleven Communist leaders, 1949; joined in protest against United States Treasury Department's withdrawal of tax-exempt status from International Workers Order, Red adjunct, 1948; co-signed the denunciation of the anti-Communist film, The Iron Curtain, which was based on exposure of the Canadian atomic spy ring; sponsored in 1951 the testimonial dinner to Dr. W. E. B. DuBois, who has been identified as a leading Communist Party member; and co-signed the letter to President Truman supporting Moscow "cease fire" propaganda in mid-1951.

That Wolfe has many avenues by which he can bring his viewpoint to play upon others is attested to by his appointment for the second time in 1951 to the high office of Chief Justice. (This pro-Communist record of Justice Wolfe is taken from many reports of the House Committee on Un-American Activities, including those on the *Civil Rights Congress as a Communist Front Organization,* 1947, the *Scientific and Cultural Conference for World Peace,* 1949, *The March of Treason —a Study of the American "Peace" Crusade,* 1951, and the *Communist "Peace" Offensive—The Attempt to Disarm and Defeat America,* 1951.)

These are but samples of hundreds of similar cases in the Communist front field that could be cited. It is of importance to recognize that the member of a Communist front is in control of an area of influence on his own account. His name and authority help to attract lesser people to views similar to his own and thus expand the confusion upon which Moscow feeds. Whenever a new line is introduced under orders of the Kremlin, the normal Communist fronter is expected to plug for that line at once and as best he can in the area in which he operates. That is, if he is on a newspaper, he will do his utmost directly or indirectly to get that paper in whole or in part to echo the line. If he is an artist, he will lend his work to drawing people together in small groups so that they may become converted to that line. A well-known pianist, for instance, has frequently given house recitals, which prove to be merely the vehicle for a discussion favorable to Communist causes.

The multifold activities of the Communist fronter on a national scale are reflected in the work of concealed Communists and their friends in community organizations. Here the effort has often to be carried on in a more circumspect manner, but it is not unusual to find several persons busy in a number of local community groups, all posing as non-Communists but forwarding what happens to be the current program set down by the Kremlin.

As to the captive organizations, how they are entered and controlled will be reviewed in those chapters dealing with infiltration respectively in government, labor, education, and among the Negro people. For a succinct account of how the Institute of Pacific Relations was taken over and employed for penetration into the State Department, the reader should study Chapter III of my *The Cry Is Peace*. A large labor union which is a classic example of becoming captive to the conspiracy is the United Electrical, Radio, and Machine Workers Union. Shut out from membership in the CIO because it is Communist controlled, its influence and that of its fellow Red-ruled unions lingers on. This is demonstrated by the statements of certain CIO leaders against Congressional investigations of the Communists and against the Smith Act, helpful in curbing the conspiracy. By these expressions, such leaders as President Walter Reuther of the CIO and President James B. Carey of the International Union of Electrical Workers, who are fighting the Communists, actually weaken their own fight. The result has been Communist gains in the labor field.

Pro-Communist lawyers, and lawyers who are allies of the Communists are readily used by the conspiracy in its infiltration work. John Abt, notorious member of the Ware cell in Washington, did much to persuade Sidney Hillman, president of the Amalgamated Clothing Workers, to take up stands which helped Red capture of the American Labor Party. This and other moves by the ACW leadership which aided the Communists took place while Abt was counsel for that organization. Lee Pressman, another member of the Ware cell, had for a number of years an equally damaging influence within the top circles of the CIO. At the present time, Harold Cranefield is counsel for the United Automobile, Aircraft, and Agricultural Implement Workers Union, CIO, of which Walter Reuther is president. Cranefield is also an active and devoted member of the National Lawyers Guild, which has been called by the House Committee on Un-American Activities "the legal bulwark" of the Communist conspiracy. The Guild has followed the Party line for many years, and its key officers have been cited by the House Committee as repeaters on Communist fronts.

The National Lawyers Guild

In no case is Communist penetration into non-Communist circles through a front organization presented more strikingly than in the instance of the National Lawyers Guild. After an extensive study, the House Committee on Un-American Activities could state: "The National Lawyers Guild is the foremost legal bulwark of the Communist Party, its front organizations, and controlled unions. Since its inception it has never failed to rally to the legal defense of the Communist Party and individual members thereof, including known espionage agents. It has consistently fought against national, State, and local legislation aimed at curbing the Communist conspiracy. It has been most articulate in its attacks upon all agencies of the government seeking to expose or prosecute the subversive activities of the Communist network, including national, State, and local investigative committees, the Department of Justice, the FBI, and law-enforcement agencies generally. Through its affiliation with the International Association of Democratic Lawyers, an international Communist front organization, the National Lawyers Guild has constituted itself an agent of a foreign principal hostile to the interests of the United States. It has gone far afield to oppose the foreign policies of the United States, in line with the current line of the Soviet Union."

Citing the Communists' acclaim for the Guild at the time when it was founded, the Committee quotes from my testimony of July 20, 1948: "In the National Lawyers Guild there is a complete duplicate of the Communist Party's hopes and aspirations in that field, although there are a number of non-Communists in the National Lawyers Guild. In fact some of their lawyers locally are not Communists, but they play the Communist game either wittingly or unwittingly." (*Report* on the National Lawyers Guild, House Committee on Un-American Activities, Sept. 17, 1950.)

It is thus, by working out an interlocking relationship with men in high positions, that the Communists and their allies are effective. They often persuade these men to a line of conduct which affects the thinking of thousands of people. Walter Reuther, criticizing Henry Wallace, stated a few years ago that the Communists will be willing to do all your work for you, write your speeches, and perform other services—if you will let them do your thinking for you. That is a very apt expression.

Communist infiltration continues with much success in this country. It is still a power in the land. It can be halted, however, by an intelligent understanding of how the conspiracy operates, and by the will and courage to defeat it.

CHAPTER IX

WORK IN LABOR AND INDUSTRY

In 1950, several committees of the Congress of Industrial Organizations presented reports on Red-ruled unions recommending their expulsion from the C.I.O. The heart of these reports is contained in the following paragraph:

"The committee finds that the fundamental purpose of the Communist Party is to promote the interests of the Soviet Union. It finds that, although the Communist Party has claimed to champion unionism and organization, it has always done so in order to carry on Communist work within trade unions and in order to pervert their policies to the advantage of the Soviet Union. The Communist Party, the committee finds, does not believe in trade unions. It believes in using trade unions. And it believes in using them for the purposes of the Soviet Union."

The deep truth in this statement can be grasped from the nature of Soviet Communism. Since no genuine freedom is possible (as Lenin states in *State and Revolution*) until the classless society has been won, and since the classless society cannot be gained without the dictatorship of the proletariat, all mass organizations are expendable in that effort. The trade unions are of no consequence in themselves; they are for the Communist merely convenient agencies to achieve the aims of the vanguard. Whenever Soviet power is established, these trade unions are crushed, and caricatures of them are created which are solely speed-up machines for the Soviet bureaucracy.

For Soviet Communism the extensive work within the trade unions of the non-Soviet countries is most essential for two outstanding reasons. First, since the Communists contend that they are striving for "a dictatorship of the proletariat," alleged interest in the problems of the working class becomes of prime importance. With that goes the necessity of having Red representation among certain segments of the workers and their unions. Second, by getting control of certain unions, particularly in the basic industries, or by establishing cells there which can expand in an emergency, the Communists lay the foundations for disruption of production when it serves the Kremlin's purposes. Since the political strike, beginning as an economic strike, is one of the chief initial steps toward armed insurrection, it is urgent that Communists be well planted in the unions. It gives them a great advantage in stirring up the workers to engage in those bloody struggles that lead to the Soviet dictatorship.

It is because of these considerations that Lenin wrote in 1920: "It is necessary to agree to any and every sacrifice . . . to resort to all sorts of devices, maneuvers, and illegal methods, to evasion and subterfuge, in order to penetrate the trade unions, to remain in them, and to carry on Communist work in them at all costs." (*Left Wing Communism, An Infantile Disorder*, Lenin, International Publishers, 1934, p. 38.)

This emphasis on working within trade unions does not prevent the Communists from seeking also to enter the ranks of management and to find allies and friends in big industry. A knowledge of the philosophy of Communism is of value here, since its primary dedication to militant atheism drives it to make adherents in every avenue of life. Comparatively speaking, the Soviet fifth column in this country has not made as much headway among the working people as among industrialists, educators, scientists, and other professional groups.

The extensive efforts of the Reds to get into the unions in order to secure a "proletarian" coloration, and their lengthy directives on union work, make it necessary to give first consideration to this field of infiltration. A helpful introduction to the story of Red successes in this field can be obtained from the history and background of "boring from within" in the United States.

Before the Bolshevik revolution in Russia, which created Communist fifth columns in all countries, those who worked for the overturn of the current social order could be roughly divided into three groups—the disciples of anarchism, of syndicalism, and of social democracy. The anarchists regarded the state in itself as the fundamental evil, and sought its complete overthrow. They were divided into two schools, the anarchists of the deed and the philosophical anarchists. The former regarded it essential to resort to terrorism, bringing the state into chaos by the assassination of those at its head. As late as 1901, a small group of anarchists in Paterson, New Jersey, worked out the assassination of President William McKinley through one of their numbers, Leon Czolgosz. The philosophical anarchists relied on "non-resistance" to the state, to carrying on propaganda, and in seeking to undermine confidence in all institutions—religion, the family, and the law. Prince Peter Kropotkin of Russia was perhaps the best known champion of anarchism on the international scene, being first an advocate of "the deed" and then becoming merely a propagandist for anarchist philosophy.

In the late 1880's, the anarchists drew much attention in the United States, being very active in issuing a number of publications. They received particular prominence in the Haymarket affair, when several of their leading activists in the Chicago area were charged with responsibility for the bomb killing of police officers, in connection with a strike at the McCormick farm machinery plant. By the 1900's, the anarchists were of small consequence in the American scene, establishing and maintaining a few colonies where their philosophy was taught and which were subsequently to be invaded by the Communists and thrown into turmoil by them.

From anarchism stemmed the syndicalists, who were equally set upon the destruction of the state. In its place, instead of the nebulous "society" of individual unrestraint as planned by the anarchists, the syndicalists hoped to put the rule of the revolutionary industrial unions. After the triumphant issue of the class war, which they sought to forward as eagerly as the Communists did later, the champions of this viewpoint expected the setting up of an industrial government, ruled by the workers and based on their control of all industry. It was the unions alone, organized by industries and not by crafts, and brought to a revolutionary pitch, which would overthrow the state by violence and set up a new society. The syndicalists looked with contempt upon any effort to engage in parliamentary action or "to take over" the state, by whatever means.

In contrast, the social-democrats, or Marxists, as their movement developed, relied more and more upon the ballot box as the means to take over the state machine and convert it to socialism. There were in every country "left socialists," of course, who affirmed that Marxism stood for violence in the capture of the state. What Lenin did, specifically in *State and Revolution*, was to blend certain aspects of anarchism, syndicalism, and social democracy into "the theory and tactics of the dictatorship of the proletariat." With the social democrats, he held that the state machine must be captured, but he derided their "ballot boxing" with even more contempt than did the syndicalists. The capture could take place only through "the violent shattering of the bourgeois government," as Marx had previously declared. With the anarchists and syndicalists, he predicted the end of the state, but through the withering away of the proletarian dictatorship after it had smashed all bourgeois governments and bourgeois thoughts. By this move, Lenin "restored Marxism" and expanded it; it must be borne in mind that Marx and Engels had stressed the necessity of the dictatorship as early as the Communist Manifesto of 1847. And by this manner of presentation, Lenin gained the adherence of many former syndicalists, so that it is not very surprising that a considerable number of them in the United States became Communists after the year 1918.

"Boring From Within"

Conspicuous among those adherents of syndicalism who eventually enrolled under Lenin's banner was William Z. Foster, a congenital leftist, who was later to be reprimanded by Stalin for that tendency. As a syndicalist, however, Foster was to champion a tactic which fit in with the Communist method of infiltration—"boring from within." The Industrial Workers of the World, the organized representation of syndicalist thought and action in this country, were opposed to any relations with "the old line" American Federation of Labor unions. The IWW denounced the AFL in bitter terms as "betrayers of the working class." Determined to set up its own industrial unions of a revolutionary character, the IWW succeeded only in organizing the migratory workers, although conducting large-scale and violent strikes in the textile industry. The IWW views were shared by a comparatively small but active number of men who were members of the AFL unions, and these became "two card carriers," with membership both in the IWW and the AFL.

Observing this development, and also the uncertain foundation on which the IWW was based, Foster became the mouthpiece of those who favored the carrying of the revolutionary syndicalist ideas into the regular trade unions. In 1912, he left the IWW and joined the Brotherhood of Railway Car Men. Simultaneously, he joined with others in forming the Syndicalist League of North America, and then the International Trade Union Educational League, both dedicated to boring from within the regular unions but unsuccessful on the whole in getting any foothold in the American Federation of Labor. Through friends and allies he made in Chicago, Foster and his syndicalist colleagues were able to win a leading role in organizing drives among the packing house workers and steel workers. In the latter campaign, Foster—through his good relations with John Fitzpatrick, president of the Chicago Federation of Labor—succeeded in becoming secretary of the national committee established by the AFL for conducting the strike of 1919. Five years later, Fitzpatrick was to get his dose of Communist perfidy, in their assaults upon him when they formed an abortive Federated Farmer Labor Party against his sounder views.

After the steel strike of 1919, Foster received unexpected encouragement for his boring from within policy in Lenin's pamphlet, *Left Wing Communism, an Infantile Disorder*, which appeared in 1920. The Communist Party here docilely endorsed Lenin's view that the "old line unions" should be penetrated, "by deceit and subterfuge" if necessary. As a result, Foster was invited to attend the first Congress of the Red International of Labor Unions, held in Moscow in 1921. En route from Chicago to Moscow, Foster stopped in New York and visited my office at *Labor Age*, of which I was the editor. Rather naively I warned him against becoming a Communist, not knowing that he had already pledged himself to Soviet allegiance. In Moscow, he definitely affiliated with the Communist International, and the Trade Union Educational League (TUEL) was established as the American section of the Red International of Labor Unions (RILU). The directing head of this RILU was Solomon Lezevsky, who appeared in World War II as a director of public relations for the Soviet dictatorship.

The RILU combined the attempt to build revolutionary unions under complete control of the Comintern with penetration of the regularly established unions. For the United States, the TUEL was permitted to concentrate on the latter program, and it proceeded to do so by creating turmoil and wreckage in many union fields, and specifically in the needle trades. The International Ladies Garment Workers Union, where the invading Reds allied themselves with the gangster Arnold Rothstein, was brought almost to ruin. Its officers managed to hold control of the national union, however, and were able in time to rebuild it on firm foundations. Because of the universal disruption on which they had engaged, the Communists were expelled in many instances from the unions and were excluded from any positions of leadership.

Then, in 1928, came the command from Moscow to set up separate Red-ruled unions, a procedure which was in line with the consolidation of world revolutionary tactics laid down by the Sixth Congress of the Communist International under Stalin's leadership. (The Sixth Congress produced the program of the Communist International, the resolutions and theses for concentrating on Communist insurrections in the Orient, and the definite instructions to Communists everywhere to oppose their own governments in case of war. The main theme of the Sixth Congress was the division of the world into two camps—the one led by "the Dollar Republic," the other by Soviet Russia.)

The Trade Union Educational League obediently complied with Moscow's command and transformed itself into the Trade Union Unity League (TUUL), supposedly a center for Red-ruled unions. Among those alleged unions which were set up by the TUUL were the Steel and Metal Workers Industrial Union, the National Miners Union, the National Textile Workers Union, and the Needle Trades Industrial Union. Other affiliates were the Marine Transport Industrial Union, the Cannery and Agricultural Workers Industrial Union, the Food Workers Industrial Union, and the Shoe and Leather Workers Industrial Union. While the TUUL worked up a number of strikes on its own account, and claimed 125,000 members in 1933, a chief feature of its work was to enter AFL strikes and try to bring about their collapse. Many of their alleged unions were mere shells, with their local headquarters in the same offices as local headquarters of the Communist Party, and frequently some active comrade doubled as a representative of the "union" and the local Party organization. The service of the TUUL to the Stalinite cause was actually to come later, in the enrollment of many of its former activists in leading positions in the CIO.

This development is something to be remembered carefully, since it gives a measure of the true extent of Red infiltration and how it is conducted. A comparatively small number of fanatical Reds, who had been unable to organize the American workers when they were traveling under their true colors, man-

aged to assume positions of power in the labor movement when
they concealed themselves under the banner of the CIO and
were backed up by CIO funds.

By 1935, the time had come for another about-face, again directed by Moscow, and in March of that year, the Trade Union
Unity League was dissolved. Although Foster admits that "the
TUUL unions did not succeed in building up powerful organizations numerically," and that their "membership was loose and
subject to violent fluctuations, hence exact estimates of their
numerical strength were difficult to make," the dissolution move
was not the direct result of these failures. It was part of the
preparation for the new line initiated by Moscow, which was
to be registered in the same years at the Soviet capital by the
Seventh Congress of the Communist International. The seizure
of power by Hitler, which the Communists in Germany had
aided greatly, had proved to be more permanent than Stalin had
expected, and it became necessary to woo the democratic nations
in order to get them to aid in defending the Soviet dictatorship.
Therefore, the "united front" became the order of the day, and
this naturally entailed entry into the regular trade unions.

The Moves Into the CIO

Never was the complete control by Moscow of everything the
Communist Party of the United States did in relation to the
trade unions more clearly demonstrated than in the 1935-36
episodes. With the same unanimity with which they had assailed
the AFL unions, the Communists now entered them with the
motley array of workers still loyal to the remnants of Red unionism. As an instance, Ben Gold, veteran Communist, led his fur
workers division of the Needle Trades Industrial Union into the
International Fur Workers Union, and immediately became the
chief officer in the New York Joint Council. Shortly thereafter he
was to be made president of the entire organization, as it became
the International Fur and Leather Workers Union. The transport
workers, who had been only partially organized through Com-

munist initiative, walked into the International Association of Machinists. And so it went in other fields.

But 1936 saw the birth of the Congress of Industrial Organizations and the beginning of its big organizing campaigns. John L. Lewis, at its head, needed organizers to extend the CIO and to oppose the AFL. The new movement had huge funds at its disposal, furnished largely from the treasury of the United Mine Workers. The Communists saw their big opportunity in this development, and with the consent of Moscow the American Politburo ordered all those Red-ruled groups who could make the move to join the CIO. They had scarcely got settled in the AFL when they walked out of it. (From the Communist viewpoint, these events are recorded by William Z. Foster, in his two books, *From Bryan to Stalin* and *The History of the Communist Party of the United States*, both International Publishers, N.Y.)

The rapidity with which the Communists moved can be gauged by the fact that in 1949 at least twelve international unions of the CIO were under their complete control. If we add Local 65 of the Wholesale and Retail Workers Union—which in many ways acted at that time as an international union of its own—thirteen should be the total. In addition, the Reds controlled a number of key locals in other CIO affiliates, specifically in the United Automobile, Aircraft, and Agricultural Implement Workers Union. Among these were the big Ford Local 600 with its 80,000 members, in which they had a large share of the leadership, and the highly skilled Tool and Die Makers Union.

In the AFL, whose penetration they had not abandoned, even though the task was much harder, they had leadership in the New York and Cleveland District Councils of the International Brotherhood of Painters, Paperhangers, and Decorators, and had taken over a number of locals in the hotel and restaurant industry, including several joint councils. Jay Rubin, who had been an itinerant representative of various Red unions, became the chief executive of the New York Council. There was also a considerable number of cells in other AFL and CIO unions, specifically, in the powerful United Brotherhood of Carpenters and Joiners. In this instance, the Communists had no hope of gaining any immediate control internationally, but their cells were of value in gaining recruits for the Party and also in keeping Red ideas alive for any possible emergency.

The "UE"

The outstanding illustration of Communist tactics in gaining complete control of a large union is furnished by the United Electrical, Radio, and Machine Workers Union. Composed of about 300,000 members, and located in a number of sensitive positions connected with American defense, this is the largest of the labor organizations under Red domination in 1953. To get an intelligent grasp of how this has come about, we can turn back to the period of the TUUL. The Steel and Metal Workers Industrial Union had been one of the least successful of the Red creations in gaining membership. It had, however, established a light metal trades workers union in New York City, headed by James Matles, veteran Communist. The Reds had also located in Schenectady one Julius Emspak, also known as Comrade Juniper. These two were to play the big parts in the capture of the large union in the electrical and radio field that was to come out of CIO organizing activity. (These events and the Red control of the UE are related in many reports of the House Committee on Un-American Activities, down to the annual report of 1952; hearings of the House Committee on Labor under the chairmanship of Representative Charles J. Kersten, 80th Congress; and are related in *Men Without Faces*, Budenz, Harper & Brothers, N.Y., specifically Chap. VIII.)

When Moscow commanded the move into the AFL in 1935, Matles led his small local of metal workers into the International Association of Machinists and was welcomed by the New York District Council of the IAM. Approximately a year later, again under orders, he had to move the local out of the IAM into the newly formed United Radio Workers of America, CIO. Here he received an even warmer welcome, and under an arrangement with president James B. Carey became national organizer. This was just what the Communists wanted, since in a new organization those who are doing the organizing work are in a position to affect the attitudes of the officers of newly formed locals. Matles loaded his staff with faithful Reds, a number of whom had been in the previous TUUL movement. Although this gave the Soviet fifth column domination over an increasing number of local unions, it did not yet assure national control. Carey had been in on the ground floor, at the very birth of the UE, as it came to be known, having been active in unionizing the Philco plant in Philadelphia. He still had the prestige of being its first president. However, his eventual doom was settled by that addition of Matles as national organizer, and his agreement to the selection of Emspak as national secretary-treasurer.

During the Hitler-Stalin Pact, the question of leadership in the UE first became an issue. The Communists had specific instructions to create strikes everywhere, for the benefit of Hitler, and they did succeed in cutting down American defense production in the big walk out at Allis-Chalmers, Milwaukee, in 1941 and in the shutting down of the North American Aircraft plant at Ingleside, California, in the same year. They were also responsible for instigating a number of other stoppages, with a view to preventing the United States from defending itself, or affording such aid to Britain as would save it from Nazi conquest. The UE, although so extensively penetrated by the Communists, was not able in any large measure to respond to this Red command. In part, this was due at that time to an uneasy feeling on the part of the union members that they should not put themselves in the position of blocking American defense preparations. It was also due to Carey's objections, since as national secretary of the CIO he was in close touch with Philip Murray who did not approve of striking at American defense.

The Communists, accordingly, decided to get rid of Carey at the next national convention, which was scheduled to be held in Camden, New Jersey, in September, 1941. They conducted an intensive campaign of vilification against him, but when the time for the convention rolled around, the Red line had changed. In June, 1941, Hitler had attacked Soviet Russia. With all their efforts thereafter directed to getting the United States into the war in order to save Stalin, the Reds would have dropped their opposition to Carey if he had gone along with them. By that time, however, he was alarmed. Instead of working with them, he introduced resolutions barring Communists from office in the union. Thereupon, the Reds made an alliance with the representatives of the big Lynn local, which had differences with Carey on purely trade union problems and had a considerable following among other locals. It was agreed that Albert E. Fitzgerald, head of the Lynn group, should be the candidate for president, and that Emspak and Matles should retain their posts. This arrangement proved victorious, and Carey was defeated.

The UE has consistently followed the Communist line on every occasion, and its strategic location at the General Electric plant at Schenectady, which is connected with atomic manufacture, and in other like places, constitutes a serious threat to American security. (For an account of the capture of the UE, and for other descriptions of Red maneuvers within the unions, consult Chapter VIII, "Red Web in Labor," Budenz, *Men Without Faces*.)

When the Kremlin opened up its so-called "cold war" against the United States, which in reality is the beginning of World War III, the Communists entered upon an anti-American campaign which brought them into collision with the CIO leadership. At that time, they were well entrenched in the national office of that labor center. Lee Pressman was general counsel, Len De-Caux was editor of the *CIO News*, official CIO publication, and the Fowlers, husband and wife, were respectively in charge of research and of the national women's auxiliary. The CIO national officials, duly alarmed, got rid by degrees of these pro-Communists and Red agents at the centers. They were also compelled to move for the expulsion of those unions which preferred Red domination to going along with CIO policies. The United

Electrical, Radio, and Machine Workers Union anticipated its expulsion by dropping affiliation through non-payment of dues. This move was considered to be the safest way to hold on to the largest possible membership. It proved successful. While the CIO did organize the International Union of Electrical Workers, now again under Carey's presidency, the UE held a substantial part of its membership. In 1953, it apparently increased this following, with victories in several NLRB elections.

Red-Ruled Unions

An index of Red strength in the labor movement, with its possibilities of serious harm to American defense in any emergency, can be gleaned from the list of the unions which were under Communist domination in 1949 and have largely remained under that domination. These CIO unions were:

The American Communications Association, headed by Joseph Selly, veteran Communist.

The Food, Tobacco, Agricultural, and Allied Workers of America, headed by Donald Henderson, who headed the old Red-ruled union in this field.

The International Fur and Leather Workers Union, headed by Ben Gold, open Communist.

The International Longshoremen's and Warehousemen's Union, headed by Harry Bridges, convicted of perjury for swearing he was not a Communist.

The International Union of Mine, Mill, and Smelter Workers, headed by Morris Travis.

The United Public Workers of America, headed for years by Eleanor Nelson.

The National Union of Marine Cooks and Stewards, headed by Hugh Bryson.

The United Furniture Workers of America.

The United Office and Professional Workers of America. (*Communist Domination of Certain Unions*, Report of Senate Sub-Committee on Labor and Labor-Management Relations, Document 89, 82nd Congress, 1st Session.)

All of the above unions were expelled from the CIO in 1950. Among those not expelled were the following:

Transport Workers Union of America, which under the leadership of Michael Quill broke with the Communist Party.

The National Maritime Union, which under the leadership of Joseph Curran likewise repudiated previous Communist control.

The United Electrical, Radio, and Machine Workers Union, actually led by James Matles, official representative of the Politburo in that union, which dropped affiliation before charges could be filed.

In addition, as has been stated, there was Local 65 of the Wholesale and Retail Workers Union, headed by Arthur Osman, who is now head of the newly formed Distributive, Processing, and Office Workers of America (DWOPA).

After the break with the CIO, the Communists knew that certain of the unions they controlled would not be able to stand on their own feet. These unions had largely been built up by CIO cooperation and CIO funds. Under orders of the Politburo, they were merged into the DPOWA, around the strong center of Local 65, the most successful of them all. In this manner, the old United Office and Professional Workers of America and the Food, Tobacco, and Agricultural Workers were blended into the new organization. Several small locals of the Wholesale, Retail, and Department Store Union, of which Local 65 had also been a part, were likewise put in the new grouping.

Since this was the weakest link in the chain of Red unionism, it is not surprising that the DPOWA has worked itself back into the CIO. It has, it is true, a rather large treasury and controls thousands of workers in offices of big and little corporations, in the wholesale and retail store field, in banks and insurance companies, drug chains, welfare work, the food processing field, the tobacco and other agricultural industries. This does put a strain upon it, however, in its far-flung organization work, a strain which would be relieved by entry into the CIO, from which it could get much help. CIO affiliation would also remove it as a security problem for many business concerns.

While the reasons for the return of the DPOWA to the CIO are clear, the relationship of its leaders to the Communists is more obscure. The leaders have openly defied the House Committee on Un-American Activities, but *Political Affairs* of June, 1953, denounced them as "renegades." These two events indicate that they have broken with the Communist Party organizationally, but have some Communist hangovers. (*Counterattack*, July, 1953.)

A careful analysis of the character of the unions under Red domination today would make clear that they are good handles for Communist subversive purposes. The Mine, Mill, and Smelter Workers Union (formerly the Western Federation of Miners) has under its wing the copper miners of the country and also many thousands of workers engaged in processing copper and other kindred metals into finished products. These metals are all vital to war production, and the grip which the Soviet fifth column has on the organized workers who handle them will yet constitute a serious weakness. The unionization of office workers, whether in private or in public occupations, serves the conspiracy well. One of the chief methods of underground information for the fifth column are secretaries and those similarly employed, who may advise the appropriate Communist functionary of the contents of files and the nature of correspondence. More than that, they can also tamper with files, and that practice is not unknown in Communist history. The fur workers, while not engaged in an industry which is vital in itself, give considerable aid to those penetrating more sensitive industry. The funds and personnel of Ben Gold's union have been freely expended to spread Communist influence into more basic industrial areas.

In this connection, we must constantly remind ourselves that the Communist never remains confined to his own field of work. The Party expects of him the fullest cooperation in every possible direction. The control by the Soviet fifth column of specific unions goes far beyond those particular organizations. It entails aid to cells often working far beyond the periphery of these unions. The strong position of the American Communications Association in the telegraphic facilities in the Port of New York, which endangers our military communications, is only part of the ACA's power. It also encourages many other Red activities. (The specific story of the American Communications Association appears in *The Cry Is Peace*, Budenz, Henry Regnery Co., pp. 20, 21.)

The Concentration Policy

The main feature of Red infiltration into the labor movement is the concentration policy formulated in 1933 upon direct orders from Moscow. It is an outstanding part of the extraordinary conference held by the Communist Party at that time and of the *Open Letter* which that conference issued. It consists of the concentration of forces, funds, and activities first in those basic industries—steel, rubber, automobile, coal, maritime, transportation—which are particularly essential to American production. This has been the subject of constant emphasis in the National Committee Meetings of the Party and in its official theoretical organ, first known as *The Communist* and now as *Political Affairs*.

At the Fifteenth National Convention of the Communist Party, held secretly in December, 1950, this continued stress on concentration in the large-scale industries was expressed by the resolution which stated: "The Party National Convention calls upon the whole Party to establish guarantees that a real policy of industrial concentration will be carried forward, and that major attention is given to the workers in the stronghold of trustified capital. . . ."

The chief objective in concentration was most simply defined by John Williamson (member of the American Politburo and one of the eleven Communists convicted in 1949) in his report to the 1945 convention which deposed Earl Browder from leadership. Williamson gave the basic item in "tasks of concentration" as follows: "To mobilize the entire Party membership to direct its work in such a way as to be conscious at all times of the needs to strengthen our position in basic industries."

This program involves selection of specific industries for concentrated work in each state or district, but above all (as Williamson explains) it entails specifically the throwing of the greatest weight into work in the big industries of six states— New York, California, Eastern Pennsylvania, Michigan, Illinois, and Ohio. These are the so-called "concentration districts." When we consider what would be America's fate if the Communists could paralyze the Port of New York and the California ports, the steel industry of eastern Pennsylvania and Illinois (including the Calumet region of northern Indiana), the tank and aircraft manufacturing of Ohio and Michigan, we get a good picture of the reason for this pattern. To strengthen the plan still further, there is to be additional concentration in the industrial towns of intermediate size, such as McKeesport, Schenectady, Youngstown, Akron, Flint, Gary, and towns in the anthracite region and West Virginia. (*Political Affairs*, September, 1945, "The Reconstitution of the Communist Party," John Williamson, p. 814.)

The plans to entrench the conspiracy in those vital spots through which America could be destroyed are the preparations demanded of the Communists by the *Program of the Communist International*. Among its chief directives for bringing about armed insurrection out of politicalized strikes are the following steps:

"This mass action includes: a combination of strikes and demonstrations; a combination of strikes and armed demonstrations and finally, the general strike conjointly with armed insurrection against the state power of the bourgeoisie. The latter form of struggle, which is the supreme form, must be conducted according to the rules of military science; it presupposed a plan of campaign, offensive fighting operations and unbounded devotion and heroism on the part of the proletariat. An absolutely essential prerequisite for this form of action is the organization of the broad masses into militant units, which, by their very form, embrace and set into action the largest possible numbers of toilers (Councils of Workers' Deputies, Soldiers, Councils, etc.), and intensified revolutionary work in the army and the navy." (*The Program of the Communist International*, reprinted in *Blueprint for World Conquest*, Henry Regnery Co., p. 239; originally in the 1928 vol. of *International Press Correspondence*.)

In case the Soviet dictatorship should engage in war against the United States, it will be the duty of the Communists here to instigate armed insurrection, if that will facilitate the progress of the Red armed forces. This they must do even though the prospect of success in the insurrection is small or even none. The test must be solely whether the Soviet military operations against this country will be aided or not.

With such a compulsion upon the Soviet fifth column, the successful advancement of concentration in the basic industries becomes a Red "must" of the highest priority. (See *The Struggle Against Imperialist War and the Tasks of the Communists*, Resolution of the Sixth World Congress of the Communist International, July-August 1928, Workers Library Publishers, 1932, p. 10; also in 1928 vol. of *International Press Correspondence*. See also *A Century of Conflict*, Stefan T. Possony, Henry Regnery Co., Chap. IV.)

Since the CIO unions were so widely located in the basic industries, the Communists' effort to make headway in the CIO was not only due to the opportunity given them from 1936 on. It was also in accord with the concentration policy.

At the Fifteenth National Convention of the Communist Party, held in December, 1950, "concentration in all industry"

was decided. This decision aimed at getting a foothold in any
union or shop, with the view to use it as a base for wider infiltration, into the mass production areas. But the program of infiltrating the large-scale and heavy industries remains; indeed,
it was in order to forward it that the "concentration in all industry" was adopted.

The Yardstick

During 1950, Red controlled unions had been expelled from the
CIO. The yardstick used by the CIO committees in judging specific organizations to be Communist-ruled was the correct one:
the parallel between the line of the Party at each stage and turn,
and the program of the union.

The conclusions found in each case can be exemplified by the
recommendation of the committee dealing with the Mine, Mill,
and Smelter Workers Union. It states in part:

"It is abundantly clear not only that the leadership of the
Mine, Mill, and Smelter Workers Union consistently follows
the Communist Party line, but also that it does so in response
to a carefully organized mechanism by which the decisions of
the Communist Party are translated into Mine, Mill policy.
. . . The only defense of leaders of Mine, Mill has been epithet,
vilification, and confusion. They assert that they are defending
the autonomous rights of their union. But false claims of auton-
omy cannot justify adherence to the foreign policy of the Soviet
Union and a betrayal of the interest of the American working-
men. The false cry of democracy cannot justify the existence of
a secret apparatus, undisclosed to the members of the union,
by which orders of outsiders become the policy of the union's
leadership. The bogus defense that this union is interested only
in the economic gains of the membership cannot justify the building of an organizational structure, 90 per cent of it manned by
members or adherents of the Communist Party.

"The false cry of freedom to criticize cannot justify the Communist tactic of systematic assassination against the national
CIO, its officers and all affiliated unions who oppose the policies

of the Communist Party." (*Communist Domination of Certain Unions*—Report of the Sub-Committee on Labor and Labor Management Relations, U.S. Senate, 82nd Congress, pp. 107, 108. See also *The Cry Is Peace*, Budenz, pp. 228, 229.)

In 1952, the Communists were given new directives for infiltration into "Right-led unions," that is, the CIO and AFL affiliates, together with the railroad brotherhoods. The Stalinites reviewed with satisfaction their continued domination of hundreds of thousands of workers, through the organizations expelled from the CIO. It was pointed out that they were in control of the copper industry and allied manufacturing, and that they had a considerable hold in the maritime field through the International Longshoremen's and Warehousemen's Union headed by Harry Bridges. The victory attained by their slate in the powerful Ford Local 600 of the United Automobile, Aircraft, and Agricultural Implement Workers Union, CIO, was also noted—a victory considered of great importance because it followed on the heels of President Walter Reuther's attempt to dislodge the Communists. The hold of the Reds on strategic plants in the electrical industry, and specifically in the key General Electric Corporation works at Schenectady, was also significant.

From these and other vantage points, the Stalinites were ordered to begin the renewed penetration of those unions which had rejected them. It is well to underline the tactics they adopted. The infiltrators were instructed to base themselves on Lenin's *Left Wing Communism*, which stresses the necessity for subterfuge and deceit. The outstanding slogan which was to be raised was "labor unity." As the mysterious John Swift—the pseudonym of an important Communist leader—declared in giving these directives: "Labor solidarity and unity must be fought for daily, not just on special occasions." (*Political Affairs*, April 1952, "Some Problems of Work in Right-Led Unions," John Swift, p. 39. See also *Political Affairs*, Nov. 1952, "The Ford Local Union Election," John Swift, pp. 18-35.)

The cry of "labor unity" is skillfully designed to strike at the Achilles heel of many labor leaders opposing Communist infiltration of the unions. The standard argument of the Communists, which is taken up by their friends and serves to intimidate some of their opponents, is that any curb on the conspiracy will endanger the liberties of the mass of the people in this country. In the unions, the variation of that argument is that the Communists are a part of the labor movement. Both assertions, our studies have shown, are false. From the Communist view, according to which "genuine liberty" can be won only in the Communist society, the so-called bourgeois civil liberties are to be used for the protection of the Soviet fifth column in order to destroy all freedom through the dictatorship. In like manner, the sole purpose of the unions is to serve as the bases for such agitation and political strikes as will lead to the overthrow of the non-Soviet government and the destruction of the unions themselves. For the Stalinite, this view is logical. But it is amazing to observe that even those who do not accept the Communist premises often echo the Communist conclusions.

Reuther and Carey

Both President Walter Reuther of the CIO and President James B. Carey of the International Union of Electrical Workers, CIO, are engaged in a grim fight with the Communists. But, unfortunately, both Reuther and Carey give ammunition to the Red cry for "labor unity" and to the contention that any curb of the Communists injures labor. At the convention of the American Association of School Administrators on February 17, 1953, Mrs. Agnes E. Meyer, wife of the publisher of the *Washington Post*, made an extreme attack on the investigation of Communist professors and teachers. The Red press, its allies and friends, made Mrs. Meyer's speech the occasion for widespread propaganda to cover up and defend the conspiracy. Walter Reuther followed Mrs. Meyer on the speaker's platform and advocated the same anti-anti-Communist line. Said Reuther: "The growing attack by the apostles of fear, hatred, and hysteria against academic freedom and civil liberties generally must be met by an effective counter-offensive." His words seem to imply that all attempts to uproot the infiltrators from our educational system must be halted.

As the news-letter *Counterattack* states in its issue of March 20, 1953: "It makes sense when the CP plugs this line and gives publicity to Reuther when he does . . . just as it has given publicity to his attacks on the Internal Security Act of 1950 and the Smith Act, under which the Politburo and other CP leaders have been tried and convicted of conspiracy. But it doesn't make sense when Reuther plugs it. When he does he is actually, though unintentionally, identifying the interests of the CIO, the UAW, and all labor with those of the CP."

At the 1950 convention of the CIO, Reuther sponsored a resolution criticizing the Smith Act, which had been upheld by the United States Supreme Court and which is one means of halting the Soviet fifth column. This criticism was repeated by the 1953 convention of the UAW under his leadership. The Communists, while playing up in their press this anti-anti-Communist attitude, at the same time assail Reuther for breaking "labor unity" by opposing them within the UAW. It is small wonder that, with such a convenient cover as Reuther's own statements, they were able to rout his forces in the big Ford Local 600, the spearhead of their drive into the UAW. This victory they gained despite the exposure of specific officers of Local 600 as members of the Red conspiracy by the House Committee of Un-American Activities.

In view of the way in which the Reds, Communist fronters, and those influenced by them work from the top of organizations to attain their ends, it is significant that the counsel for the UAW is Harold Cranefield, leading member of the National Lawyers Guild, which the House Committee on Un-American Activities declared to be "the legal arm" of the Communist Party.

With President James B. Carey of the IUE, the story has been the same. In February, 1953, for instance, Carey appeared on the American Forum of the Air, to assail Congressional investigations and to indicate that a greater threat to the United States than Communism was the attempt of "reactionaries" to destroy it. He claimed that this led to lack of faith by the American people in one another, and in their institutions. Carey has made other statements to the same effect. This has given another convenient cover to the Communists. As a result, the CP-directed United Electrical, Radio, and Machine Workers Union won a National Labor Relations Board election at the North American Cyanimid Company plant at Niagara Falls, and at the Richmond, Indiana, plant of the International Harvester Company, early in 1953. The Red-ruled union also made marked headway among electrical workers in Pittsburgh and Erie, Pennsylvania, and in parts of New Jersey.

The attitude expressed by Reuther, Carey, and some other labor leaders along this line is in strange contradiction to the statement repeatedly made by the CIO committees that "the Communist Party does not believe in trade unions. It believes in using trade unions. And it believes in using them for the purposes of the Soviet Union." If that is so, then the Communists are the enemies of the free labor unions, as they have proved to be by their splitting tactics in non-Soviet countries and by their complete crushing of genuine unionism wherever the Soviet dictatorship is established. If it be true that the Communists are in service of no one but the Soviet Union in penetrating trade unions, then they are likewise solely serving Moscow when they infiltrate government, colleges, and schools. In self-defense, the government acts through Congressional investigations, through safeguards on loyalty and security, and through the prosecution of the criminal acts of the conspiracy. That is the true way to defend the liberties of the American people, and to protect the integrity of the free trade union movement.

Conclusions

From these considerations, a summary and conclusions can be drawn:

1. Since Soviet Communism is the chief foe of free trade unionism, it is impossible to combat Stalinism effectively without supporting the rights and development of the trade unions. By the same token, it is impossible to defend the unions for any period of time without opposing Communism fully and overcoming all anti-anti-Communist viewpoints.

Support to labor's right to organize and extend its organization are not given primarily in order to defeat Communism. That support arises positively out of the need to strengthen free organizations and institutions within our republic, and is also based on the workers' natural right to organize. There is need to do more toward bringing labor and management together on a permanent basis of collective bargaining, with government cooperating, through industry councils. This would give a firm foundation to industrial relations. (Consult *Seven Pillars of Industrial Order*, Bishop Francis J. Haas, Catholic Conference on Industrial Problems, Washington, D.C.)

In the course of advocating the rights of the free trade unions, it becomes very essential, however, to bring out fully the Communists' contempt for them, and to show in detail the great slave labor empire which has been erected by the Kremlin. This Red contempt for the unions arises out of the very nature of Communism itself—out of the ruling caste concept that only Marxist-Leninists can lead the "backward masses" to progress, and that all organizations are expendable in order to reach the stage of "genuine freedom," the classless society. It is well expressed in Lenin's statement that the workers, left to themselves and their own "spontaneity," could never get above "the trade union level." (Issues of the monthly *News From Behind the Iron Curtain*, National Committee for a Free Europe, 110 W. 57th St., New York, 19, N.Y., frequently carry translated quotations from Communist publications in Soviet Russia and the satellite regimes which show conclusively that the "trade unions" have been converted into speed-up agencies for the Soviet bureaucracy. Also consult the report of the American Federation of Labor on slave labor in the Soviet Union.)

2. The presence in industrial management circles of pro-Communist influences or complacency toward Communists can be recognized. The officers of the International Union of Electrical Workers, CIO, have repeatedly charged that the management of the General Electric Corporation is helpful to the Red-ruled UE. This is not surprising when we note that Gerard T. Swope, former chairman of the board of General Electric, has defended the Institute of Pacific Relations against the now-proven charges that Communists infiltrated the Institute on a large scale. Gerard Swope, Jr., counsel for International General Electric, was one of the character witnesses for Alger Hiss in his second trial, and the president of the same corporation was cited by Owen Lattimore as supporting his attitude which favored a soft policy toward the Communists in the Far East. These facts are cited not for the purpose of castigating anyone, but to indicate sharply that a misunderstanding of Communist philosophy and objectives has many repercussions. It is noteworthy that management on the whole has not shown the same zeal in public against Communist infiltration as has been evident when objections to demands of legitimate labor unions are involved. (See panel discussion on "Communist Threat in Industry," *Management Record*, April, 1952, National Industrial Conference Board.)

3. Because of the vital necessity of dislodging Stalinites from the control of labor organizations, it becomes essential that a genuine demand be made, from all parts of the country, that the National Labor Relations Board change its policy of refusing to look behind the non-Communist affidavits of those labor leaders who technically resign from the Communist Party in order to maintain their dominance over the Red-ruled unions. Coincident with this move could go a parallel campaign for legislation to deal firmly and forthrightly with this matter.

4. Since the Communists endeavor to show that the workers are constantly being worsted in American labor management relations, it is important to develop educationally the possibilities of equitable and expanded collective bargaining. Harding

College, under the auspices of the Disciples of Christ at Searcy, Arkansas, has issued a booklet in its Freedom Forum series, entitled *How We Work Together for the Common Good*, which can be of value in this connection. There is also the series issued by the National Planning Association, Washington, D.C., entitled *Causes of Industrial Peace Under Collective Bargaining*, containing case studies of successful collective bargaining in various corporations and industries.

5. Down in the local unions as well as local management, there can be an intelligent. alertness in regard to those who follow the Communist line. That is the acid test as correctly applied by the CIO committees in 1950, and well illustrated by the following words from the report of the CIO committee which dealt with the International Fur and Leather Workers Union:

"The Communist Party's single minded devotion to Russia controls its position on domestic issues, as well as on matters of foreign policy. During the collective security period, when the Communists supported Roosevelt's foreign policy, they also supported his domestic policy as progressive and pro-labor. In the next period, however, when the German-Russian Pact was in effect, Roosevelt was seen by the Communist Party as a reactionary and a Fascist, and his domestic program was roundly attacked as being anti-labor. As soon as Germany attacked Russia, Roosevelt became once more, in the eyes of the Communist Party, a great and far-sighted leader. Since his foreign policy was now acceptable, his domestic program was once more praised by the Communist Party." (*Communist Domination of Certain Unions*, p. 69.)

The Communist line can be studied today in a like manner, and those who are interweaving "immediate demands" with that line will be found to be serving Soviet interests within the labor movement or within management. Since the Communists, either themselves or through those whom they can make their puppets, produce their line in labor and management circles by resolutions or by a series of suggestions, the antidote is to take a stand, through all resolutions and suggestions, for the United States. Those who are aiding Soviet Russia can be smoked out by the simple device of offering proposals directly opposed to the main features of the current Communist line. The pro-Reds will react by directly or indirectly seeking to defeat such pro-American proposals.

The defeat of the Communists within labor and management takes effort, because of their devious and concealed methods. But it can be achieved by intelligent study and vigorous action.

CHAPTER X

INVADING EDUCATION

IN UNDERMINING a nation such as the United States, the infiltration of the educational process is of prime importance. The Communists have accordingly made the invasion of schools and colleges one of the major considerations in their psychological warfare designed to control the American mind. By such "cultural" work, the Soviet fifth column obtains an influence, directly or indirectly, over at least a portion of American youth. Some of the young men entering our armed forces, and some of the young women who must support them, are brought within the orbit of pro-Communist thinking, to the detriment of our national security. Future community leaders are also affected. Many by-products beneficial to the conspiracy arise from this infiltration, since concealed Communists in education or their friends become sponsors of Communist fronts, aid in financing Communist causes, and sometimes play a part in influencing the attitudes of certain scientists, specific church circles, and government agencies.

As early as 1924, in lectures delivered at the Sverdlov University in Moscow, Stalin specified "cultural and educational organizations" as valuable allies in the Communist battle for world dictatorship. These Stalin lectures are now the famous *Foundations of Leninism*, published and studied widely by the Communists. It was in 1933, however, that extensive infiltration began in the schools and colleges of this country—encouraged

208

by American recognition of Soviet Russia, and stimulated by the *Open Letter* to the Party. The Trojan horse policy of the People's Front, which had been initiated at the Seventh World Congress of the Communist International in 1935, gave added impetus to this activity. By May, 1937, the conspiracy considered that enough progress had been made in the schools and colleges to justify a special article of directives in that month's issue of *The Communist*, then the official theoretical organ of the Party. This article, "The Schools and the People's Front," laid it down as a necessity that "Marxist-Leninist analysis must be injected into every class." In order that this might be accomplished successfully, "the Party must take careful steps to see that all teacher comrades are given thorough education in the teachings of Marxism-Leninism." It was stressed that "Communist teachers are faced with a tremendous social responsibility." They must affect the children's thinking, and they must mobilize other teachers. But all of this was to be done—from the work in the classroom to the agitation among other teachers —*"without exposing themselves."* (Italics mine.)

This is the instruction which runs through all directives to the infiltrators of our schools and colleges: they must exercise their Communist influence "without exposing themselves." In this very article of May, 1937, an added precaution is given: "Only when teachers have really mastered Marxism-Leninism will they be able to inject it into their teaching at the least risk of exposure."

The article by John Williamson in the November, 1950, issue of *Political Affairs*, dealing with general infiltration but referring specifically to trade union work, makes much of the same necessity. The Red infiltrators are there counseled to perform their task in such a way as not to be "exposed" and dislodged from their positions.

This method must be thoroughly understood. If it is not constantly kept in mind, the Red techniques of entering education and influencing its course will be completely missed. Those who contend that Communists should be permitted to teach in our schools "as long as they do not teach Communism openly in the classroom" have not acquainted themselves with the ABC of Red infiltration. And yet, the late Senator Robert A. Taft of Ohio, who represented a considerable section of conservative opinion, has made this grave error.

In the classroom, the Communist teacher or professor very rarely, if ever, teaches Marxism-Leninism openly. There are hundreds of indirect ways of reaching the same end. Books by Howard Fast, the author who has refused to state whether or not he would fight against Communists if drafted, are proposed as suggested or recommended readings. The works and statements of many other "authorities" who invariably take a pro-Soviet position, such as Professor Frederick L. Schuman of Williams College, can be freely used. The Red instructor has many other "non-Communist" sources to draw on—those leading figures in public life who always follow the Communist line and whom Stalin has designated as the "reserves" the conspiracy should call upon. An entire syllabus which would inevitably lead a student either to embrace Marxism-Leninism or to be sympathetic to the Communist line, can be drawn up without one notably or openly Stalinite reference in it.

Building on that foundation, the Communist teacher or professor notes the pupil or student most susceptible to pro-Red ideas. This student is cultivated privately, with a view to drawing him toward the conspiracy. In like manner, colleagues on the faculty who indicate sympathy for pro-Communist ideas are influenced by personal association to join the Communist Party. The influence of the teacher who is committed to Marxism-Leninism goes far beyond these contacts—into parent-teachers associations (often working behind the scenes with Communists in those groups), in the preparation of books, the presentation of lectures, the voicing of opinions, the raising of finances for the conspiracy.

Anyone who doubts the widespread character of Communist infiltration into education needs only to consult the Congressional investigations over the years. Specifically, the report of the House Committee on Un-American Activities of April 1, 1951, is most helpful. Entitled *The Communist "Peace" Offensive: The Attempt to Disarm and Defeat America*, it cites scores of educators who have aided the Kremlin's peace partisans. Many of these have been sponsors or members of Communist fronts on a great number of occasions. Robert Morss Lovett, long with the University of Chicago and former American Governor of the Virgin Islands, is there cited as being a member of at least eighty-five Communist fronts. Dr. Harry F. Ward, Professor Emeritus of Christian Ethics at Union Theological Seminary, is reported to be a member of sixty Communist fronts. The late Dr. Walter Rautenstrauch, well-known professor of engineering at Columbia University, is reported to be affiliated with fifty Communist fronts. Dr. Henry Pratt Fairchild of New York University has been associated with forty of such organizations; Colston E. Warne of Amherst and Frederick L. Schuman of Williams College, with thirty, and that is the record also of Dr. Robert S. Lynd of Columbia.

Each student should examine this report carefully, since it gives an indication of the scale on which the peace partisans (so valuable to the Kremlin) have penetrated our educational institutions. Dr. J. B. Matthews, after careful examination of the records, declares that since 1935 "the Communist Party has enlisted the support of at least thirty-five hundred professors— many of them as dues paying members, many others as fellow travelers, some as out-and-out espionage agents, some as adherents of the Party line in varying degrees, and some as the unwitting dupes of subversion." (*American Mercury*, May, 1953, "Communism and the Colleges," by J. B. Matthews.)

Look for the Record

In the fall of 1952, there appeared before the Internal Sub-Committee on Internal Security a number of professors who refused to state under oath whether they were members of the Communist conspiracy (or in some cases espionage agents) on the grounds that their answers would tend to incriminate them. Among these were: Dr. Bernhard J. Stern, sociologist, Columbia University; Dr. Bernard F. Riess, psychologist, Hunter College; Drs. Moses Finley and Saul Heimlich, then of Rutgers University; Dr. Clarence A. Hiskey, Brooklyn Polytechnic Institute, and Dr. Gene Weltfish, Columbia University. These are a few of those who took this attitude. What we should note about them is not only the leading educational institutions to which they were attached for years, but also that their records have been known for a long period of time. There are bulky dossiers in the reports of the Congressional committees, dealing with these individuals time after time. Their constant sponsorship of subversive organizations forwarding the Communist line has been cited on innumerable occasions.

When they refused to testify as to their Stalinite affiliations or espionage activities, they merely confirmed what had been known all along from their performance in the past. This should be sharply noted, for it is what can be observed in scores of other cases. So far as the American public is concerned, therefore, it is the record of the teacher or professor in aiding Communist fronts and other aspects of the conspiracy that should count, and not an attempted proof of membership in the Communist Party. Since 1948 and 1949 (the arrangement being made over a period of time) no Communist has had any vestige of membership. It was the same during the Hitler-Stalin Pact period. George Blake Charney, State secretary of the Communist Party for New York, confirmed this arrangement under oath, in his testimony in 1953 before the New York Board of Regents. Charney then stated that there was no record of any individual Communist Party membership, that the members were now known only as numbers. This conforms with the explanation presented by John Lautner, former head of the State Control Commission of the New York Communist Party, before the Senate Sub-Committee on Internal Security on October 13, 1952. Lautner showed in detail how the Communist teachers were divided into small groups, as they were organized for underground Party work. (Report in the volume of *Sub-versive Influences in the Educational Process* which covers the hearings from Sept. 8 to Oct. 13, 1952.)

Even before 1948, and through most of the history of the conspiracy in this country, those individuals who joined the Communist Party when they were already in key or delicate positions were ordered by the Party not to have any trace of membership, and not to attend any branch meetings. This rule applied specifically to certain professors who either were conspicuous because of being alleged authorities in subjects affecting government, or held governmental posts.

It is important to recognize at once, then, that by and large it is impossible today to prove that any teacher or professor is a member of the conspiracy. Courts and Congressional inquiries have an obligation to seek for evidence of such membership. But for the American public and community leaders, the question that should be raised is: Does the record of this teacher or professor disclose constant aid to the Soviet dictatorship and the Soviet fifth column in this country?

That this should be the test is illustrated by the responses of Dr. Bernard J. Stern of Columbia University before the Sub-Committee on Internal Security. Stern denied that he was a Communist on the day of his appearance before the Sub-Committee. He also denied that he was a Communist the year before. But he refused to answer, on the grounds that it would tend to incriminate him, the question whether he had been a member of the Party several years before. There is only one explanation for such a stand, namely, that in the period about which he refuses to answer the Party had not yet gone underground. Ex-Communists like Bella Dodd might be available to prove his membership then, and also some record of his affiliation might have been produced. A perjury conviction would have followed, and it was clearly to avoid this that Stern took his peculiar position.

Stern's record of active participation in Communist causes goes back before the big infiltration of 1933. As early as 1931, he was a member of the early Communist fronts. In the spring of 1932, he met with a select group, called together by the veteran Communist, A. A. Heller, to institute the Red-created "Congress Against War," out of which grew the first big front organization, the American League Against War and Fascism. In all, up to 1951, he was a member or sponsor of forty Communist fronts.

Under the name of Bennett Stevens, he taught at the Workers School, and under the same name he wrote Marxist-Leninist books. At the time of his appearance on the witness stand in 1952, he was editor of the Stalinite organ *Science and Society,* a quarterly publication for intellectuals. Stern's record of consistent aid to the conspiracy over twenty years makes it unnecessary to prove legally that he is a Communist. He has done everything that a Communist would do. (For Stern's record in full, see *The Red Decade,* Eugene Lyons, 1941. Numerous reports of the House Committee on Un-American Activities, including specifically that of April 1, 1951. *Counterattack,* vol. VII, no. 14, April 3, 1953. These publications should also be consulted on the pro-Communist activities of other teachers and professors.)

Pragmatism—Aid To Infiltration

The Communists have had a number of advantages in the penetration of schools and colleges. Outstanding among these is the philosophy of pragmatism, as enunciated by Dr. John Dewey, which dominates the present educational process. Pragmatism is not a Communist philosophy, but it serves as a convenient cover under which the Reds may operate and also under which they may win many allies in the educational field.

The philosophy of pragmatism rejects the supernatural and declares there is no absolute good or absolute truth, and that morality is growth and growth is morality. The Communists believe that there is an absolute truth, Marxism-Leninism. But with Stalin, they can pick up where the pragmatists leave off, asserting that that which is new and developing is right and moral, and that which is dying and decaying is wrong and immoral. And of course, the rising and developing force today (as the Communists emphasize) is Soviet Communism itself. The Soviet dictatorship, from this viewpoint, represents the highest morality—no matter what crimes it commits, what slavery it establishes, and what terror it institutes. (See Chap. IV of the *History of the Communist Party of the Soviet Union,* Joseph V. Stalin.)

This conception, that everything new is right, flies in the face of history, which has witnessed many retrogressions and which has registered many setbacks for mankind by those who had the power, and were rising and "developing." The concealed Communist can utilize this meeting ground with pragmatism as a means to pose as a non-Communist, to widen the circle of his influence, and to implant himself in school or college. From pragmatism (or instrumentalism, to give a more precise title to Dewey's version), there flowed progressive education. First proposed by Dewey forty years ago, progressive education became centered in Teachers College, Columbia University, and from there reached out to change and color the entire method of teaching from nursery school to university. Progressive education has been an attempt to get away from formal methods of teaching, and to depend on "spontaneous" activities brought about by group discussions. The child is to be freed of discipline, and the program is to be initiated by the student rather than the teacher. Competition and rewards are to be eliminated, and the character of the pupil's work is not to be a major consideration. The theory is that in this manner the child's abilities will be released. In practice, the result has been on the whole confusion and chaos.

Of the sharp criticisms of progressive education, as it is administered, one of the most cogent is "Common Sense in the Classroom" by Marguerite Gretzinger, English teacher in Pershing High School, Detroit. In the *Michigan Education Journal* of 1950, Miss Gretzinger writes: "John Dewey pragmatism has confused the entire teaching profession from the college professors to the textbook writers, the boards of education, the school administrators, and the classroom teacher. None of us is sure of anything. The old methods have been declared authoritarian; the new methods have been preached about, but no one has demonstrated a working plan which anyone, except an angel, could administer. The results are disastrous." (Miss Gretzinger's full experiences, and her analysis of the chaos resulting from progressive education, were reprinted in *The Wanderer*, 112 E. 10th St., St. Paul, Oct. 30, 1952.)

The Soviet dictatorship would not permit progressive education within any of its schools or colleges. It requires a super-military discipline, based on blind acceptance of Marxism-Leninism, beginning in the kindergarten. Such has been the rule for educational standards both in Soviet Russia and under all the satellite regimes. But in the United States, the Soviet fifth column favors this "new education" because of the general confusion, chaos, and breakdown in morale which it can bring about. Dr. Bella Dodd, in her testimony before the Senate Sub-Committee on Internal Security, stated that the Communists constantly plugged progressive education, inspiring and instructing the Teachers Union to do the same. A book praised by the *Daily Worker* and written by a man in close association with that Red organ has taken a similar position. This work, widely hailed by the Communists, is *The Public School Scandal*, by Earl Conrad, New York, 1951.

The apparent contradiction in this stand has a logic of its own. It is paralleled by the Red outcry for an extreme interpretation of "bourgeois civil liberties"—amounting to anarchy—in non-Soviet countries, while defending the degradation of terror and slavery in the Soviet domains. Chaos and confusion are what the Communists seek in every non-Soviet nation, to make its conquest easier; this was the prescription long ago insisted upon by Lenin and then by Stalin. The Stalinite teacher also sees in the loose methods of progressive education a rare opportunity to advance pro-Communist thinking. Being definitely under instructions and having a specific goal, he can so arrange the group discussions and "social study projects" as to bring about conclusions helpful to the Communist line.

The Two Streams

These two streams—the pragmatic philosophy, initiating progressive education, and Communist infiltration—have moved along together. Distinct from each other, they nevertheless have frequently fused, and the Communists have taken full advantage of the opportunities which the pragmatic viewpoint and practices offered them.

The two tendencies—one favoring Dr. Dewey's teachings, the other sharply pro-Soviet—were originally combined in the person of Dr. George S. Counts of Teachers College, Columbia University. In the early thirties, Dr. Counts wrote several books highly laudatory of the Soviet dictatorship, and indicating that it had introduced a new era. At the same time, he was an outstanding figure in the Progressive Education Association, and author of the book *Dare the Schools Build a New Social Order?* which attained great popularity in progressive education circles. In this work, as its title indicates, Counts proclaimed the doom of the present social order, a doom that should be forwarded by the schools. He declared: "That the teachers should deliberately reach for power and then make the most of their conquest is my firm conviction. To the extent that they are permitted to fashion the curriculum and procedures of the school, they will influence the social ideals and behavior of the coming generation." This influence was to bear in the direction of bringing about collectivism.

A good illustration of how the thinking of the pragmatists about "building a new social order" could be shot through with pro-Communist purposes was given in the panel discussion in 1933 among the leaders of progressive education. Participants in this panel were, among others, Dr. William H. Kilpatrick, upon whom Dewey's mantle has fallen; Dr. Jesse H. Newlon of the New Lincoln School, Teachers College; Dr. Harold Rugg, author of the allegedly "collectivist" textbooks; and Dr. Goodwin Watson, psychologist, of the staff of Teachers College. There was much discussion back and forth on how the schools could overturn the present social order. Dr. Watson gave the answer. It was, he said, by linking the schools up "with socialist or communist agitators." And that is precisely what happened to a serious degree. The "agitators" to whom Dr. Watson referred were not soap boxers nor the picket line variety of Communist; they were the infiltrators, ordered that very year by the Open Letter to the Party to penetrate the school system.

Dr. Watson's thinking was in accord with his record of membership on numerous Communist fronts, including the vice-chairmanship of the committee on the Peekskill riots, which presented a distorted picture of the events, favorable to Howard Fast and Paul Robeson, Communists. (Reference to this panel discussion is made in the article, "Your Child Is Their Target," by Irene Corbally Kuhn, *American Legion Magazine*, April, 1952. A photostat of the discussion is in my possession.)

In the beginning—that is, in the early thirties—it was not only Dr. Counts who lauded Soviet Russia, although he did it most extensively, but also John Dewey himself. In his *The Red Decade*, Eugene Lyons could write: "Professor Counts of Columbia produced a eulogy of his largely subjective Russia and the foremost living American philosopher, John Dewey, hailed the mirage, adding, of Russia: 'In some respects, it is already a searching spiritual challenge as it is an economic challenge to coordinate and plan.' The spiritual challenge, presumably, was in the current arrests and liquidations of philosophers, historians, and professors accused of 'rotten liberalism' in their thinking." (Lyons, *The Red Decade*, 1941, p. 107.)

Both Dewey and Counts were to modify their pro-Soviet views later, Dewey to head the committee which exposed the gross character of the Soviet trials of 1937 and 1938, and Counts to criticize sharply Soviet practices. But their initial infatuation with Soviet Russia, shared by a number of their colleagues, was not lost upon the Communists; they rushed in, under such favorable circumstances, to place themselves in education from which they have not yet been successfully dislodged.

Other assistance came to the Reds. In 1933, the very year in which the Open Letter to the Party counseled such infiltration, a special committee of the Progressive Education Association issued *A Call to the Teachers of the Nation.*

While some of the criticisms of the then current social conditions, contained in this document, were worthy of consideration, its open call for "collectivization," and its insistence that the teachers promote collectivist ideas, gave the Communists those opportunities which they sought. The key thought of the report was contained in the statement: "Cumulative evidence supports the conclusion that, in the United States as in other countries, the age of individualism and laissez faire in economy and government is closing and a new age of collectivism is emerging." This vague over-simplification, with its stress on "collectivism," encouraged the Reds to use such statements for their own purposes and their friends to give them aid. (*A Call to the Teachers of the Nation,* issued in 1933 by the Committee of the Progressive Education Association on Social and Economic Problems. Members of this committee included Dr. Sidney Hook of New York University, Dr. Jesse Newlon of Teachers College, and Dr. Goodwin Watson of the same institution. This "call" is reviewed in the pamphlet, *Is There a "Subversive" Movement in the Public Schools?* being the speech of Hon. Paul W. Shafer of Michigan in the House of Representatives, March 21, 1952.)

The "call" was the signal for a flood of discussions and articles in leading educational circles on the possibility and desirability of "socialism." This discussion favoring "socialism" is found, in effect, in the official records of the National Education Association for 1933 and 1934. It was expressed by Granville Hicks, then a Communist and prominent educator, in *Progressive Education,* issue of January–February, 1934. It was encouraged by Dr. Harold Rugg, professor of education at

Teachers College, and was channelized into admiration for Soviet Russia by Dr. Goodwin Watson in *Social Frontier*, publication of the Dewey school of educators, for February 1937. Reporting on an educators' tour of the Land of Socialism, Dr. Watson declared that the tourists "had been aware of a society directed toward the sustenance of major human values." He continued: "One question lingered in our minds. Anna Louise Strong had stated it to us. 'I wish I knew,' she said, 'whether it will take longer for the Russians to develop efficiency or for America to develop socialism. Then I'll know where I want to live.'"

Miss Strong, one of the most notorious of pro-Soviet propagandists, did not get to decide the question eventually; the Soviet dictatorship threw her out of her "paradise" with the accusation that she was a "spy." Dr. Watson remained in the United States, to continue his pro-Communist work on a number of Communist fronts and in various areas. (Reference to all these events and discussions is contained in the speech of Hon. Paul W. Shafer of Michigan, House of Representatives, March 21, 1952.)

The Case of Dr. Brameld

This interlacing of Red penetration and pro-Communism with pragmatic thought in education has marched down the years. There is the case of Dr. Theodore Brameld, professor of education at New York University and right-hand man of Dean Ernest O. Melby. Dean Melby is perhaps the most conspicuous champion of progressive education, and also most vocal in his criticism of any investigation of subversion in education. His pamphlet, *American Education Under Fire*, which will be analyzed later, was written with the cooperation of Dr. Brameld, who has been a consistent member of Communist fronts for the past twenty years.

Brameld was an outstanding supporter and sponsor of the Communist created American League Against War and Fascism, denounced by the Attorney General of that time as set up to advance the interests of Soviet Russia. Its program, adopted in the fall of 1933, to which Dr. Brameld necessarily subscribed, said in part: "The black cloud of imperialist war hangs over the world . . . only in the Soviet Union has this basic cause of war been removed . . . therefore, the Soviet Union pursues a positive and vigorous peace policy and alone among the governments proposes total disarmament. . . . The government of the United States, in spite of peaceful professions, is more aggressively than ever following policies whose only logical result is war."

Dr. Brameld joined in that program, supporting a statement which the House Committee on Un-American Activities has denounced as "demands for outright treasonable activity." This was the pledge: "To work toward the stopping of the manufacture and transport of munitions and all other materials essential to the conduct of war, through mass demonstrations, picketing, and strikes . . . to support the peace policies of the Soviet Union . . . to win the armed forces to the support of this program."

When the American Politburo decided to change the name of the Workers School to the Jefferson School of Social Science, it became necessary to give the "new" institution an apparently non-Communist sponsorship. This would be one of the effective ways to disguise in part its completely Marxist-Leninist character, that is, its dedication to teachings and plans for the overthrow of the government of the United States by violence. Among the prominent sponsors who took on themselves the responsibility for launching the so-called Jefferson School was Dr. Theodore Brameld. In 1949, when the eleven Communist leaders were on trial, Brameld was one of those who came publicly to their defense. In that same year, he was one of the prominent sponsors of the Waldorf-Astoria Peace Conference— the so-called Scientific and Cultural Conference for World Peace. At this notorious conference, the United States was denounced and Soviet Russia hailed as a citadel of peace, civil disobedience against the United States was recommended to the point where it was said by Richard Boyer, writer for the *New Yorker Magazine*, who spoke openly for the Communist Party: "It is the duty of Americans to defy an American government intent on imperialist war." Brameld made no objection to any such seditious statements, although opportunity was given to him to do so. By 1949, Dr. George Counts and Dr. Sidney Hook had a different view of Soviet Russia, although they seemed to weaken their new attitude by anti-anti-Communism. They were among those, however, who signed an open letter to the conference, pointing out the plight of culture under the Soviet system which Brameld and his associates were praising so highly. "Over the last three decades," the letter stated, "the Soviet dictatorship has mercilessly imprisoned, exiled, or executed distinguished men of letters in that country." The letter asked "when the delegates from the Soviet Union appear at your conference, to make inquiry of them as to what happened to the purged artists, writers, and critics of the Soviet Union." Neither Dr. Harlow Shapley of Harvard, to whom the open letter was addressed, nor Dr. Brameld, who was one of those to whom its inquiries were directed, could or would answer it. Both of them stood for Soviet purging of scientists; both of them had clearly only one view of "academic freedom," that it should cover the Communists alone in their penetration of American education. There is no other explanation for their silent championship of the barbarities of the Kremlin.

Brameld is one of those who have woven in and out, sometimes contributing to the Deweyite organ, *Social Frontiers*, and sometimes writing for the Stalinist *Science and Society*. In the fall issue of 1936 of the latter publication, Brameld expressed the belief that Marxism "would applaud" the statement of Professor Jesse Newlon that "teachers must prepare to join in an organized army with the liberal forces seeking to build a better society—in the struggle of the people against special privileges." Brameld, in the name of Marxism, in the pages of a Stalinist publication, is stating here the formula by which the

Communists and pro-Communists took advantage of the vague plans and declarations of the Dewey school to overturn the social order.

In November, 1935, writing in the organ of the Dewey school, *Social Frontiers*, Brameld went farther along this line in his article on "Karl Marx and the American Teacher." He defended the necessity for the violent overthrow of the present social order on the same grounds that Lenin and Stalin declared to be necessary. That reason, heard from the defense in all the trials of the Communist conspirators, is that those in control will resort to violence inevitably, and therefore violence and illegality are essential to overthrow "capitalist society."

Following up this thought of illegality which he defended, Brameld proceeded to declare that, consistent with Marxist strategy, teachers who wish to conduct their activity "within the school and without in behalf of the collectivist ideal must influence their students, subtly if necessary, frankly if possible, toward accepting the same position." That is so clear an explanation of Communist methods in the classroom, and so definite an exhortation to follow those methods, that it deserves careful re-reading. If a lighter note were permissible in such a serious background, this distinguished professor of education at New York University should historically become known as "subtly if necessary, frankly if possible" Brameld. Such a title would serve to high-light his case history as one of the most illuminating in regard to the interlacing of pro-Communist ideas, seditious activities, and Marxist-Leninist tactics with the pragmatic school in education. (Dr. Brameld's record is contained in part in two important documents: *Review of the Scientific and Cultural Conference for World Peace*, prepared and released by the House Committee on Un-American Activities, Washington, D.C., April, 1949, and in *Is There a "Subversive" Movement in the Public Schools?* printed speech of Representative Paul W. Shafer of Michigan, March 21, 1952.)

This interlocking of the progressive education movement with the penetration by the Communists and their allies could be extended to a far degree and will be increasingly apparent as the reader examines the history of Communist fronts and the many uses to which educators have been put by the Communist conspiracy. To cite another instance, Professor John J. DeBoer of the University of Illinois was one of the outstanding panel speakers at the seditious Waldorf-Astoria "peace" conference. He has been a member or sponsor of from five to ten other Communist front organizations. In the movement which arose from Dr. John Dewey's views, Professor DeBoer was also most active, being one of the well-known presidents of the Progressive Education Association. This association of the two tendencies was not surprising on the campus at Champaign, where the Soviet fifth column has made marked inroads into the adherence and thinking of a considerable section of the faculty. There has been a flourishing and effective cell of at least thirty Communist professors there, with the usual much more extensive influence than even that number indicates.

In order to keep a sense of proportion, a two-fold consideration must be borne in mind. As I stated in my article in the *American Legion Magazine* for November, 1951, "We must first recognize, in order not to get into a panic, that the overwhelming majority of our educators are patriotic and desirous of serving America. Sometimes in their educational organizations, they are too easily buffaloed by the Communists with the cry of 'academic freedom,' not realizing fully that all Reds are under direct instructions and serve as soldiers of an invading army. But when we consider the comparatively modest remuneration they receive for the important services they perform, we can pay a tribute to their devotion to the United States.

"But the second reality is this: That there is a strong, aggressive and growing minority among our educators who are committed to the Communist cause and who serve repeatedly on Communist front organizations. What is more to the point, they are well organized, function secretly, and have influence far beyond their numbers." ("Do Colleges *Have* to Hire Red Professors?" Louis F. Budenz, *American Legion Magazine*, Nov. 1951.)

It is unfortunate that up to the present, this strong and aggressive minority has intimidated the overwhelming majority of educators with new cries of "fascism" and "McCarthyism," so that a considerable part of the vocal expression from educational circles has tended to favor the seditionists.

Culture Under One Roof

The Communists have another advantage, which must be understood if their invasion of education is to be properly estimated and combated. It is expressed by a phrase which I used in Communist discussions, and which still holds true, that they place "culture under one roof." By this we mean that every "cultural activity" is designed to support all others. Anyone who examines carefully the report of the Cultural Commission of the Communist Party, *Let Us Grasp the Weapon of Culture,* will be made aware of this fact. Everything of a "cultural character" is there blended together. It can be readily seen from its pages how the Communists use lectures, entertainers, the placing of books in the libraries, the penetration of parent-teachers associations, women's clubs, local men's groups, and community organizations in their work of influencing the educational process. (This report, made under the name V. J. Jerome, was presented to the Fifteenth National Convention of the Communist Party in December, 1950, and first printed in *Political Affairs* for February, 1951. In 1953, it was reprinted as a pamphlet by the Communist Party and distributed in thousands of copies, in the drive to strengthen Communist infiltration of "the cultural field.")

A variety of methods is thus used to reach into education and affect it, and so to help in throwing the American mind into confusion or pro-Communism. Most desirable of all, necessarily, is the placing of Communist teachers in the schools and colleges. In this, the conspiracy has been very adroit. Dr. Bella

Dodd has testified, before the Senate Committee on Internal Security, of 1500 Communist teachers in the elementary or high schools whom she knew to be in the Communist camp. At first blush, this would seem a small number. We must constantly remind ourselves, as Dr. Dodd and I agree, that two or three Communists on any faculty are normally enough to dominate the school or campus. They do not act alone, but have aid from the outside. They work under the directives of Communist functionaries who seek out ways to influence trustees of the college involved or members of the board of education. It is not unusual that certain men of wealth on the board of trustees give protection to the subversives on the faculty, to the detriment of those who are genuinely patriotic; these trustees being influenced by the cries of academic freedom, by a gross ignorance of the Communist methods, by personal considerations, or by partisan interests.

Beyond all this, the Communists on the faculty have the loud support of specific organizations in the community which other concealed Communists infiltrate and control. Nor do the Reds hesitate to resort to whispering campaigns against the character of an opponent, which frequently terrorize non-Communist teachers or professors. This goes far beyond the outspoken cry of "McCarthyite"; it extends into sly and organized gossip, reflecting on the work, the morals, and the integrity of the person under attack because of his patriotic position. Here, again, the gangster character of the Communist philosophy, carried on by non-gangsters, serves as a potent weapon. When to all of this we add the ease with which the subversives can persuade the champions of progressive education to come to their aid, the formidable character of even a small number of Communists can be properly measured. It is in this manner that the Reds, working through the Teachers Union (which received high praise in the report of the Party's Cultural Commission), were able to wield great influence in the elementary and high schools.

In the colleges, we can start with the 3500 professors who are members of Communist fronts or in allied activities. The over-

whelming number of these, probably, are direct adherents of
the conspiracy. They are well scattered through the colleges
of the country. Although there were concentrations in the larger
universities, such as Columbia, Harvard, Yale, the University
of Chicago, New York University, there was also a considerable representation on smaller faculties. In addition to the
Communists who are members of fronts, there are substantial
cells of less well-known teachers and professors, not only at
such places as the University of Illinois, but also at Smith,
Bryn Mawr, Vassar, Sarah Lawrence, Cornell, Brooklyn Polytechnic, Massachusetts Institute of Technology, Boston University, and Haverford.

Libraries—Red Target

The school and college libraries are other targets of the Reds.
For a number of years, cells have existed among librarians, and
the Communist influence has not been small in the American
Library Association. At the local level, the big effort is to get
the works of concealed Communists into the libraries, and if at
all possible to have them placed on the required or recommended reading lists. There are several objectives in this maneuver other than the effect the books themselves (apparently
non-Communist in character but many slanted in a Communist
direction) will have on the students. The Soviet fifth column is
keenly aware of the value of prestige, of getting its concealed
members recognized as "authorities." So bitter an anti-American and disciple of Stalin as Howard Fast does not do damage
solely through his books. When he is recommended to students
as an authority on American history, as has been done in a
great number of school libraries throughout America, the Communists can count on a certain sympathy for his views when he
defiantly tells Congress in effect that he will not fight the
Chinese Communists even if drafted. His works in themselves are
carefully prepared to lead the immature mind to a pro-Stalinite
position, or at least to the point where he will be an easy victim of the Communist line. And yet, on June 20, 1953, Otto E.

Dohrenwend, chairman of the Scarsdale Citizens Committee, which has been opposing Red penetration of the schools in that community, could report: "Howard Fast's books, earlier this year, were banned from the libraries of information centers of the State Department throughout the world. . . . But, believe it or not, a book by this Communist is still recommended reading in the tenth grade of the Scarsdale High School."

Langston Hughes, the Negro poet who had been a member of eighty-five Communist fronts, finally agreed before the Senate Permanent Investigations Committee headed by Senator Joseph R. McCarthy that none of his works written in his "pro-Communist period" should be read or studied. And yet, those works have been widely promoted by concealed Communists and have been kept on the shelves of school libraries in many cities. The whole school of "Far Eastern experts," who betrayed the United States into a Chinese policy that has led to bloody Korea, are still popular as school references. The works of Owen Lattimore; Annalee Jacoby; Theodore White; Edgar Snow; Richard Lauterbach; Albert Rhys Williams; Kate Mitchell, *Amerasia* editor; Guenther Stein, the Soviet espionage agent; Israel Epstein, the Soviet espionage agent; and Agnes Smedley, the Soviet espionage agent—all these have been shown to be the result of planned propaganda to deceive American opinion on the Far East. That has been established beyond doubt by the hearings and findings of the McCarran Sub-Committee on Internal Security. Other pro-Soviet writers who have been especially favored are Vilhjalmur Stefansson, Clifford Odets, Dorothy Parker, Lillian Hellman, Otto Kleinberg, Harrison Forman, Dr. W. E. B. DuBois, Carey McWilliams, Corliss Lamont, and George Seldes. Even such well-known Marxist-Leninists as James S. Allen and Herbert Aptheker are listed on high school and college libraries reading lists.

Other transmission belts used by the conspiracy include PTA speakers, assembly programs for children, career conferences for students, in-service workshop courses for teachers, and adult school lecturers.

The Scarsdale story illustrates what has happened in a great number of other communities. Scarsdale is one of the wealthiest suburbs in the United States; when we understand the materialistic philosophy of Communism, we can comprehend that this would be one of the fruitful centers of Red infiltration. The Communists laid plans as early as 1944 to invade Scarsdale and the other conservative precincts of Westchester County, New York. Lecturers and program directors brought into the school system there included Dr. Bernard F. Riess of Hunter College, whose pro-Communist record filled pages of Congressional hearings, and Dr. Bert Loewenberg of Sarah Lawrence College, sponsor and panel speaker at the notorious Waldorf-Astoria "peace" conference. Among the entertainers and speakers brought into Scarsdale, either to perform before the school children or to speak at PTA meetings and other community organization affairs, were: Paul Draper, the dancer, member of fifteen Communist fronts; Lisa Sergio, also with a Communist front record; Pearl Primus, who was built up as a dancer by the Communists; and Louis Dolivet, notorious Stalinist agent. Even to this day, the school board defends the exposure of the children's minds to these pro-Communist influences. The Town Club education committee, composed of business executives, whitewashed the scandalous conditions in the Scarsdale schools in a report published in the spring of 1953. At the very time when the Town Club education committee was preparing its report, Professor Irving Goldman of Sarah Lawrence College was appearing before the Senate Internal Sub-Committee, where it was brought out that he has been a member of the Communist Party and of Red cells at Columbia University and Brooklyn College. He knew individuals who have been exposed as espionage agents for Soviet Russia. But the Town Club report ignores Goldman's record, although he was one of the lecturers at the off-campus courses for Scarsdale teachers. (Address of Otto E. Dohrenwend, chairman of the Scarsdale Citizens Committee, before the Larchmont Knights of Columbus; printed in the *Brooklyn Tablet*, June 20, 1953.)

In the colleges, much of the same picture appears in too many instances. At Princeton University, Professor H. Hubert Wilson is conspicuous in defending subversives in education and in supporting fronts. When the Communists organized the Emergency Civil Liberties Committee, Professor Wilson became associated with it. More than that, when an anti-Communist organization, the American Committee for Cultural Freedom, called his attention to the character of this front, he replied with a sneer. Professor Wilson became one of the speakers at the conference held at Carnegie Hall on January 30, 1953, which took up the cudgels in defense of the subversives. This is not surprising, since Professor Wilson was one of the prominent contributors to the smear-America issue of *The Nation*, in 1952. (*Counterattack*, vol. VII, no. 4, Jan. 23, 1953.)

In 1949, Professor Wilson was the author, along with Richard Carlton Snyder, of a "textbook" which enjoyed unusual popularity in the government and political science departments of many universities. This book, *Roots of Political Behavior*, has been described by an eminent lawyer and professor as "poison." The reviewer is Ben W. Palmer, member of the Minneapolis bar, lecturer at the University of Minnesota, and member of the advisory editorial board of the *American Bar Association Journal*. The poisonous character of the work is the impression it conveys "that man is an irrational animal, that morals are relative, religion outmoded." It also conveys the idea that the Constitution of the United States is "a bar to progress, respect for it mere 'fetish-worship,' American government a means for the exploitation of the masses by the rich, and on its record a colossal failure." Logically, it includes an apologia for violence as a means of overthrowing the American government. Mr. Palmer's judgment is supported by the five columns of quotations from the book's pages, which show it to be a ground breaker for Communism. At least fifty leading colleges and universities use this text, including Columbia, Haverford, Massachusetts Institute of Technology, New York University, Rutgers University,

Swarthmore College, and Williams College. (*The Educational Reviewer*, 112 E. 36th St., New York 16, N.Y., Oct. 15, 1950.)

Corliss Lamont, most consistent of pro-Soviet propagandists, teaches philosophy at Columbia University, and his works on that subject are used in other colleges. Lamont has been named as a Communist before Congressional committees, and was for years head of the leading Communist front first known as the Friends of Soviet Russia and then as the National Council for American-Soviet Friendship. He has been on more Communist fronts than any other member of the academic profession. Frederick L. Schuman of Williams College is lauded as an expert in international affairs, although his record (which has been given) shows that his works have been written in collaboration with the Soviet foreign office, and that one of them was published by the Communist Party itself, designed to show that the United States is "mad" in defending itself. The much-touted work by Sydney and Beatrice Webb on Soviet "civilization" has received an almost reverential attention in many colleges and universities, although it is now known that vital sections of it were prepared by the Soviet secret police.

On the faculties of some of our larger universities, the following are conspicuous for their presence on Communist fronts through the years and by their aid to other Communist causes:

From Yale: Thomas I. Emerson, Fowler V. Harper, Halford E. Luccock, Dr. John Peters.

University of Chicago: James Luther Adams, Rudolf Carnap, Dr. John B. Thompson, Kermit Eby, Edith Abbot, Dr. Anton J. Carlson, Wayne McMillen.

Columbia University: Corliss Lamont, Robert Lynd, Dorothy Brewster, Bernhard J. Stern, Walter Rautenstrauch (now deceased), Clark H. Foreman.

Harvard: Harlow Shapley, Kirtley Mather, Ralph Barton Perry, Dr. Alben Butler.

Smith College: Dorothy Douglas (retired after many years as full professor), S. Ralph Harlow, Mervin Jules, Oliver Larkin.

At Princeton, N. J., we find Dr. John A. Mackay and Paul H. Lehmann at the Theological Seminary, and Dr. Irwin Panofsky and Albert Einstein at the Institute for Advanced Study.

We could also include many others, adding Montague Francis Ashley Montague, chairman of the department of anthropology at Rutgers University; Maurice Halperin, head of the Latin-American department of Boston University, who confesses in effect that he has been a Soviet espionage agent for years; Louise Pettibone Smith of Wellesley College; Eda Lou Walton of New York University; Ephraim Cross and Abraham Edel of the City College of New York; and Derk Bodde of the University of Pennsylvania. (The names of these educators appear in a number of reports of the House Committee on Un-American Activities, including *The Communist "Peace" Offensive—a Plot to Disarm and Defeat America; The March of Treason; The National Lawyers Guild, Legal Bulwark of the Communist Party;* and *Civil Rights Congress as a Communist Front Organization.* They are all mentioned in "Communism in the Colleges," J. B. Matthews, *American Mercury,* May, 1953.)

If we would go into the less conspicuous cooperators with the conspiracy in each of these institutions, the list would grow to formidable proportions. The smaller colleges are not immune from the pro-Communist poison. On June 1, 1953, as an indication of this, Dr. Charles J. Turck, lawyer and president of Macalester College at St. Paul, made an impassioned attack on all Congressional inquiries. Dr. Turck was doing a piece of special pleading. He was a prominent member of the Communist-created Mid-Century Conference for Peace, and has been a familiar name on other Communist front lists. The faculties of Oberlin, the University of Miami, Kentucky, Nebraska, Kansas, Oregon, West Virginia, Reed College in Oregon, Bible College in Missouri—to mention only a few—furnished sponsors or members to front organizations and to cooperators with Communist causes. Other women's colleges than those mentioned hitherto, namely Mt. Holyoke and Bryn Mawr also were represented, and of course, Hunter College in New York.

Methods of Using Educators

In addition to serving the Kremlin in the classroom and the academic world, educators are valuable to the Soviet fifth column in the following ways: by raising finances for the Communist Party and Communist causes; by influencing governmental circles; by invading the field of science, where Moscow knows America is strong, to undermine that strength by subversion; by entry into the church and church organizations; and by encouragement of and participation in undercover work, specifically in espionage assignments to obtain American defense secrets.

Dr. Dorothy Douglas, until 1952 full professor at Smith College with great influence upon the students, furnishes a case illustrating the relationship of certain educators to Party finances. Dr. Douglas is a woman of some wealth. Before the House Committee on Un-American Activities, she refused to state on the grounds it would tend to incriminate her whether she had given $600.00 per month for three years to Robert William Weiner, head of the "secret fund" of the conspiracy. This fund is used for many purposes, including the trips of secret Soviet agents to Latin America, European countries, and Moscow. It has also been used to bring secret agents into this country. The case of Dr. Douglas could be multiplied a number of times. Red educators are also often in a good position to raise funds from wealthy persons for Communist conspiratorial purposes.

Professors have a facility for getting into government posts, often in an advisory capacity. Those who bear allegiance to Stalin and to Stalinite fronts have not neglected this golden opportunity. Colston E. Warne of Amherst College, one of the Communist front veterans, was an adviser for several years to the Economic Advisory Council to the President of the United States. Marshall Dimock of Northwestern University was consultant to the Department of Defense since 1948, although he was praised by Howard Fast in *Political Affairs* in 1949 for his work at the seditious Waldorf-Astoria "peace" conference. (The pro-Communist records of Warne and Dimock are given in various reports of the House Committee on Un-American Activities, including *The Communist "Peace" Offensive*, 1951; *The Review of Scientific and Cultural Conference for World Peace*, 1949. See also *The Cry Is Peace*, Budenz, pp. 145, 149, 162.) Maurice Halperin, now at Boston University, was advisor to the United Nations at the first conference at San Francisco, held many important posts with the United States and the United Nations in Europe and Latin America, finally becoming advisor to Secretary of State Acheson. Of Halperin, the Senate Sub-Committee on Internal Security said: "In the course of its investigation into Communists in government, the Sub-Committee had in its record Elizabeth Bentley's testimony that a member of a Soviet espionage ring in Washington during the war was Maurice Halperin, who had been head of the Latin American division of the Office of Strategic Services and of Latin American Research Analysis in the State Department. It also had the information that Nathaniel Weyl, an ex-Communist, who later testified fully before the Sub-Committee, had known that Halperin was a member of the Communist Party of Texas and Oklahoma who had been sent to Mexico for the Communists to attend meetings of the Communist Party there. In addition, a top secret memorandum circulated among security authorities, dated November, 1945, was made known by the then Congressman Richard M. Nixon in 1950, and this listed Maurice Halperin as a member of a Soviet espionage ring." And yet, when Halperin appeared under oath before the Sub-Committee, he refused to answer on any of these points, on the grounds that it would tend to incriminate him. Since fear of disgrace or embarrassment or a desire to protect one's associates is no ground for the plea of self-incrimination, as will be noted below, Halperin's refusal to answer at this moment of peril to the United States can be interpreted only in one light. That is, that if he were to answer truthfully, his answer would have to be "Yes" both to the inquiries about Communist Party membership and espionage. But in the face of this defiance of Congress by Halperin, Boston University merely censured him and then retained him as head of the Latin American Department.

Owen Lattimore of Johns Hopkins University and T. A. Bisson, now of the University of California, were conspicuous in working for those policies which would lead to the victory of a Red China. Although Mr. Bisson was shown clearly by the McCarran Sub-Committee on Internal Security to have joined with men like Frederick Vanderbilt Field, Israel Epstein, Guenther Stein, and Harriet Lucy Moore—veteran Communists—in bringing on the catastrophe that led to the killing of thousands of Americans in Korea, he had no difficulty in becoming a member of the faculty of the University of California. (For Bisson's and Lattimore's records, consult hearings of Senate Sub-Committee on Institute of Pacific Relations and that committee's *Report*, entitled *Institute of Pacific Relations*, *82nd Congress, 2nd Session*.) Thomas I. Emerson, at present professor of law at Yale University, and a consistent supporter of pro-Communist causes, worked with Nathan Witt, a Communist, in the legal department of the first National Labor Relations Board, and moved from there to many other spots in the government. Virginius Frank Coe, until recently secretary of the International Monetary Fund, got his start on the staff of Johns Hopkins Law Institute and was also at the University of Toronto, before he moved into the United States Treasury Department. Despite Coe's being in six successive important government posts, the Senate Sub-Committee on Internal Security can state: "Coe refused to answer, on the grounds that the answers might incriminate him, all questions as to whether he was a Communist, whether he was engaged in subversive activities, or whether he was presently a member of a Soviet espionage ring. He refused for the same reason to answer whether he was a member of an espionage ring while Technical Secretary of the Bretton Woods Conference, whether he ever had had access to confidential Government information or security information, whether he had been associated with the Institute of Pacific Relations, or with individuals named on a long list of people associated with that organization." He took this stand in the face of sworn testimony by Elizabeth Bentley and Whittaker Chambers that he had been in the Communist conspiracy and had served as a Soviet espionage agent. (*Activities of United States Citizens Employed by the United Nations,* report of Senate Sub-Committee on Internal Security, Jan. 2, 1953, p. 7; also see hearings and report of this Sub-Committee on the Institute of Pacific Relations.)

These references give only a superficial glimpse of professors of a Communist or pro-Communist persuasion who found their way into government and would naturally have influence in those circles.

Pleading the Fifth Amendment

Since one of these men mentioned, Virginius Frank Coe, has been conspicuous in refusing to answer questions concerning his Communist affiliations or activities, some consideration must be given to the claim of privilege under the fifth amendment of the United States Constitution. The overwhelming majority of professors, teachers and government officials who were charged with pro-Communism have resorted to this plea before Congressional inquiries, particularly in 1952 and 1953. One of the first persons to make this plea was the notorious J. Peters, head of the Soviet espionage apparatus in this country for the Communist International and the man who directed the activities of Whittaker Chambers and Alger Hiss. Under the assumed name of Alexander Stevens, one of his many aliases, Peters refused to answer all questions which touched on Soviet espionage in this country or on his association with the Communist conspiracy, although a letter of his was introduced into evidence which showed that he was acting representative of the Communist International here during the absence of Gerhart Eisler. (*Hearings Regarding Communist Espionage in the United States,* House Committee on Un-American Activities, 1948, pp. 1267-71.) Under the super-military organization and discipline of the Red conspiracy, what a Communist leader of Peter's stature does is a signal for others to follow. The pattern which has been established since, and which has been loudly supported by the Communist Party, is therefore significant.

The portion of the fifth amendment upon which those charged with Communist affiliation or espionage must rely is that provision which states that no person "shall be compelled in any criminal case to be a witness against himself." The Senate Sub-Committee on Internal Security which is a subdivision of the Senate Committee on the Judiciary has stated definitely that "fear of disgrace, embarrassment, or exposure of one's past associates is not proper grounds for the invocation of the privilege." The Sub-Committee states: "The legal effect of such a claim of privilege on the part of a witness was that it constituted an affirmation that if he answered the particular question truthfully, he would be providing at least a link in a chain of circumstances that could lead to his conviction for a crime against which the statute of limitations has not run." To which the Committee adds: "Moreover, the Sub-Committee could not fail to observe that in virtually every case the witness invoked his privilege against self-incrimination only when it became apparent that the evidence available to the Sub-Committee was so concrete and substantial that a denial would expose him to possible prosecution (for perjury); otherwise, he unhesitatingly denied membership."

From all this, the Sub-Committee concludes: "For these reasons, the Sub-Committee considered the claim of privilege, particularly on the question of Communist membership, extremely significant in the determination of those who were Communists." (Report of Sub-Committee on Internal Security, United States Senate Committee on the Judiciary, *Subversive Influence in the Educational Process*, pp. 6-8.)

The Commission of Jurists, appointed by the Secretary General of the United Nations, reviewed this matter and came to the same conclusion. Dealing with those who refuse to answer on charges of espionage, the Jurists declare: "The officer has refused to answer the question on the only lawful ground open to him, namely, that in answering he would become a witness against himself. In our opinion such a person is just as unsuitable for continued employment by the United Nations in the United States as one who had actually been convicted, and his employment in the United Nations should not be continued." The same opinion was also given regarding anyone who claimed privilege and refused to answer concerning his Communist Party membership. (*Activities of United States Citizens Employed by the United Nations,* Report of Senate Sub-Committee on Internal Security, pp. 8-12.)

In other words, both the Senate Sub-Committee on Internal Security and the United Nations Commission of Jurists declare that if any teacher, professor, or government employee refuses to answer concerning Communist Party affiliations or espionage work, it is because a "yes" answer on his part would be a link which would convict him of a crime connected directly with the answer. The Senate Sub-Committee states that the law is that the plea must be made "in good faith," that is, that it not be made to avoid testifying about someone else or to avoid personal embarrassment. The reader can readily see that if this were not the law, witnesses could defy courts and Congress on behalf of criminals of any kind, specifically where conspiracies were involved. The whole structure of our legal procedure would be destroyed, and the courts and Congress made powerless.

The Senate Committee states that it gave all witnesses the benefit of the doubt about their "good faith," although it gives as its opinion that they did not act in such good faith. Under the super-military discipline of the Communist conspiracy, "good faith" in this case is impossible. Every Communist must act according to orders and establish a pattern of conduct. Therefore, although the Sub-Committee, in order not to appear unfair, recognized the plea under the fifth amendment, it is evident from the case of J. Peters to the latest case that men and women have been in this way breaking down the authority of the courts and Congress.

Both under the law and Communist practice, therefore, the man in the street is correct in regarding the person who refuses to answer as being guilty of criminal Communist affiliations or of espionage activities or both, as the case may be. Senator Joseph R. McCarthy has established the fact that for the fifth amendment to be pleaded, the witness must state that if he truthfully answers the question about Communist affiliation, this truth would tend to incriminate him. The "inference" of guilt which cannot be drawn in a criminal proceeding in court does apply, the Senator has stated emphatically as chairman of the Sub-Committee on Permanent Investigations, to Congressional inquiries or in public opinion. (This was stressed at the appearance of Harriet Lucy Moore before the Sub-Committee on September 28, 1953.)

Among Scientists

As to the field of physical science, the United States excels so greatly in that area that it became the chief target of the fifth column's infiltration. The breakdown of morale in this field, the stealing of our defense secrets by scientists turned into espionage agents, and the employment of certain scientists to create public confusion were all involved in Soviet designs.

The importance of this penetration was emphasized by William Z. Foster, national chairman of the Communist Party, in a leading directive article appearing in *The Communist* for September, 1938, entitled "The Communist Party and the Professionals." It contained a specific and significant instruction to "our scientists" to bestir themselves on behalf of the conspiracy. When the Fifteenth National Convention of the Party in December 1950 hailed six leading scientists for their service to the cause of "peace," it registered at the same time that Foster's instruction had been taken seriously. Great emphasis was laid on the progress made among scientists, but also on what had to be done to extend Red control of scientific America. The six scientists hailed by the Party included Linus C. Pauling, atomic physicist of California, Philip D. Morrison of Cornell, Harlow

Shapley and Kirtley Mather of Harvard, Anton J. Carlson of the University of Chicago, and Dirk J. Struik of the Massachusetts Institute of Technology. Each one of these men deserved the Red accolade, for each is a veteran member of Communist fronts and has aided Communist causes in other ways. Of Dr. Linus C. Pauling, the House Committee on Un-American Activities reported on April 1, 1951: "His whole record given below indicates that Dr. Linus Carl Pauling is primarily engrossed in placing his scientific attainments at the service of a host of organizations which have in common their complete subservience to the Communist Party, USA, and the Soviet Union. Professor Pauling has not deviated a hair's breadth from this pattern of loyalty to the Communist cause since 1946." (*The Communist "Peace" Offensive, the Attempt to Disarm and Defeat America*, House Committee on Un-American Activities, 1951, pp. 85-87.) To support this indictment, the committee shows that "despite his eminence in scientific circles, his association with subversive organizations are numerous." The list of those organizations and causes is then given, from the hearings and records of the House Committee, including his sponsorship of the seditious Waldorf-Astoria peace conference in 1949, his participation as speaker and vice-president at the Communist-created "American Continental Congress for Peace," his association with the Civil Rights Congress, and his joining in a number of statements on behalf of Communist leaders.

Of Dr. Philip D. Morrison of Cornell, the second scientist praised by the Communists, the House Committee declares from its records that he is an "important pillar of the Communists' 'peace' campaign." It adds: "Professor Morrison travels up and down the country on his Red missions." Then the committee lists Morrison's pro-Red activities, including his being a sponsor and member of the program committee of the Waldorf-Astoria peace conference in 1949, his signing of many statements on "world peace," initiated by the Communists, his sending greetings to the *Daily Worker* in connection with May Day, the international Communist holiday. The committee also discloses that Morrison sponsored a conference "of the subversive National Council of the Arts, Sciences, and Professions," and attacked the Federal Bureau of Investigation in the *Daily Worker* of May 12, 1947. Summing up its indictment of Pauling, Morrison, and other pro-Communist scientists, the House Committee states: "The examples of the pro-Communist sympathies and affiliations of certain scientists cited above pose a grave problem for the security of our country. It requires serious study and action." (*The Communist "Peace" Offensive*, p. 90.)

Dr. Harlow Shapley of Harvard, the third scientist praised by the Communists, has been a member of fully twenty Communist fronts, including organizations cited as subversive by the Attorney General, such as the Joint Anti-Fascist Refugee Committee and the League of American Writers. Shapley was an active participant in the seditious Waldorf-Astoria Peace Conference and was officially praised by the Communist Howard Fast for his work in that connection. To show how far Shapley has gone along the way with the Communists, his signing of statements in defense of Communist cases for both the Council of the Arts, Sciences, and Professions and the National Federation for Constitutional Liberties can be cited, together with his association with the Progressive Citizens of America when the Reds supported and dominated that organization. (*Review of the Scientific and Cultural Conference for World Peace*, 1949, House Committee on Un-American Activities, pp. 18, 28, 29, 33, 39; also the *Communist Peace Offensive*, 1951, especially p. 107.) The wide variety of Shapley's affiliations with Communist causes is again illustrated by his sponsorship of the Spanish Rescue Ship Mission, a Red-created group to aid the Communists in Spain, and which by degrees developed into the Joint Anti-Fascist Rescue Committee. (*Daily Worker*, Feb. 6, 1941, p. 4.)

Dr. Anton J. Carlson of Chicago University, also praised by the Communists, is a member of fully ten Communist fronts, including the American Peace Mobilization, which picketed the White House in 1941 in behalf of Hitler. That was during the

Hitler-Stalin alliance. (*Daily Worker*, March 10, 1941, p. 2.) He also supported the Spanish Rescue Ship Mission in 1941 and eight years later signed a public statement to President Truman which "repeated the fraudulent 'peace' propaganda being issued from Moscow," as the House Committee designates. Carlson urged the defeat of the American "arms program" and was a leading sponsor of the Mid-Century Conference for Peace, another notorious Communist front in which he was associated with Shapley. The Chicago scientist became a sponsor of the seditious Waldorf-Astoria Peace Conference of 1949 and of the Moscow-created Stockholm "Peace" Appeal. (Carlson's record can be found in many issues of the *Daily Worker* but is summed up in two leading reports of the House Committee on Un-American Activities, that on *The Scientific and Cultural Conference for World Peace*, 1949, and on *The Communist Peace Offensive*, 1951.)

Professor Kirtley Mather of Harvard has shown like devotion to Stalinite causes, with membership in or sponsorship of an impressive number of Communist fronts. For four years he was national president of the American Association of Scientific Workers (AASW), part of an international movement to enlist scientists in support of Communist causes. This was the World Federation of Scientific Workers, cited by the House Committee on Un-American Activities as "another international Communist front organization." Its leading officers were Frederick Joliot-Curie of France and John Desmond Bernal of England, two notorious Communist scientists. Joliot-Curie boasted that scientific workers in the United States had been affected by Communist propaganda, making this statement in a broadcast over the Moscow radio on March 24, 1950. He had also encouraged "espionage in behalf of the Soviet military machine," as the House Committee directly charges. (Section of report of April 1, 1951, House Committee on Un-American Activities, "Subversion of Scientists Through the 'Peace' Movement," pp. 83, 84.) The President of the Canadian Association of Scientific Workers, one of the companions to the AASW, was Professor

Raymond Boyer, exposed as a member of the Canadian Red atomic spy ring and sentenced to prison for his crime of espionage. The *Report of the Royal Commission,* which is based on the documents taken by Igor Gouzenko from the military espionage department of the Soviet Embassy at Ottawa, declares that Communist control of the Canadian organization of scientific workers was a means by which espionage was furthered. The Royal Commission asserts, from evidence produced in its hearings, that the Canadian group maintained "liaison with corresponding organizations in other countries," including Professor Mather's organization. (*The Report of the Royal Commission,* June 27, 1946, Ottawa, p. 70.) Since the connection of the AASW with the World Federation and with the Canadian group was brought out in official documents in the United States and Canada, it is an eloquent fact that Professor Mather and his organization of scientists did not condemn the Canadian Soviet spies and did not demur against the "siren call to treason," as the House Committee on Un-American Activities terms Joliot-Curie's broadcast. Quite to the contrary, he immediately associated himself with Communist-created "peace" movements which were stimulated by Joliot-Curie's World Peace Congress. (Report of House Committee on Un-American Activities, April 1, 1951, pp. 83, 149.) And in 1952, Mather was denounced by the House Committee on Un-American Activities for his letter commending Dirk Struik, sent to "thirty ministers of the Gospel in Massachusetts," when Struik was indicted for his Communist activities. The House Committee states that Mather "exerts an influence over thousands of students at Harvard University," and then adds: "With individuals like Professor Struik and Mather teaching in our leading universities, your committee wonders who the Professor Struiks were at Harvard who led Alger Hiss along the road of Communism until he committed espionage against his country." (*Annual Report,* House Committee on Un-American Activities, year 1951, Feb. 17, 1952, pp. 16, 17.)

The sixth scientist publicly praised by the Communists, Dr.

Dirk J. Struik of the Massachusetts Institute of Technology, has the longest pro-Communist record of those mentioned. He is a member or sponsor of fully fifty Communist fronts, as the House Committee on Un-American Activities shows in its report of April 1, 1951. These cover every possible variety of aid to the Communist cause in the United States and follow every twist and turn of the Communist line. Conspicuous among his pro-Red acts are his sponsorship of the "open" Communist Party School, the Jefferson School of Social Science. Especially to be noted also was his joining in the Statement in Defense of the Communist Party during the Hitler-Stalin alliance, reported in the *Daily Worker* of March 5, 1941. Of Dr. Struik the House Committee on Un-American Activities reports in 1952, on the basis of testimony given by Herbert A. Philbrick, undercover agent for the FBI: "Among those Philbrick identified as being members of the professional section of the Communist Party was Dr. Dirk J. Struik, a professor of mathematics at the Massachusetts Institute of Technology. According to Philbrick's testimony, both before your committee and during his appearance as a Government witness in the trial of the 11 Communist leaders, Dr. Struik taught courses at the Communist Samuel Adams School in Boston, in addition to teaching violent overthrow of the capitalist state to members of the professional section of the Communist Party. During this same time, Dr. Struik was teaching his students at the Massachusetts Institute of Technology." (*Annual Report,* Committee on Un-American Activities, for year 1951, Feb. 17, 1952, pp. 15, 16.)

As I have stated on several occasions, specifically in my book *The Cry Is Peace,* the use of the names of outstanding scientists was of great value to the conspiracy in persuading lesser men in this field to engage in espionage as well as infiltration. We have the anomalous situation in the United States that we send the Rosenbergs to the electric chair but heap honors on those who helped to breed the Rosenbergs. Dr. Harlow Shapley of Harvard was chosen in 1952 to present the Westinghouse Awards to those students in science who had won scholarships

But Oliver Carlson has shown conclusively in the *Freeman Magazine* for October 30, 1952, that the first bond issue was defeated merely to get rid of Goslin, and that upon his resignation, a second bond issue was passed by an overwhelming vote. Among Dr. Goslin's acts, incidentally, had been the bringing in of Dr. Theodore Brameld, veteran Communist fronter, to lead the summer workshops for teachers.

Third, the claim is made that "dissent" will be confused with "disloyalty," a plea which flows from the academic freedom argument. (But, as Dr. Matthews points out, if an investigation of the use of marihuana by teen-agers would be charged as a "drive against coca-cola," the person making that charge would readily be seen to be incompetent. So it is in this case. And Dr. Harry Gideonse, President of Brooklyn College and a distinguished champion of civil liberties, came directly to the point when he stated under oath, referring to the hearings of the Senate Sub-Committee on Internal Security: "I appreciate that you are not concerned with the liberal, with the right to be critical, with the right to hold unpopular views; that is not your interest at all. That you are concerned, as a matter of fact, with protecting genuine freedom of thought against the temptation of some few who have sold their birthright as Americans for a mess of intellectual potage, to a foreign power." Professor Harry Allen Overstreet, an experienced educator, author of *The Mature Mind*, strengthened this view by declaring that it is only by ridding our schools and colleges of Communists that we can protect genuine dissent or, as he put it, "the freedoms of investigation and the integrity of investigation that we require in our educational processes." [*Subversive Influence in the Educational Process*, report of Senate Sub-Committee on Internal Security, July 17, 1953, pp. 6, 28.])

Fourth, statements are prepared and signed by leading officials of big corporations, "defending" the college or school in which subversive influences are found. This is the common practice, and the presence of the vice-president of a big radio corporation or a big manufacturing concern on such a list is supposed to impress those who want to clear the schools of Communist penetration. The community is supposed to ask the question: "How could these industrialists ever be sympathetic to Communism?" But that is becoming an outworn practice, as it is becoming more widely known that among a number of representatives of management, pro-Communist influences do play a part. For some of these men are often bound up in a pragmatic and materialistic philosophy akin to that which forms the basis of Communism. A striking illustration of a leading industrialist who has aided the Communist line, though undoubtedly he did this unwittingly, is Ernest T. Weir, president of the National Steel Company of Weirton, West Virginia. Mr. Weir is known as a bitter opponent of organized labor. At the same time, he has been prominent in advocating recognition of Red China and in urging "negotiations" of a general character with Soviet Russia, going to the extent of issuing pamphlets on a nation-wide scale in support of these pro-Soviet proposals. His arguments are not based on moral grounds, but on strictly "practical" considerations which do not apply when confronting Soviet Communism.

In the same manner, officers of corporations can sometimes be induced to sign statements "defending" a certain educational institution when subversive influences are shown to exist on its faculty. The actuality is that the best way to support the school or college in question is to cleanse it completely of these subversive influences.

Fifth, the "smear" tactic, which the Communists have always used on a big scale, is brought to bear in various forms. Those who are protecting the Reds often borrow Red methods, and so it is in this case. Sometimes there is a misrepresentation of facts, as when Dean Ernest O. Melby states in regard to Scarsdale that the Citizens' Committee "was challenged to prove its charges—but presented only vague accusations and a sense of hysteria. The charges were dropped." This is completely untrue, both as to the nature of the charges and as to the statement that they were dropped. The "smear" may take the form of crying "McCarthyite" or "book burner" at those who present the facts about Red teachers, books, lecturers, or entertainers. It may go further and lead to a whispering campaign against the sanity of the person or persons alleging the presence of subversive influences; this being an old device of the Communists in locality after locality.

These, and other similar methods of attack, can be defeated by carefully bringing out the facts, basing every statement on the record in the case. This is essential to offsetting Communist tactics in all situations but is of prime importance in the educational field.

It may be added that the American Association of Universities (not to be confused with the American Association of University Professors) set down as a matter of policy that Communists or those who follow the line would be excluded from American college faculties. Until mid-1953, very little had been done to implement this excellent statement, and, except for those professors who had been thoroughly exposed by congressional inquiries, few Communists or followers of the Communist line had been disturbed in their academic positions.

In certain areas there were honorable exceptions to this rule. New York City educational authorities received special commendation from the Senate Sub-Committee on Internal Security for the methodical manner in which they were proceeding to rid the school system of subversive teachers. Out in California, to all appearances, definite steps were being taken in the same direction. The Senate Sub-Committee, wishing to avoid Federal intervention on too large a scale, placed the responsibility for getting rid of subversive influences in the educational process in the hands of the college authorities and local school boards. That is where the case remained in the Fall of 1953.

CHAPTER XI

USE AND ABUSE OF MINORITY GROUPS

IN THE Communist strategy for world conquest, "minority groups" receive large consideration. This is particularly true of the "colonial question," with which is blended the agitation among the Negroes in the United States. In his last book, written just before he died, Lenin stated that "in the last analysis, the outcome of the struggle (for world control) will be determined by the fact that Russia, India, China, etc. constitute the overwhelming majority of the population of the globe." By taking advantage of the colonial peoples' desire for independence and linking it up with Soviet Russia, "the final victory of Socialism" would be "fully and absolutely assured." ("Better Fewer, But Better," *Lenin's Selected Works,* vol. IX, p. 400.)

Lenin's last thought made itself felt at the famous Sixth World Congress of the Communist International, held in Moscow in 1928, where the resolutions and theses were adopted which still guide the Communist plan for establishing the world Soviet dictatorship. One of the outstanding guides which became part of this Congress was the "Theses on the Revolutionary Movement in the Colonies and Semi-Colonies." The "first-rate" international importance of China in the Soviet scheme of things was the first point made in this document. Its basic theme was the linking up of "the emancipatory struggle of all colonial and other dependent peoples" with the leadership of the Soviet Union. "The revolutionary emancipatory movements of the colonies and semi-colonies" were to be channelized toward Soviet control, so that they would "more and more rally around the banner of the Soviet Union." This was considered to be a basic measure, guaranteeing victory in the wars, foretold in this document, between "the imperialists," including specifically the United States, and the Soviet dictatorship. It was this linking of the people of China, India, "and similar colonial countries" with Soviet Russia and its fifth columns that would offer "the surest guarantee of victory over imperialism": the achievement of world dictatorship.

Nothing could express more definitely Lenin's dream that Asia was to be the Soviet base for subjugation of all other nations, than did the pages of this document. The important condition for Soviet success in this area was necessarily the penetration of the "colonial independence movements" in order to bring them under the complete influence and control of the Kremlin. Accordingly, this document not only explains how Communists are to be developed in China, India, Korea, and other like places, to stimulate armed uprisings under Soviet direction. It also devotes much space to charging the Communists throughout the world to oppose to the death all "reformist" efforts at independence.

This determination to destroy all "reformist" or "bourgeois" attempts by the peoples of Asia to win national liberation is a key to Soviet strategy in this respect. It states quite clearly— and commits the Communists quite definitely to the statement —that there is an obligation to make certain that spontaneous movements for independence do not succeed. The Soviet fifth columns are to take advantage of the desire of the Asiatic peoples for independence to chain them to the Soviet despotism.

This statement explains the course of the Communists in China, in Korea, and in other like countries. It is unfortunate that more leading Americans were not acquainted with this fundamental attitude of the Kremlin. If they had been, history would not have recorded the ready American acquiescence to "coalition government" in China, the indifference to the fate of

Chiang Kai-shek, and the readiness to agree to the partition of Korea. Under the Communist program, the Kremlin would never rest until it had sovietized China completely, nor will it rest until it has "unified" Korea under Soviet rule. The only alternative to the Soviet achievements was their outright defeat by a strong, clear, open-eyed policy of opposition at all points to any Soviet maneuvers by the United States.

The Communist determination to bring the colonial movements under Soviet dictation is expressed sharply by Stalin in the section of his *Foundations of Leninism* entitled "The National Problem." Stressing the great importance of "the national liberation movement of the oppressed and dependent peoples," Stalin adds: "This does not mean, of course, that the proletariat must support *every* national movement, everywhere and always, in every single concrete case. It means that support must be given to such national movements as tend to weaken, to overthrow imperialism, and not to strengthen and preserve it. Cases occur when the national movements in certain oppressed countries come into conflict with the interests of the development of the proletarian movement. In such cases, support is, of course, entirely out of the question. The question of the rights of nations is not an isolated, self-sufficient question; it is a part of the general problem of the proletarian revolution, subordinate to the whole, and must be considered from the point of view of the whole." (*Foundations of Leninism*, Little Lenin Library edition, p. 79.)

Now, "the development of the proletarian movement" is ineradicably founded upon the "interests" and guidance of the vanguard, the Communist Party. And "the problem of the proletarian revolution" can only be solved, from the Stalinite point of view, by constant direction from the Kremlin and the complete victory of the Soviet dictatorship in the Kremlin. The Communists everywhere, studying Stalin's words meticulously and zealously, understand thoroughly that the genuine desire of peoples for independence must be snuffed out in favor of complete subordination to Soviet Russia.

For the Communist, this position is logical. In the eyes of the members of the vanguard—that ruling caste of the chosen few possessing the secret of Marxism-Leninism—all groups are expendable. The rights of the workingman, the yearning for independence on the part of Asiatic peoples, pale into nothing for the Communist in comparison to his real goal: First the world dictatorship, then the classless society. All such movements and demands are merely to be used; their grievances are to be exploited, for that goal which according to Lenin is the sole state and era in which "genuine freedom" exists. What is more difficult to understand is the ready acceptance by many a non-Communist of the Red claims that they are seeking the "independence" of colonial peoples. In the Bolshevik Revolution in Russia, Lenin's cry was "land to the peasants." The victorious Soviets proceeded to take the land away from the peasants. In like manner, Moscow outlined the battle for "colonial liberation," and then makes the colonial people subject to its dictatorship. Here, as in all other cases, we note that the Communists are taking advantage of the shortsightedness, or exploiting policies of the Western powers, to obtain dominance over the Asiatic and African people.

The Kremlin also employs the desire of some of these Western powers to hold on to colonies as an agency to advance appeasement. Thus, in 1953, Great Britain championed the recognition of Red China—which will eternally threaten the United States—in order to hold on to Hong Kong. The irony of this position is, of course, that a permanent Red China will easily take over Hong Kong. We can observe a similar tendency of the British to consider favorably the "neutralization" of West Germany, which means its eventual sovietization, in order that Britain may extend its military operations for the protection of its colonies in Africa. The United States, which has no such reason for appeasement of Soviet Russia, yet favors a policy of "containment" which leads to the same end. Here the Communist infiltration of advisory posts in the government, and the specious argument that the only way to hold our "allies" is to surrender to their weaknesses and appeasements, become decisive. (A study of the Hiss case, the hearings and report on the Institute of Pacific Relations, and the proceedings of other Congressional investigations will reveal how widespread has been this Red infiltration of American government agencies. See Chapter XII, p. 278. The testimony on June 29, 1953, of J. Anthony Panuch, former Deputy Assistant Secretary of State, reveals another aspect of Soviet domination of this nation's foreign policy after World War II, and indicates that Red infiltration of the State Department continues. See hearings of Senate Sub-Committee on Internal Security for June 29.)

One of the great features of Soviet psychological warfare within the United States has been the constant suggestion that Soviet Russia stands for "the welfare and independence of colonial peoples." This has been one of the most flagrant hoaxes practiced on the American mind, and it has even been advanced by public figures such as Supreme Court Justice William O. Douglas and by newspapers such as the *Louisville Courier Journal*, which in 1953 came out for recognition of Red China.

Communists and the Negro

The same considerations apply to the Communist attitude toward the Negro in the United States. Any examination of American Communist documents will attest to the huge amount of attention given in words and acts to "the Negro problem." No matter what set-backs they receive, the Reds keep at it— with the sole illuminating exception of the period when Soviet Russia's existence was endangered by the German military offensive. This notable exception, when the Negroes were counselled by the Reds to forget their problems and grievances in order that the United States could help the Kremlin win the war, lights up at once an interesting fact. Just as the CIO committees have demonstrated that the Communist attitude on the unions was dictated solely by the interests of Soviet Russia, so the line of the Communist Party on the Negro has been tailored to a like purpose.

The Negro is just as expendable, his real interests are just as indifferent to the conspiracy, as are the colonial peoples and their welfare. The Negro is to be used, the cry about his rights to be abused on behalf of the Soviet dictatorship.

There are two chief reasons why the Negro question is considered important for the conspiracy. First of all, it can be the occasion for creating those "contradictions" or divisions within this country that would have serious consequences if Communist propaganda were to prevail. Nothing underscores this point more than the Red demand for "self-determination in the Black Belt," that is, the carving out by force of a separate Negro republic in the heart of the South. A moment's reflection reveals that such a demand, if it were to get enough momentum to be taken seriously, would injure the Negro people by giving an excuse to those who want to continue their exploitation.

The second leading reason for Communist interest in the Negro is the effect that reports of discrimination in the U.S.A. can produce among the Asiatic and African peoples. Throughout the world, it is one of the constant themes of Red psychological warfare against the United States. Even Hitler made use of it to gain prestige in Japan.

For these two reasons, the Communists (in the words of William Z. Foster, their national chairman) consider the Negro problem "the Achilles heel of American imperialism." That is, it is the weak spot which they can strike at in order to bring about the downfall of the United States. But there are other advantages in the drastic exploitation of this problem. Among them is the possibility of swaying "liberals" by accusing those who will not go along with the Communists of being enemies of the Negro people. Another is the discipline that can be exercised over otherwise recalcitrant members of the conspiracy, by charging them with "white chauvinism" when they have not fully lived up to the dictates of Moscow.

The Communist line on the Negro has changed from time to time according to the exigencies of the Soviet dictatorship, but two factors stand out through the years. These factors have not always been pressed forward and have sometimes been blurred over or apparently cast aside; but they have always been revived at the first opportunity.

The first of these factors, which is peculiarly Communist and not at all acceptable to Negro Americans, is "self-determination in the Black Belt." It is significant that the same "Theses" of the Sixth World Congress (1928) which dictated the Communist course in China, India, and Korea, also stated the following: "In those regions of the South [in the United States] in which compact Negro masses are living, it is essential to put forward the slogan of the Right of Self-Determination for Negroes." (*International Press Correspondence*, vol. 8, no. 88, Dec. 12, 1928, p. 1674.)

In October, 1928, John Pepper (or Pogany, his correct name) explained in the pages of *The Communist* that this slogan called for "the establishment of the Negro Soviet Republic." Since Pepper was at that time the Communist International Representative in this country, his declaration was that required by Moscow. This was confirmed two years later by the renewed demand for a Negro Soviet Republic, put forward in the famous 1930 Party resolution to which James S. Allen (Sol Auerbach) refers in the December, 1946, *Political Affairs* as "the full national program" on the Negro question. Allen's judgment has more weight, since he is one of the leading Communist theoreticians in this country.

The boundaries and extent of this separate republic in the South have been forecast on several occasions. The Negro Communist leader, James W. Ford, and his comrade James S. Allen, present it as follows: "The actual extent of this new Negro Republic would in all probability be the present area in which the Negroes constitute the majority of the population. In other words, it would be approximately the present plantation area. It would be certain to include such cities as Richmond and Norfolk, Virginia, Columbia and Charleston, S.C., Atlanta, Augusta, Savannah, and Macon, Georgia, Montgomery, Alabama, New Orleans and Shreveport, La., Little Rock, Arkansas, and Memphis, Tennessee." (James S. Allen and James W. Ford, *The Negroes in a Soviet America*, N.Y. Workers Library Publishers, 1935, p. 39.)

In March, 1952, one Charles P. Mann (a fictitious name) wrote the following description: "The submerged *nation* is located in the Black Belt, where 5,000,000 Negroes constitute today the majority of the population of a contiguous stretch of territory (recorded in county units) forming a crescent moon shaped pattern through at least five southeastern states with port outlets at Charleston on the Atlantic and Mobile on the Gulf, encompassing the bulk of Mississippi and a good section of South Carolina, Georgia, and Alabama." It is this area which he decribes as the "physical, material, heart-land base of the Negro nation." (*Political Affairs*, March 1952, "Mr. I. F. Stone and the Negro Question," p. 23.)

Apparently the area of this separate country torn from the United States has shrunk in Communist estimates during the past seventeen years. Negro migration to the North, and the coming of whites into certain sections of the South, have robbed some regions of the claim that the Negroes are actually the majority of the population. Nevertheless, James S. Allen, in the *Political Affairs* for November, 1936, contends that certain localities where the whites are in the majority shall be incorporated in the Negro Republic, in order to establish a common territory.

This plan for setting up a separate Negro nation in the South, born in bloodshed and turmoil, has aroused strong and continuous opposition among leading Negroes in the United States. It has been rejected by the Negro people as a whole, as the Communists admit, though they seek to explain this away by saying that the Negroes "are essentially a young nation, a developing nation." When Benjamin J. Davis, Negro Communist, wrote in approval of self-determination in the Black Belt in the *Daily Worker* for July 22, 1945, there was an outburst against it in Negro journals and in Negro expression in general. Even when the plan was first proposed at Moscow in 1928, it drew the fire of certain Negro comrades on the grounds that the American Negro wants to be a part of the American community, not severed from it.

Why do the Communists persist in this proposal for a separate Negro nation in the South, torn from the United States? In the first place, it is in accord with Stalin's concept of the Negroes as a "nation" as he has defined the term. Indeed, William Z. Foster is content to give this as the sole reason why "self-determination" has to be urged for the Black Belt. In January, 1947, when the slogan was revived fully by the Communists as a feature of the "cold war," Foster stated: ". . . the Negro people in the Black Belt are a nation . . . they possess the essential qualities of nationhood, as elaborated in the works of that great expert on the national question, Stalin. This lays a firm basis for the self-determination slogan. So I will not deal further with this basic matter of whether or not the Negroes in the Black Belt are a Nation." (*Political Affairs*, Jan. 1947, "On the Question of Negro Self-Determination," William Z. Foster, p. 54. The preceding quotation about the youth of the Negro nation is from the same source.)

Stalin's definition of a nation, to which Foster refers, is given as follows: "A nation is a historically evolved, stable community of language, territory, economic life, and psychological makeup manifested in a community of culture. . . . It is only when all these characteristics are present that we have a nation." (Joseph Stalin, *Marxism and the National Question*, International Publishers, New York, 1942, pp. 12, 13.)

The Communists are very much engaged in fitting the Negroes into this definition, leading to many discussions on the difference between "race" and "nation," and the relation of one to the other. But the Stalinite view of "the Negroes as a nation" and for "self-determination" always prevails in the long run, as it is bound to do. Thus, as late as October, 1952, Harry Haywood, a leading Negro Communist, wrote: "In saying that the Negro people are oppressed primarily as a nation in the South and as a national minority in the North, the original Memorandum [of the National Committee] was, of course, correct. With the exception of the brief period of Browder revisionism, this has been the Communist Party's position since 1928 and was reaffirmed in 1946." (*Political Affairs*, Oct., 1952, Harry Haywood, "Further on Race, Nation, and the Concept 'Negro,'" p. 47.)

The 1946 reaffirmation to which Haywood refers was the Resolution on the Question of Negro Rights and Self-Determination, adopted by the special plenum of the National Committee of the Communist Party in December, 1946. Three years later, in September, 1949, it was officially endorsed anew as having "reaffirmed the national character of the Negro people's struggle." The new resolution frankly declared: "This movement (for Negro rights) provides the basis for the full realization of Negro nationhood, whether it be achieved under capitalism or socialism. The Communist Party supports the right of self-determination for the Negro people, that is, their right to realize self-government in the Negro majority area in the South." (*Political Affairs*, Sept., 1949, p. 52.)

This leads us to the second reason for the Communist persistence in holding to the objective of a "Negro nation." A moment's thought will bring out the violence and turmoil that would follow any loud raising of this issue, particularly in times of crisis. If the Soviet Union in its scheme for world domination were to attack the United States by military means, it would be of great aid to the Soviet armed forces if civil warfare were to break out in the United States. If the Negroes themselves did nothing about this demand for nationhood, but if the Communists would raise it in such a form as to cause narrowminded whites to assail the Negroes physically, Soviet purposes would be well served. For, from the Kremlin's viewpoint, the Negro is expendable. (The map of the proposed "Negro Republic" in the Black Belt is reproduced from the Communist official pamphlet, *Negro Liberation*, in the testimony of Manning Johnson, *Hearings Regarding Communist Infiltration of Minority Groups*, Part II, House Committee on Un-American Activities, 1949.)

There have been some writers who have thought that the Communists hold to this purpose solely because Stalin enunciated it, and that Stalin maintained it solely to vindicate his dictatorial position. The first is largely true, since Stalin and now his successor in the Kremlin rule Communist thought and action. But Stalin has changed a number of his directives when they were found unfit in a particular time or region, always from an alleged Marxist-Leninist-Stalinist base. The fundamental reason for not changing in this case is due to the "club in the closet" which the issue provides for the American Communists, and which can be taken out and used when an hour of emergency arises.

It is in that light that we must understand the official Party declaration on Negro nationhood: "The Communist Party does not attempt to impose any specific solution in advance of the form in which the right of self-determination will be exercised; nor does it prematurely raise self-determination as an immediate slogan of action." Such words are clearly inserted into the official resolution in order to make the concept more palatable to the Negro people, while still retaining it for any big crisis. It is another case of Aesopian language. "The right of self-determination" is not to be made an immediate occasion for action; the Communists do not mean by that term a mere guarantee of voting rights to the Negroes in the Black Belt. They mean a separate nation, as they have always meant, torn from the United States by force, or made the occasion for internal violence.

Nothing demonstrates this reason for the demand more clearly than the history of its varied public use by the Communists. Invariably, it is brought forward stridently when the conspiracy is seeking to create difficulties within the United States because Soviet Russia is openly hostile to this country. But in all Trojan Horse periods, when the Kremlin has as its purpose to persuade the American people that it has changed from a wolf to a lamb, "self-determination in the Black Belt" sinks into the background and is even sometimes explained away.

The very time of "Browder revisionism," to which Haywood refers, comprises those years when Communist infiltration made its great gains, first, through the Trojan Horse policies of the "people's front" which followed the 1935 World Congress of the Communist International, and then in the years of World War II. To penetrate the agencies of American government and opinion making, the Soviet fifth column had to present a pretty picture of itself, and emphasis on bloody uprisings in the South and the tearing asunder of the United States would have marred that picture. (For a detailed study of the gyrations on the public use of "the Negro nation in the Black Belt," see the excellent *Communism Versus the Negro* by William A. Nolan, Henry Regnery Company, Chicago, 1951.)

"The Fight for Negro Rights"

Another dominant phase of Communist work on the Negro problem is the continued emphasis on "the struggle for Negro rights," which runs all the way from battles against discrimination in housing to widely publicized defenses of individual Negroes accused of crimes. Here we have again the advancement of social reforms, many of which are justified, not for the sake of the reforms themselves but as a "screen" or "cover" for the illegal activities of the conspiracy, as Stalin prescribed in *Foundations of Leninism.* Through this agitation, and particularly by carrying it on sometimes more loudly than anyone else, the Communists seek to win prestige and allies among certain Negroes as well as among "liberal" whites. These allies provide the conspiracy with those "reserves" who come to its defense when its subversive purposes and measures of espionage and violence are exposed. It is with this in mind that at every trial of the Communists for conspiracy to advocate the overthrow of the government of the United States by force and violence—under the Smith Act—their outstanding "defense" has been that they are "in the forefront of the struggle for Negro rights, the labor movement, women, youth, and all oppressed groups." Federal Judge Harold R. Medina ruled, and was upheld in his ruling by the United States Supreme Court, that this was not a genuine defense. Even if the Communists' contention were true, which it is not, their interest in these "reforms" would not offset the proof that their objective is the violent overthrow of the United States government under the Constitution. (*Trial Transcript, United States of America vs. Eugene Dennis, et al.*)

In the second big trial of the Communist leaders at Foley Square in 1952, under Judge Edward J. Dimock, the defense was permitted to introduce extensive quotations on the Party's stand for these "reforms," at least when such passages appeared in books or other documents setting as the Communist goal the violent overthrow of the government. This protracted the trial for weeks and perhaps months, providing the Soviet fifth column with those delays which it regards so important in its strategy. "The fight for Negro rights," as for "labor rights" and other like proposals, gives the conspiracy valuable by-products at the occasion of legal defense.

The complete subservience of the Communists' loudly proclaimed interest in the Negro people to the purposes and exigencies of the Soviet dictatorship is also illustrated by the changes in tempo which have occurred over the years in forwarding this "struggle." During the depression, when the Kremlin solemnly looked forward to a revolution in America, the Communists rushed into the Scottsboro case, elbowed aside those who were originally engaged in defending the Scottsboro boys, and engaged in one of the most extensive national campaigns they have ever waged. By their bitter anti-religious attitude at that time, their attacks on Negro ministers as "social fascist misleaders of the masses," and by their failure to take up the immediate demands of the Negro people, they alienated thousands of Negroes in this drive. There were also bitter accusations in the Negro press that millions of dollars raised for the Scottsboro defense by the Reds had actually been used for Communist propaganda. (For a study of this case, and for an examination of the twists and turns in the Communist line on

"Negro rights," see again *Communism Versus the Negro*, William A. Nolan, Henry Regnery Co., Chicago, 1951.)

In contrast, when the United States joined hands with Soviet Russia in World War II, the Soviet fifth column counseled the Negroes not to agitate for their "rights," going to the extent of digging up statements of Frederick Douglas made during the Civil War and allegedly to that effect. Even more than in its public pronouncements, the Communist Party in action sought to put a brake on movements to improve the conditions of the Negro. Everything had to be sacrificed to save the Land of Socialism, "the Fatherland of the toilers of the world."

At the conclusion of World War II, when Stalin opened what is actually World War III, the Communists went to another extreme. They assailed all "bourgeois nationalist" organizations and tendencies among the Negroes, that is, all organizations and tendencies which are not Communist. They rushed again into every case where a Negro was accused of a crime, and devoted a great amount of time and space to "the struggle against white chauvinism." (See in particular the issue of *Political Affairs*, June, 1949, devoted entirely to the subject "The Struggle Against White Chauvinism." It was followed by a number of articles in subsequent issues on the same theme.)

This problem of "white chauvinism," which is the exhibition of "white superiority" over the Negroes in any form, has long plagued the ranks of the Communists. In 1931, a public trial was staged of one Yokinen, a Finnish comrade, who was expelled from the Party for "white chauvinism," as a horrible example, even though he pledged that he would do anything the Party required. All through its subsequent history, right down to the present (except for the World War II period), the Party has complained of the continuance of this "virus" among its membership.

But in the days following World War II, when Stalin launched his war against the United States, the Communists demonstrated that this excitement about "white chauvinism" was merely a stratagem to enable them to further Soviet propaganda among the Negroes. This was nowhere shown better than in the rash and untrue declaration by Paul Robeson in 1949 at the Soviet-controlled peace conference in Paris, that the American Negroes would not fight for the United States against Soviet Russia. The Negro press in this country blasted Robeson for his outburst, which could not have been made without direction from Moscow. Jackie Robinson, the noted Brooklyn second baseman called before the House Committee on Un-American Activities, repudiated and refuted Robeson's slander against the Negroes, and asserted what is the fact: the Negro people are loyal to the United States. Since Robeson would know in advance that such would be the reception of his remarks, it is evident that he did not make them in order to win over the Negroes. He made them, coldly and by premeditation, in order to create among the whites in this country the suspicion that the Negroes were disloyal, and thereby to increase racial friction in this country.

With Soviet aggression on the march, the value of the Negro problem for agitation among the peoples of Asia was not forgotten by the Kremlin. In 1951, William L. Patterson, leading Negro Communist in the United States and secretary of the Civil Rights Congress, was sent to the Paris sessions of the United Nations. There he presented a report, charging the United States with "genocide" bcause of excesses against the Negro people. Immediately, this report was published in pamphlet form and distributed throughout the world as an indictment against the United States. It is a sample of the blunders of the State Department while Dean Acheson was Secretary of State, that Patterson was permitted to go to Paris to make this attack upon the American nation, so helpful to Soviet aggression, which assumed a semi-official character by having been presented to the United Nations.

This incident reminds us again that the Communists are not interested in the Negro people but only in using them for the advancement of Soviet aims. The Negro problem in the United States is one that challenges American democracy. Soviet propaganda did not create it, and it is something to which we as Americans have given too scant attention. But at this time, when the Stalinite dictatorship is sending long lines of men and women into slave labor and is oppressing people of all origins, to charge the United States with "genocide" is to distort the whole course of current history.

Fronts in Negro Field

Early in its history, the Communist Party laid plans for penetrating the National Association for the Advancement of Colored People, and other "bourgeois" or "reform" organizations among the Negroes. Lenin's *Left Wing Communism: An Infantile Disorder*, published in 1920, had provided the key for such infiltration. But the early Communists, with an underground mentality and with "revolutionary goals" stressed more than "immediate demands," were handicapped in entering and influencing "reformist" mass organizations. In the Thirties, after the Open Letter to the Party had shown them the way, and the United States recognition of Soviet Russia had given them the opportunity, they began to enter the NAACP more successfully.

As usual, the comrades also relied upon "transmission belts" which they would create themselves, Communist fronts in this field. The first step along this line was embodied in the American Negro Labor Congress, founded in 1925. Because of its narrow attitude, devoted almost exclusively to the "revolutionary" aspect of Communism, it made little headway. In 1930, it was succeeded by the League of Struggle for Negro Rights which began with assaults on lynching but ended up by merging into the International Labor Defense, the legal or defense arm at that time of the Communist conspiracy. With the adoption of the "people's front" policy, dictated by the Seventh Congress of the Communist International in 1935, the conspiracy in this country was able to launch a much more successful front, the National Negro Congress. It was part and parcel of those other large Communist fronts which arose during these years, resorted to the same methods of playing upon the fear of "fascism," and made headway among college professors and professionals in general. The NNC, indeed, was the first big foothold obtained by the conspiracy among Negro intellectuals. This was not a phenomenon peculiar to the Negro people, whose "masses" remain aloof and indifferent to Red blandishments; Communist progress among white intellectuals was comparatively much greater.

The Soviet-Nazi pact gave the death blow to the National Negro Congress. By their new line in support of Hitler, the Communists were compelled to introduce resolutions against "imperialist war," attacking the United States and praising Soviet Russia, which the Third National Negro Congress of 1940 could not adopt. The Reds so persisted in their "rule or ruin" tactic that all those delegates representing organizations of any consequence withdrew, and the NNC became a mere paper organization.

One Communist-created venture that went on to some degree during the war was the Southern Conference for Human Welfare, which had a benevolent and mild aspect and attracted a considerable number of Negro ministers and Southern white "liberals" like President Frank P. Graham of the University of North Carolina. (Mr. Graham was for a short period Senator from that state, having been appointed to fill a vacancy but being defeated in the subsequent primaries.) The secretary of that Conference was Clark Foreman, subsequently identified before Congressional committees as a Communist, and the *Daily Worker* admitted carefully the Red influence in founding and nurturing that organization. Its mild appearance might have seemed at first blush to make it of little value to the Communist cause, but that appearance had to be put on in order to give it some standing among Southern "liberals." The importance of the Conference to the conspiracy lay largely in the alliances that were made, the newspapers that were persuaded to a position helpful to the Communists, and the help that came to other

Red undertakings from some of those influenced by their contact with concealed Communists. The good effects of these relationships show down to the present. (An instance of this that might be cited is the assault upon ex-Communists who testify for the government by the Charlotte, N.C. *News,* which has been of marked aid to the conspiracy.)

During the war, there was also brought into existence the Council on African Affairs, headed by Paul Robeson. It was designed to appeal to Negro intellectuals and to draw their interest toward the peoples of Africa and, of course, the Communist activities on that continent. While its membership was limited and its influence not so great as the Communists expected, it provided new allies and propaganda which could be of value to the international conspiracy. In our estimate of Soviet plans and purposes, we must never forget this extension of propaganda through the Communist organs in all parts of the globe, and then into non-Communist newspapers or agencies. There is no doubt that the Council on African Affairs gave a lift to the Kremlin's designs on creating turmoil in Africa.

When the so-called "cold war" was initiated by Moscow, the conspiracy in the United States went back to the original idea by bringing into being the National Negro Labor Conference. Its first secretary was William Hood, who at that time was secretary of the powerful Ford Local 600, United Automobile, Aircraft, and Agricultural Implement Workers Union, CIO. Meanwhile, assailing the leaders of the National Association for the Advancement of Colored People as "reactionaries" and "bourgeois," the Communists intensified their attempts at infiltration of the NAACP. Here they were successful to the extent of working into the control of certain branches, ironically enough through "colonizing" white comrades in those local groups. The NAACP is composed of both Negro and white members, but this influx of white Communists caused the leadership to instruct branches to check carefully on white persons admitted. In 1949, the national leadership felt obliged to grant to the local branches the right of initiative in such matters as police brutality, lynching, and other grievances. This was intended as a practical step, since the national office could not handle all such questions, but the Communists saw in it a great opportunity. They created so much agitation in certain branches that the 1950 convention of the NAACP gave power to the national office to "expel any unit" which after investigation would be found to be Communist controlled. The vote on this resolution was 309 to 57, and the fact that one out of seven delegates voted against the resolution indicated that the Reds had made headway. (Chapter 12 of *Communism Versus the Negro*, William A. Nolan.)

The impossibility of proving today that any person or group is a Communist Party member, because of the underground character of the whole membership, has handicapped the NAACP in carrying this resolution out to the full. But Red control can easily be distinguished by the resolutions a local unit adopts and by the measures it supports. If that rule is finally applied to the NAACP, more progress may be made in coping with infiltration.

Under the new Trojan Horse tactics brought forward in 1953, as a result of Stalin's international directive to create "contradictions" among the Western Powers, the Communists are concentrating on penetration of all "reformist" organizations, including, specifically, the NAACP.

The directive for this renewed reliance on the Trojan Horse was given specifically in December, 1952, in the draft resolution on "Situation Growing Out of Presidential Election," issued by the national committee of the Communist Party. Emphasis was placed on infiltration of "reformist" groups, including (by name) the NAACP. In the following month, an article of directives on the Negro question was issued, in which appeared the following: "What is needed among our leading Negro cadre is the very conscious mobilization to fight to carry out the line of the Party, to work with the masses in the Right-led, reformist organizations and, in the first place, the NAACP. It is only in this way that the program of the Party can be brought into life and result in the development of mass united front action in the struggle for Negro rights." (*Political Affairs,* Jan., 1953, "White Chauvinism and Negro Bourgeois Nationalism," Samuel T. Henderson [an apparently fictitious name], p. 62. The draft resolution to which reference has been made appeared in *Political Affairs,* Dec. 1952.)

Although the Communists admit in effect that they have not been able to make much headway among the mass of the Negro people, whom they label "backward," their determination to get a strong hold within the NAACP is attested by deep Red interest in the 1953 convention of that organization. They hoped to make NAACP, or at least a number of its branches, a sounding board for Communist propaganda and a channel to reach the Negro people.

The 1953 convention of the NAACP set as its major goal the ending of race discrimination in all forms in the United States within ten years, that is, by 1963, the Centennial of the Emancipation Proclamation. This is a goal which all Americans can endorse. Discrimination weakens the fabric of our American communities, whether it be exercised against the Negroes, the Mexican-Americans, or the Puerto Ricans. But the *Daily Worker* of July 7, 1953, announced that it intended to get into this NAACP campaign, which the Communists can be counted on to attempt to distort for Soviet purposes. In the past, they have done so with the proposals for Fair Employment Practices Acts, their loud and conspicuous championship of these measures doing them much more harm than good. (An enlightening discussion of Communist methods to penetrate organizations of the Negro people is contained in the testimony of Manning Johnson, *Hearings Regarding Communist Infiltration of Minority Groups,* Part II, House Committee on Un-American Activities, 1949, especially pp. 511-19.)

Action by Americans

All patriotic Americans have an obligation to evince as much interest and zeal in bringing about a solution to the Negro problem in the United States as do the Communists in their perverted way. We have said that this is an American problem, of which the Soviet fifth column takes advantage for Soviet purposes, just as it seeks out any other weakness or grievance for a like end. The patriotic American must give attention to ending discrimination in the United States, but not primarily because it is essential to do this in order to combat Communism. His responsibility is deeper than that. It concerns the strengthening of the American Republic. In the course of activity along this line, he will be confronted with the Communists (almost always concealed), and will have to deal with Communist maneuvers and propaganda. In local branches of the NAACP or in his local community generally, he can soon detect Red influences by the resolutions and causes they interlace with the Negro work, the tone in which they forward their proposals, and their constant effort to bring about friction and conflict. For instance, at the time when the Reds engineered the Peekskill riot, a number of local units of the NAACP were pressed by Communist members to defend Paul Robeson and Howard Fast, Communists, and to denounce the authorities of Westchester County, N.Y. Concealed Reds, active in local community work among Negroes, also sought to persuade Negro ministers and others interested in that work to sign petitions in favor of the atom spies, Julius and Ethel Rosenberg. With an understanding of the current Communist line during any particular period, and with some study of how Communists operate, it is not difficult to detect their hand.

In considering the positive side, the reader must bear in mind the statement by Lester B. Granger, Executive Secretary of the National Urban League, before the House Committee on Un-American Activities. Mr. Granger stated: "Authentic Negro leadership in this country finds itself confronted by two enemies on opposite sides. One enemy is the Communist who seeks to destroy the democratic ideal and practice which constitutes the Negro's sole hope of eventual victory in his fight for equal citizenship. The other enemy is that American racist who perverts and corrupts the democratic concept into a debased philosophy of life. In opposing the one enemy, Negro leadership must be careful not to give aid and comfort to the other.

"Those white leaders of stature in this country, those who exert widespread influence in Government, industry, business, and politics, will be very badly advised if they seek to increase the difficulties of reputable Negro leadership as it stands precariously on defense against these twin enemies." (*Hearings Regarding Communist Infiltration of Minority Groups*, Part I, Committee on Un-American Activities, 1949, p. 464.)

That being the case, it seems essential that these measures at least be encouraged and participated in:

1. The creation of interracial councils or conferences, in which representative Negro and white citizens in the community can meet together on the basis of their common citizenship, to work out the problems of Negro-white cooperation locally. Among the first considerations of this endeavor should be necessarily the ending of discrimination—in housing, employment, and related fields.

2. Participation in the local units of the National Association for the Advancement of Colored People, to advance the work it is doing to end discriminatory practices without community conflict.

3. To forward educational endeavors in human relations, so that there will be a better and wider understanding of the need for working together of the Negro and white communities for the benefit of life in each city, state, and the country as a whole.

The reader is urged to give the utmost attention and extended study to this series of proposals. In varying forms, he would also apply kindred measures to the vitally needed work in relation to Puerto Ricans, now coming into New York in such large numbers, and to the Mexican-Americans who present themselves first in the Southwest and California, but who are also now being brought into other parts of the country.

The Mexican-Americans are becoming a large numerical unit

among agricultural workers, cannery workers, and in migratory work generally. The exploitation to which they often are subjected presents an opportunity to the Communists. At the Fourteenth National Convention of the Communist Party, held in 1948, the Mexican-Americans came in for special consideration. Here, again, the Soviet fifth column adopted an attitude which was designed to promote conflict in the United States and to make the Mexican-American issue one that could promote Communist agitation in Latin America against the United States.

The very first words of the special Resolution on Party Work among the Mexican-American people read as follows: "The special historical development of the Mexican people in the United States as a conquered people, victim of American imperialist expansion, with close ties to Latin America, requires a new and special approach of our Party to the Mexican problem." On this foundation, which could easily lead to a demand for "self-determination" such as was raised for the Black Belt, the Communists officially proceeded to take steps. The idea of the conquest of the Mexican people by the United States was to be given further study so as to be further developed—and it could develop into a demand for a separate Mexican-American nation in the southwest. Immediately, Red literature was to be made available on a large scale in the Spanish language, training schools for Mexican-American cadres were to be instituted, and "a struggle" to be forwarded to advance certain grievances of the migratory workers. (*Political Affairs*, May and July, 1949, "The Plight and Struggles of the Mexican-Americans.")

There would seem to be a fruitful soil for Communism among the Mexicans in this country. In many places, discrimination against them is great. "No Mexicans Need Apply" is a sign sometimes seen in connection with certain better types of work. "No Mexicans Can Eat Here" appears frequently in southwestern restaurants. Often whole families move northward with the fruit and vegetable crops, working in the fields and orchards for the canneries. They live under the most primitive conditions, sometimes a family of ten to twelve living in one barrack-like enclosure. But Communism as such has not made great progress among them, partly due to their religious beliefs. It is through "mass organizations" such as the Communist-controlled union in the food and cannery industries that the Reds get their interest, and from that base they seek to win selected Mexicans for special training as members of the vanguard.

With the Puerto Ricans it is much the same. An opening for the fifth column was provided with the seating in Congress of Vito Marcantonio from a district in New York which contained many Puerto Ricans. So important did the Communist Party consider the candidacy of Marcantonio that it threw every available Party person into his district at election time, engaged in house to house canvassing on his behalf, distributed thousands of leaflets, and organized rallies. With his defeat, the Reds lost some advantage in their plans for wide penetration of the Puerto Rican migrants into the United States. But the effort still continues and is linked up with the Communist demand for the independence of Puerto Rico. The real objective is to create in that island a Soviet base against the United States. (*Political Affairs*, June, July, 1952, "Puerto and the Fight for Its Independence," Pettis Perry.)

Soviet Anti-Semitism

In contrast to the alleged championship of minority groups, which the Communists are forever claiming as their special province, the anti-Semitism fostered in Soviet Russia provides added evidence that this enthusiasm about such "reforms" is merely for the purpose of forwarding the Kremlin's aims. Although Soviet Russia has written into its basic law that anti-Semitism is a capital offense, this is to be considered in the same light as the whole Soviet constitution, which also "guarantees" freedom of assemblage and demonstration. These provisions have been shown by history to be mere window dressing to clothe the dictatorship with the outer garments of democracy. But anti-Semitism has persisted in Soviet Russia and existed there even before the official use of it in the campaign against "Cosmopolitanism" in the late Forties and the open denunciation of "Zionist plotters and spies" in 1952. (For a scholarly discussion of this matter, read *The Jews in the Soviet Union*, Solomon M. Schwarz, Syracuse University Press, 1951, and an article by the same author in *Commentary*, June 1949, "The New Anti-Semitism of the Soviet Union.")

Back in the Thirties, the Communists in the United States were compelled to engage in gross anti-Semitism, under the guise of attacking Zionism, a tactic made necessary at that time by Soviet Russia's wooing of the Arab States. Cartoons derogatory to the Jewish people and to their alleged characteristics were to be found in the pages of the Communist press and, as usually, the Jewish Communists were required to publish these cartoons first in the pages of the Yiddish daily, the *Freiheit*. (One of these cartoons is reproduced, as a sample of the others, in the testimony of Rabbi Benjamin Schultz, Secretary of the American Jewish League Against Communism, *Hearings Regarding Communist Infiltration of Minority Groups*, Part I, House Committee on Un-American Activities, 1949, opp. p. 440.) The record of anti-Semitism under Soviet auspices in the satellite regimes can be examined in the 1952 and 1953 issues of the magazine, *News From Behind the Iron Curtain*, published by the National Committee for a Free Europe, Inc., 110 West 57th St., New York, 19, N.Y.

For the Communists in this country, however, the cry of "anti-Semitism" has been most valuable. Through it, they have won many friends in Hollywood and also allies among teachers and professors, who adhered to Communist causes even after the hollowness of Red pretensions in this regard had been thoroughly revealed. These people had to swallow the Hitler-Stalin Pact, which was in reality an alliance, after they had been persuaded that the Kremlin and its followers were the foremost fighters against Hitlerism and all its works. They also had to suffer the long series of attacks upon the Jews by Soviet Russia, beginning with the opening of the "cold war." But with that agility at mental gymnastics which distinguishes the Communists, the Hitler-Stalin document was first represented as "a pact of peace" showing the peace-loving nature of the Soviet dictators, and then as a "breathing spell" to prepare for warfare against the Nazis. These arguments threw dust in the eyes of a great number of people. In a similar manner, in the later period, the brazen anti-Semitic persecutions and propaganda in Soviet Russia and under the various satellite regimes were represented as the punishment of "traitors."

Concerning the United States, a helpful delineation of Communist methods in working among the Jewish people was presented by Rabbi Benjamin Schultz before the House Committee on Un-American Activities in 1949. That record deserves careful study. Dealing with the question in general, Rabbi Schultz says: "The Jew is a lover of liberty. The American Jewish League Against Communism represents the majority viewpoint of American Jews on this subject of Communism." To which Rabbi Schultz adds: "As a Rabbi, a believer in God, a servant of mankind, I cry out against this black force of Communism which is ushering a new dark age into much of the world, and which seems to be expanding. . . . As a Jew, I consider Communism equivalent to Fascism and Nazism as a great historic evil. This country is in greater danger—because of the very subtlety of that danger—than it ever has been in all its history. And persons of Jewish faith have found more peace and prosperity in America than they ever have in any corner of the earth. Not only as Americans, but also as Jews, they must act against the enemy of America.

"But the Communists, unfortunately, will not desist from their efforts to capture us until either all the minorities are separately won over, or the Communist movement is destroyed." (*Hearings Regarding Communist Infiltration of Minority Groups*, Part I, House Committee on Un-American Activities, 1949, pp. 434, 435.)

"Language Groups"

"The language groups," those which gathered together recent immigrants from abroad who maintained their native language in America, have always been a special target for the Communists. It was in "the language federations" of the Socialist Party that the Communists originally had their strongest following, when the break came which led to affiliation with the Communist International. Over the intervening years, the conspiracy has maintained separate sections of the Party for language groups, has sought to penetrate organizations which represented various foreign language groupings, and has maintained a Red press in a number of languages in this country. Dailies as well as weeklies are among these journals, all of which are supposed to take the editorial policy from the *Daily Worker*. The Red "language groups" have also been the foundation for the International Workers Order, the adjunct of the conspiracy in the insurance field, and the source of considerable finances to the conspiracy.

From its "language" sections, the Party has been able to establish many channels of illegal communication with Communist forces abroad, and also a basis for smuggling in Communists illegally from other lands.

There is a wealth of information today to which the student can turn for data on the broken pledges of Soviet Communism to "minority groups" and to "colonial" and "dependent" peoples. For the conspiracy's false use of anti-Semitism and for detailed material on its maneuvers among the Jewish people, the American Jewish League Against Communism, Inc., 220 West 42nd St., New York, can be consulted. Headed by Rabbi Benjamin Schultz, it has performed an invaluable service in opposing the conspiracy. Direct quotations from official Communist documents and newspapers, showing the gross exploitation by Soviet power of the "dependent" peoples, can be obtained from publications of the National Committee for a Free Europe, Inc. There is now in existence a whole library exposing Soviet subjugation of the Chinese people, among which books *The Enemy Within* by the Reverend Raymond J. DeJaegher and Irene Kuhn, *No Secret Is Safe* by the Reverend Mark Tennien, and *Brainwashing in Red China* by Edward Hunter are particularly recommended.

All such accounts are given further life by the sworn testimony of Negroes who are former Communists, such as Manning Johnson and William Nowell, which can be obtained through the House Committee on Un-American Activities. This accumulated evidence underscores what we could know from the nature of dialectical materialism, which is after all a weapon for a ruling caste: That the grievances and aspirations of "minority groups" and "colonial peoples" are used by the Soviet dictatorship to abuse these groups.

CHAPTER XII

INFILTRATION OF GOVERNMENT AGENCIES

WITH THE overthrow of the United States government a major goal of the Red conspiracy, the agencies of that government are logically a chief target for infiltration. In this the Stalinites have been unusually successful, as the record, which is only half disclosed, has revealed. Stalin's "law of conspiracy"—that "it takes a thousand men to build a bridge but one to blow it up"—applies neatly. If one or two Communists, or persons influenced by the Communists, work themselves into positions of trust and responsibility in any federal agency, they can create havoc. Working in non-Communist garb and always under directions from Soviet agents, they can bring about vacillation, uncertainty, and even downright betrayal of the interests of the United States. If they are in very high places, they can suggest those recommendations which will betray, and have betrayed, millions of people to the Kremlin.

Espionage, which of its very nature involves comparatively few persons, is another motive for Red penetration in government circles. Were it not for the comparative ease with which espionage was carried on in the United States, particularly during World War II, Soviet Russia would not now have the secret of the atomic bomb. Many other secrets, concerning our military planes and methods of intelligence work, would not now be in the possession of Moscow.

Deadly as espionage proves to be, it is the infiltration which influences policy that is the most threatening to American security. Whittaker Chambers, who is known above all because of his confessions of espionage work in Washington, has indicated this, and it is known to everyone who has been an active member of the conspiracy. If espionage is detected or even suspected, measures can be taken physically to guard against its effects, at least in part. American ingenuity being what it is in the sphere of physical science and production, it can establish certain safeguards against the weapons placed by espionage in the hands of the enemy. When great regions are placed under the control of Soviet Russia, through the acquiescence of the United States, the remedy is much more difficult. The United States is then bound by its own betrayal of these peoples and regions. The United States is in the sorry plight it is today because of the Red infiltration of the federal government which led us to agree to our own defeats.

If new catastrophes of this character are to be prevented, it is essential that there be an ever-growing number of men and women who understand Communist methods in government, are alert to the effects of such influences, and know how they gain strength from pro-Communist propaganda. It would have been much more difficult for Alger Hiss and his associates to betray the United States—and the biggest part of that betrayal consisted in what happened to the Chinese and the Poles—had it not been for a sympathetic attitude toward Soviet Communism created in many organs of American public opinion after the recognition of Soviet Russia in 1933. The reader should constantly remain aware of the relation between views helpful to the Communists expressed in certain newspapers, and on television and radio, and the ease of infiltration of the government by Soviet agents.

In 1953, the Soviet fifth column prepared for new penetrations of government agencies at all levels—federal, state, and municipal. The scheme was embodied in the "Resolution on the Situation Growing Out of the Presidential Elections (Final

Text)," issued by the National Committee of the Communist Party and published in *Political Affairs* for July, 1952. The directives in this Communist document are for renewed entry into positions where government officials can be influenced.

Preliminary to an examination of the many official records now at our disposal, it would be well to read *Witness* by Whittaker Chambers, and *Out of Bondage* by Elizabeth Bentley. In the former book, we might begin with Part V, in the latter with Chapter VI. Although both accounts deal largely with espionage, they refer to characters who were also agents of infiltration with a view to influencing policy. These books give an easy and vivid introduction to some of the methods by which the federal government has been entered by the Communists, and how some of their operations there are supervised directly by Soviet agents from abroad.

To this reading there should be added my own two books, *Men Without Faces* and *The Cry Is Peace*, showing with documentary evidence the character and methods of the Communist Party which is directing this infiltration and the effects produced in American public affairs. There has been so much of an uproar against the idea that our government agencies can be entered by the Communists, so much confusion created over this issue by the Reds and their friends, that it is well to establish the grave fact of such penetration right in the beginning. It would seem that even a child could grasp that the government which the Stalinites are sworn to overthrow would be an object of their attention and activity. But we must realize that it is one of the weaknesses in the American scene that so many leading political figures and forces, aided and abetted by certain agencies of opinion-making, are bent upon suppressing the truth in this phase of American life.

The Cases of Hiss and White

If you had been told that one of the most trusted advisers in our State Department, a man who was present and influential at Yalta, who was so important that he became the first General

Secretary of the United Nations, had served Stalin so faithfully that he had stolen secret American security documents for Soviet Russia, you would have been impressed with the ease of Red penetration. Max Bedacht, a member of the National Committee of the Communist Party but obscure from the public viewpoint, approached Whittaker Chambers, then also obscure, and recruited him into the underground. Chambers came under the supervision of J. Peters, illegal alien operating from the ninth floor of Communist headquarters, but thoroughly hidden from the public eye. And in the course of his labors, Chambers was introduced to Alger Hiss, already a member of the Red cell in Washington, that cell which had first entered the Department of Agriculture in 1933.

Because of the dramatic course of events which led to the conviction of Alger Hiss, his name is associated primarily with espionage. It must be remembered that he had even more damaging effects in forwarding those measures which led to the betrayal of the Chinese, the Poles, and other peoples. His position was so prominent in the work for the formation of the United Nations, that he has also come to symbolize Red influence in our government.

The role of the late Harry Dexter White deserves more consideration than it has received. Under-Secretary of the Treasury, with considerable influence over his superior Henry Morgenthau, White furnished secret information to Elizabeth Bentley for one Soviet espionage ring, and to Whittaker Chambers for another. Dispensing funds ostensibly to Nationalist China, he insisted that the Chinese representative be Dr. Chi, a Communist under the wing of Philip Jaffe, Soviet espionage agent. The American representative on this fund became Solomon Adler, another Soviet espionage agent. White's greatest crime against the United States, however, was the Morgenthau Plan, which would have made Germany a satellite of Soviet Russia. It would have kept the United States from being one of the occupation powers, agreed to all Soviet demands for the complete denuding of Germany, and sanctioned Soviet slave labor for tens of thousands of Germans. While opposition from the American people prevented this scheme from being fully adopted, an abbreviated form of the proposal appears in the Potsdam Agreement of 1945. Aptly termed "the world's worst peace," this agreement provided for the destruction of the German economy, the forced mass deportation of millions of Germans from the East to the West under conditions that made many of them die of cold, hunger, and disease, and permitted the continuance of slave labor by remaining silent on that subject. The United States also agreed with Great Britain and Soviet Russia to the division of Germany, which has now given the world "the German problem," the occasion for so much of the weakness of Europe. In other words, the United States assented, in the spirit of the Morgenthau Plan, to a prostrated Germany which could not be a bulwark against Soviet Russia as it should have been. While Harry Dexter White cannot be given sole responsibility for this degrading agreement by the United States—many hearts and hands in official positions brought it about—the terms on the whole were his brain child, particularly the severest portions. (For a full understanding of the gross betrayal of American interests and human decency at Potsdam, read *America's Second Crusade*, William Henry Chamberlin, Henry Regnery, Chicago, 1950, particularly Chap. 13.)

The case of Harry Dexter White emphasizes that one man, placed in a proper position and working secretly with others, can create havoc in American security. And there were other Whites—Lawrence Duggan in the State Department, Edwin S. Smith and Nathan Witt in the National Labor Relations Board, Frank Coe in various government posts, and finally Secretary of the International Monetary Fund. With these names, the list is only begun.

Use of the IPR

Direct penetration of the government by the Communists and those who cooperate with the conspiracy is accompanied and furthered by Red capture of organizations that can bring pressure or wield influence on United States policies. Nothing reveals this better than the carefully prepared report on the Institute of Pacific Relations, one of the great state papers of our time. Its high standing is attested to by the fact that it was published with the approval of the entire Senate Committee on the Judiciary, composed of leading representatives of both political parties and representing various trends of opinion. For anyone who wishes to be conversant with the relationship of the Red conspiracy to infiltration of our government, the report is required reading. From the conclusions to this report, supported by extensive documentary and oral evidence, we learn: "The Institute of Pacific Relations has not maintained the character of an objective, scholarly, and research organization. The IPR has been considered by the American Communist Party and by Soviet officials as an instrument of Communist policy, propaganda, and military intelligence. The IPR disseminated and sought to popularize false information including information originating from Soviet and Communist sources. Members of the small core of officials and staff members who controlled IPR were either Communists or pro-Communists."

These conclusions, based on the examination of thousands of documents and of no less than sixty-six witnesses, deal with an organization of innocent origins and innocent appearance, which the Communists captured by taking over its technical staff and active officials. It is an organization which was valuable to the Red conspiracy because it "possessed close organic relations with the State Department through interchange of personnel, attendance of State Department officials at IPR conferences, constant exchange of information and social contact." And this prestige of the IPR, particularly with the State Department, was used "to promote the interests of the Soviet Union in the United States."

When a man built up by the IPR as "our leading Far East expert," trusted adviser to the State Department, can be described by the Senate Committee in its conclusions as "a conscious, articulate instrument of the Soviet conspiracy," we begin to understand more fully where Red control of the IPR tended. The description is that of Owen Lattimore, who also was charged with having testified falsely before the Senate Internal Security Sub-Committee on at least five separate matters that were relevant to the inquiry.

Beyond that, we learn that "over a period of years, John Carter Vincent was the principal fulcrum of IPR pressures and influence in the State Department." This is the man who represented our government for a number of years in the Far East, was formerly in charge of the Far Eastern section of the State Department, and was the source of the recommendations that were to be made in regard to American attitudes in China and neighboring countries. The report also says: "The IPR was the vehicle to orientate American Far Eastern policies toward Communist objectives . . . Owen Lattimore and John Carter Vincent were influential in bringing about a change in the United States policy in 1945 favorable to the Chinese Communists."

The McCarran Sub-Committee on Internal Security found that this pressure from within the IPR on the government continued during the period 1945–1949. It was "instrumental in keeping United States policy on a course favorable to Communist objectives in China." That is, a relatively small group of Communists and pro-Communists in the IPR, working in and around the State Department, were instrumental in persuading the United States to take a course in China which led to the victory of the Communists. The whole debacle in Korea is a fruit of these connivings.

Blindness to Communist penetration of the government has been staggeringly expensive—in lives, funds, and the security of the United States. One illustrative case may be given. Among the corps of Soviet espionage agents who infested the IPR—like Guenther Stein, Israel Epstein, Agnes Smedley—one of those worth noting is Michael Greenberg. A Communist alien coming from Great Britain, he had hardly arrived when he succeeded Owen Lattimore in 1941 as managing editor of *Pacific Affairs,* the IPR organ. Lattimore, by that time, had been propelled into the Office of War Information headed by Elmer Davis, which became in itself a convenient point of penetration for the Reds. Greenberg continued the tone of *Pacific Affairs* "in the Lattimore tradition," that is, weighting it in favor of a pro-Red viewpoint on the Far East. In the latter part of 1942, nevertheless, he was appointed to a position with the Board of Economic Warfare and was assigned to and shared an office in the White House with Lauchlin Currie, executive assistant to President Roosevelt. Greenberg was one of several IPR stalwarts who made use of White House stationary in their correspondence, giving weight to their pro-Soviet recommendations.

This man, who could so easily penetrate the White House itself, has been identified as a Soviet espionage agent, and was declared by Professor George Taylor of the University of Washington to be so clearly following the Communist line that Taylor was shocked when Greenberg obtained a White House position. (*Institute of Pacific Relations, Report of the Committee on the Judiciary*, 82nd Congress, 2nd session, p. 182.)

The machinations of the Red agents within the IPR and then the State Department are so extensive that they cannot be covered here. The reader may wish to make a special study of the *Report* of the Senate Judiciary Committee on this subject. The voluminous hearings which led to that report are also of great value.

Inquiries by Congressional committees in education and other fields are constantly disclosing new information in regard to the ramifications of Communist entry into government posts during the recent past. The Office of War Information and the Office of Strategic Services were both entered by persons known today to be Communists, such as Waldo Salt, Leonard Bernovici (Berkowitz), Carl Marzani. It will suffice to give specific attention to the man who was chief of the Latin American division of the OSS, Maurice Halperin, who is now head of the Latin American Department at Boston University. Mr. Halperin went from post to post in the government with the greatest of ease, being an adviser to the United Nations Conference at San Francisco in 1945, a consultant to Economic and Social Council of the United Nations, adviser to the Secretary of State. During much of this time, according to the testimony of Elizabeth Bentley, Halperin was connected with Soviet espionage rings. During all of his government service, it is charged that he was a member of the Communist Party, a charge which he refused to answer on the grounds of self-incrimination. Boston University continues him on its faculty, adding one more to the many reasons why the United States has been so decisively defeated in so many areas by Soviet aggression. For if a man charged with espionage and subversion defies the Congress of the United States and is in effect supported in such defiance, a blow is given to national morale and a gain is made for the Red drive toward uncertainty and defeatism in American public opinion. (See *Subversive Influences in the Educational Process,* Hearings of the Sub-Committee on Internal Security, 1953, Part 6, pp. 664-75.)

Named By McCarthy

Nothing brings out more clearly the effectiveness of the penetration of the State Department by the Communists and their friends than the list of those who were removed from, or left, that department after charges made by Senator Joseph R. McCarthy of Wisconsin. This list includes John Stewart Service, who was caught by the FBI in 1945 giving top secret papers to Philip Jaffe, Soviet espionage agent. After being cleared by the State Department seven different times, Service was finally dismissed on December 13, 1951, on orders of the top Loyalty Review Board which reversed the State Department's previous clearance. Others were: Edward Posniac, who resigned after having been cleared by the State Department Loyalty Board in December, 1948; Esther Brunauer, dismissed from a key job where she was handling secret material; Stephen Brunauer, who resigned under fire from top secret work as head of the navy's high explosive section; Peveril Meigs, whom the State Department permitted to resign, but who then went with the Military Establishment, from which he was removed under the loyalty program. There were Hans Lansberg, allowed to resign by the State Department, who went to the Department of Commerce, where he was discharged in 1951 under the loyalty program; Oliver E. Clubb, director of the State Department Division of China Affairs, cleared by the Tydings Committee, ordered by the State Department Loyalty Board to be discharged but saved by the then Secretary of State, Dean Acheson, who permitted Clubb to resign with a clean bill of health so as to get a pension of $5,800 per year; V. Lorwin, suspended in 1951 under the loyalty program; William T. Stone, assistant to Assistant Secretary of State William Benton (afterward Senator Benton), associated with Frederick Vanderbilt Field and Owen Lattimore on the board of the Communist magazine *Amerasia*, who resigned when his case was to be heard. (For these and other instances of infiltration of the State Department, read *McCarthyism, The Fight for America*, by Senator Joe McCarthy, 1952.)

To all of this there was added on July 2, 1953, the testimony of J. Anthony Panuch, former Deputy Assistant Secretary of State, before the Senate Sub-Committee on Internal Security. Mr. Panuch gave the startling information that almost all the data concerning Alger Hiss' subversive connections which came out later were contained in the security files of the State Department as early as 1945. Panuch had prepared a memorandum disclosing Hiss' pro-Soviet views and acts, in which he stated: "Dr. Hiss exercises Svengali-like influence over the mental processes of Junior Stettinius." Edward R. Stettinius, Jr., had been Secretary of State when the United Nations Charter was drafted, while Hiss served as Secretary General of the first UN Conference and was at that time (1946) American delegate to the United Nations.

That Panuch's memorandum was true can be seen from the Stettinius memoirs which justify President Roosevelt's concessions to Soviet Russia at the Yalta Conference. At that conference, Hiss was Presidential adviser, and Stettinius mentions him favorably several times in his book, although by then Hiss had been indicted. The effects of Communist penetration are well illustrated in this control of Stalin's agent over the then American Secretary of State. (Testimony of J. Anthony Panuch before Senate Sub-Committee on Internal Security, 83rd Congress, 1st session, pp. 842 ff.; see also note commenting on Panuch's testimony, *Interlocking Subversion in Government Departments*, Report of Senate Sub-Committee on Internal Security, July 30, 1953, pp. 26-28.)

The Senate Sub-Committee on Internal Security, through its Counsel, Robert Morris, has brought together all the evidence that has been accumulated of federal government penetration by Communists and their allies. This is a startling complement to the previous excellent report on the Institute of Pacific Relations. But it covers only part of the ground, not bringing in the hearings and findings of other committees and departments of the government.

With so much ease in entering our own government, it is not surprising that the Communists also moved into the American technical staff in the United Nations. Much of the spotlight has been focused on Virginius Frank Coe because of his key position in the administration of the international monetary organization, and many of the others in the UN have been lost sight of. More than twenty of the technical staff, who came from the United States, refused to state whether or not they were Communists on the ground it would tend to incriminate them.

Jacob Grauman may be selected as an example of the facility with which Communists and their friends have moved from one position in our government to another, and thence into the United Nations. This man was successively employed by the United States Department of Labor, the National Research Project, the War Production Board, and became attached to the International Bank of Reconstruction and Development of the UN. On March 27, 1953, he resigned from his UN post when summoned before the Federal Grand Jury in New York.

There was no reason why he should resign in 1953 if he were

no longer a Communist. And yet, before the Senate Sub-Committee he denied Communist Party membership after January 1, 1948, refusing to answer for all the preceding years on the ground that any truthful answer would tend to incriminate him. That year 1948 is being heard of increasingly in the pleas of Communists and in the discussion of Red infiltration. It was in 1948 and 1949 that the Communists went thoroughly underground, with all their members no longer having any vestige of membership. It is evident that from 1948 or 1949 on, dependent on how fast the Party was able to move in arranging its underground organization, practically every Communist can state that he is not a member of the Party and still escape perjury charges. In 1953, when testifying before the New York Board of Regents, George Blake Charney, Secretary of the Communist Party in New York, declared that every Party member was now known only as a number and that there was no record of the names of those affiliated with the conspiracy.

Another case worth citing, because of its paramount importance, is that of Dr. Harold Glasser, former assistant to the late Harry Dexter White in the Treasury Department. Of his record the Senate Sub-Committee on Internal Security states: "The record shows, however, that in 1940, the Treasury Department sent him to Ecuador as financial adviser to Ecuador's Ministry of Finance. In 1943, he was the Treasury's representative and chief of the Financial Control Division of the North African Economic Board. He was the financial expert of the American delegation in the formation of UNRRA and in the subsequent administration of this international body 'throughout its whole life.' In this capacity, he was one of those 'with a predominant voice' in determining which countries should receive aid from UNRRA and which should not. In 1944, the Treasury Department sent him to Italy 'to make a study and develop a program for fighting inflation in the civilian liberated areas.' In 1945, he went to UNRRA council meetings in Europe. In January 1947, he participated in a Four Power study of the economy of Trieste. In the spring of that same year, he was an adviser to Secretary of State Marshall at the meeting of the Council of Foreign Ministers in Moscow."

That illustrates the ease with which Dr. Glasser moved around into strategic positions, affecting American policies with other countries. And yet, this is the man who appears in the memorandum of the then Congressman Richard M. Nixon in 1945 as being under "direct control by the Soviet representatives in this country." He was identified as a Soviet espionage agent by Elizabeth Bentley in 1951 and 1952, and Whittaker Chambers also testified under oath to Glasser's Communist adherence. This he mentions quite frankly in his book, *Witness*. (*Interlocking Subversion in Government Departments*, Report of Senate Sub-Committee on Internal Security, 1953, pp. 6, 7; see also *Witness*, Whittaker Chambers, 1952, pp. 429, 430.)

The Communist Spectrum

If we understand the various categories of Communist affiliation and activity, we will grasp the reason for the varying pleas made by those whose records show that they are Communists. Some deny membership in the Party at any time. Some refuse to testify about a certain period. Still others refuse to testify at all about their membership at any time. The cause for this variation is to be found in the different responsibilities assigned to these people by the Party in the past. When a man joined the Party while he was in a key or delicate position, he was ordered not to have any vestige of membership and not to attend branch meetings. An examination of these categories of Communists will also throw light upon the pattern of penetration of the government and its relationship to other areas of Red work.

The Communist categories can be given as follows: 1. the espionage agent; 2. the infiltrator of government; 3. the infiltrator of other organizations; 4. members of Communist fronts; 5. open rank and file Communists; 6. Party bureaucrats or functionaries.

An explanation of these degrees of responsibility to the Party, and of the different membership requirements that prevail in each case, is given in my testimony on "The Communist Spectrum" before the McCarran Sub-Committee on Internal Security in August, 1951. It runs as follows:

"We have what I call the Communist spectrum. The spectrum of Communist allegiance; that is a term I used while I was still a Communist and to some extent was adopted by other people who discussed this in the Politburo. That is to say, we will take the spy.

"Anyone engaged in espionage like Judith Coplon, and there are a number of those people trained for espionage alone, must not give any indication of any association with Communists. As a matter of fact, they are not even permitted to approach Communist branch meetings; they are ordered not to do so. They cannot have any contact with known Communists.

"That of course is quite obvious why that would be. The infiltrator of government is somewhat in a similar position and is not supposed to have any vestige of Communist membership on him and to avoid any public relationship with Communists. Beyond that he is also permitted of course within limitations to make such statements critical of the Communist Party as will assure his non-Communist standing so that he may put the burden—I use that word "burden" of his activity in the Communist cause because that was the way it was used—the weight of his activities in the Communist cause.

"Then there is the infiltrator of other organizations. They likewise have the same responsibilities, though they are not so much protected as anyone in the Government. I mean protected by the Communist Party. They likewise can misrepresent.

"You take, for example, during the one month that I was supposedly a non-Communist, though a Communist, in August, 1935. I was specifically directed by Stachel again to criticize the party to non-Communists but to do it lightly and to put the burden of my arguments in favor of cooperation with the Communists, although I was a fully admitted Communist Party member working as a non-Communist until they could decide what my function should be.

"We have also the case of even Ben Gold, the open Communist, and this was worked out while I was still in the party, though it didn't come to fruition until the next CIO convention, who as an open Communist signed a report denouncing Communist infiltration in the CIO. That was in order to ameliorate the feelings of Philip Murray.

"These special exemptions are granted by the district leader functioning as a non-Communist in infiltrating into other organizations in order that his infiltration may be effective.

"Next in the category are the members of the Communist fronts who have still another set of responsibilities, to follow out the fronts, to respond when called upon, but who again deny they are Communists, and of course in denying it have to express occasionally why they are not Communists. You just can't say, 'I am not a Communist,' you have to explain why. They are permitted to do that, although 95 percent of the members of Communist fronts, according to my knowledge, are members of the Communist Party.

"When I say members of the Communist Party I do not mean necessarily card-carrying Communists because most Communists do not carry cards but are subject to Communist allegiance.

"Then there are the open party members, the expendables as they have been called, the rank-and-file Communists, the picket-line Communists, who are supposed to be open, and they are not permitted to deviate from the line of the party because they represent the reputation of the party.

"Likewise with the bureaucrat or functionary. The word 'bureaucrat' is not used in the party. Although Lenin said our party is bureaucratic, they don't like to use that. They are functionaries. They, of course, have a deep responsibility and they cannot deviate from the party at all. Anyone who is a section organizer or a district organizer of the party or the like in his person is the party because the leadership principle is very strong.

"Among the bureaucrats, though, there are variations again. There are those illegal agents sent in here by Stalin who direct the party, who are largely underground; there are the open party representatives like William Z. Foster, today, and Browder when I was there, and the like; and then there are, of course, certain functionaries who for one reason or another, from time to time, become concealed.

"Now each one of these, at the time that they perform these different functions, have different responsibilities in regard to how much they will assert their Communist integrity. The great question that was always put in the Politburo and at State committee meetings, and I have attended a number of State committee meetings where this question came up for lesser people in the party, those people who were concerned, the question was always how far they could go in order that they could carry on their deceit of others, what scandal it will create in the party.

"According to the answer to that question they were granted a certain immunity from being quite regular from the party line or party regulations." (*Hearings on the Institute of Pacific Relations,* Senate Sub-Committee on Internal Security, 82nd Congress, Part II, pp. 558–59.)

Degrees of concealment, then, explain the distinctions made to some extent in the respective pleas by those charged with being Communists when they appear before courts or congressional committees. According to the Leninist precept, it is their duty to perjure themselves if necessary, but to protect themselves against conviction for perjury.

Pattern of Infiltration

Returning to the case of Jacob Grauman, which elicited this very important discussion, the witness admits that his references for employment on the War Production Board were David Weintraub, Edward Fitzgerald, and Harry Magdoff, all in government employment. Weintraub has been named as a member of the Communist apparatus by Whittaker Chambers who states that Weintraub gave him employment when he required a cover for underground Communist activity. Both Fitzgerald and Magdoff refused to give their Communist activities or affiliations on the grounds that truthful answers would tend to incriminate them. Fitzgerald persisted in this position even though Elizabeth Bentley had named him as engaged in Soviet espionage work.

These references for Grauman present a good picture of the pattern of Red infiltration of government, which has been followed in so many instances. One Communist or friend of the Communists recommends another, all posing as not affiliated with the Party. A claque is built up, singing the praises of this Communist or that, thus drawing the favorable attention of high government officials.

Another United Nations employee, Mrs. Eda Glaser, furnishes interesting information on another point, the ease with which Communists could move from Red agencies into the government. Mrs. Glaser refused to testify both as to her membership and as to whether she signed a number of Communist nominating petitions. In order to obtain a place with the Soviet Purchasing Commission, she went to Cornell University in 1944 to "brush up" on the Russian language, with which she was generally familiar. From that position, working directly for Soviet Russia, she went quite naturally to work for the New York Furriers' Joint Council, which is completely controlled by the conspiracy. (In addition to my personal knowledge of this matter, on which I have testified under oath, the House Committee on Un-American Activities and the House Committee on Labor have established the fact of Red control over this union. But see specifically *Communist Domination of Certain Unions*, Senate Sub-Committee on Labor and Labor Management Relalations, 1951, pp. 63-78.) Its chief officer, Irving Potash, was convicted in 1949 under the Smith Act. In 1946, the ambulatory Mrs. Glaser became attached to the United Nations Relief and Rehabilitation Administration, UNRRA, under the directorship of the Honorable Herbert H. Lehman, now Senator from New York. Immediately she was sent to Russia where she spent fourteen months aiding in the distribution of UNRRA supplies. After her return from Russia, she is immediately placed in the United Nations Security Council, being employed in its reference library.

Then, there is the strange case of Jerome A. Oberwager. Employed by the United Nations proper and then by UNESCO, its educational arm, Oberwager was such a grave security risk that the State Department passport division refused him a passport to Europe in January, 1953. This was done although Oberwager had already spent many months in Mexico for UNESCO. It also is brought out, through his plea of possible self-incrimination, that he actually took the trip to Europe secretly without a regular United States passport in his own name. He refuses to disclose what the purpose of this trip was or whom he met with while on this mission in violation of American law. That is not the end of his story, for it must be known that prior to his United Nations connections, he was engaged in preparing educational material for United States Army personnel at the Aberdeen Training Center. (*Activities of United States Citizens Employed by the United Nations*, Hearings of the Sub-Committee on Internal Security, 83rd Congress, 1953, Parts 1, 2, and 3. These data are specifically taken from Part 2.)

As to government workers in lesser posts—secretaries and clerks—the Communists did not forget them while striving to get members of the conspiracy into executive positions. The first agency set up by the conspiracy to corral rank and file government workers was the United Federal Workers, headed by Eleanor Nelson and affiliated with the CIO. In order to reach out into other and local government bodies, the Communists established the State, County, and Municipal Workers of America. In April, 1946, these two organizations were merged into the United Public Workers, under the presidency of Abram Flaxer, whose connections with the conspiracy are well known.

(See testimony of twenty witnesses, including me, reported in *Hearings* of Senate Sub-Committee on Internal Security, "Subversive Control of the United Public Workers of America," 1951; see also *Communist Domination of Certain Unions*, Senate Sub-Committee on Labor and Labor Management Relations, 1951, pp. 3-18.) The UPW was expelled from the CIO in 1950, on substantiation of charges that the organization was under Communist control. It is interesting to observe that the committee which tried the UPW not only refers significantly to the fact that its members "are in the main government employees" and that there is a "growing anxiety about Communist activity in the government"; it also emphasizes "the vilification and the slander employed by the UPW representatives" against the committee and the CIO. Such is the usual Communist pattern, whether applied to union leadership or "McCarthyism," and it cannot be passed over hurriedly. For it is unfortunate that some of the very CIO unions and leaders who condemn this "vilification" when applied to them, fall victims to it when it is hurled at Congressional inquiries into subversion.

States and Cities

In July, 1953, the House Committee on Un-American Activities established through hearings at Albany that a Communist cell existed in the government apparatus of New York State. Nothing was so surprising about this, since New York has been conspicuously slow in doing anything against Communist influences. In 1948, the State Committee on Un-American Activities in Washington established the fact that there was widespread infiltration of the State government there, including even several legislators and Representative Hugh DeLacey, then a Congressman. Meetings of the Communist cell in the State government were sometimes even held in the Capitol building at Olympia. One of the members of the legislature, Mrs. Kathryn Fogg, was not only identified as a Communist Party member but also as a delegate to a national convention of the Communist Party. Two means of entry into the State government were the Communist-controlled Commonwealth Federation, an organization purporting to support the New Deal and the Old Age Pension Union, which the Reds captured and which represented aged persons in getting their State pensions. (*First Report, Un-American Activities in Washington State*, 1948.)

Nor are municipal bodies neglected. During a number of years, Si Gerson was in a post of importance in New York City, through appointment by Stanley Isaacs, elected as a Republican to several high positions. Gerson is a notorious Communist, and Isaacs is a member of a considerable number of Communist fronts. During the unguarded years of World War II, Communists got into such posts as executive assistant to the mayor. In July, 1953, "the fantastic story unfolded," as the *New York World Telegram* put it, of how the Communists had formed a better espionage apparatus in the New York police department than the intelligence service of that department had established against the Communists. Early in World War II, the New York police through their "sabotage squad" placed twenty-eight members of the force secretly in the Communist Party. They made great headway for a while, working at Communist headquarters, writing for the *Daily Worker*, and becoming branch organizers in some instances and educational directors in others. They also attended certain closed Party conventions. But the Communist Party was not asleep, and through Bernard Chester or Zuker, better known as Comrade Chester, Communists had been placed in the police department. One of these was Lieutenant Arthur Miller. Not only did Miller and his comrades among the police discover who were penetrating the Communist Party, with the result that the Party expelled more than a dozen of them at one time, but they also succeeded in getting four Party members into the highly secret Bureau of Special Services and Investigation. This Bureau has complete charge of subversive probes and its members are selected as counter-spies. Thus, four of those allegedly penetrating the Communist Party were actually Communists penetrating the police department's secret service.

"As a result," Howard Rushmore writes in the *New York Journal-American* of July 23, "the police counter-espionage system was wrecked." The full extent of this wreckage and how it came about would never have been known had it not been for the testimony of John Lautner, ex-Communist and former head of the State Control Commission of the Communist Party in New York.

In other cities, notably Chicago, Communists wormed their way into advisory positions where they could have influence on the administration. In Hawaii they were similarly successful, working under the direction of Jack Hall, lieutenant of Harry Bridges. Hall has now been convicted under the Smith Act as an active participant in the conspiracy to advocate the overthrow of the United States government by force and violence.

In addition to direct infiltration, the Soviet fifth column also seeks systematically to influence certain political figures through playing upon their weaknesses or prejudices. This is clearly one of the directives given in the report of the National Committee published in July, 1953. In the past, it was in that way—through both open and concealed Communists—that the late Representative Adolph Sabath of Illinois was persuaded to be such a friend and champion of Communist causes. He was no mean ally—for a number of years he was chairman of the House Rules Committee. It was in a similar manner that the Reds induced Elbert Thomas, then Senator from Utah, to express himself so strongly in behalf of Soviet Russia. (For an account of these influences, and their results, consult my *The Cry Is Peace*, 1952.)

Pressure by Transmission Belts

Work within the government is accompanied by pressure from without, through the stimulation of "crusades" by either Communist fronts or captive organizations or both. The Communists are always aware that they must make all "mass organizations," religious, labor, educational, and scientific groups, "transmission belts" for the Communist line. During the first six months of 1953, they made great gains in this respect, inducing many organizations, newspapers, and other agencies of opinion to forward the Communist line in relation to government. The campaigns against "McCarthyism," "book burning," and alleged "attacks on religion" were all Communist initiated and Communist stimulated. They arose from the order given by Joseph Stalin in October, 1952, that the Communist Parties "in imperialist countries" should raise higher "the banner of bourgeois civil liberties." The arrogance of that order from a man who had crushed all liberties is colossal. And yet, transmitted in the form of cries against "McCarthyism" and the other slogans issued by the Party through the *Daily Worker*, the dead Stalin is able to control the opinion of a great segment of vocal America. The average American, the so-called common man, was least affected by these outcries, but self-appointed groups and some stable organizations, penetrated or influenced by concealed Communists, took up the Communist line and plugged it day after day. Newspapers gave them publicity notices far beyond their actual representation of American thought, and the government was induced, in part at least, to retreat and in some instances even to sanction the Communist line, making America's security more unstable.

On June 1, 1953, the *Daily Worker* acknowledged that the Communists were the "initiators" of the cry of "McCarthyism." In an editorial, "Our Crusade Hits Home," the Red organ called the roll of those who had followed the fifth column's initiative. By "McCarthyism," as can be observed in the pages of the *Daily Worker* for 1953, is meant any attempt to curb the conspiracy, including the Federal Bureau of Investigation and the decisions of the Federal Courts. It is the fifth column's tactic to personalize the assault upon any defense of the United States they want to scuttle. In that way, as per Stalin's advice, they concentrate the greatest amount of attack upon a given point at one time. Next, under the same banner or outcry, they proceed in their attempts to pick off every opponent that they have in government.

The Little Iron Curtain

The Communists could not permit the accumulation of damaging evidence by Congressional inquiries throwing light on the extensive operations of concealed Communists in education and government. They had to halt it, or at the least to create that "confusion" which they always seek, in order to bring about the paralysis of any moves against them. During the first six months of 1953, they were eminently successful in influencing our government to adopt a "soft policy" toward them internally and internationally. Their ability to bring the "reserves" into action (as Stalin has taught them in *The Foundations of Leninism*), and to get non-Communists to conduct their battle for them, is the chief explanation of their success. As the result, they have thrown a "little iron curtain" over America, so that it is impossible to discuss fully and freely the extent of Communist penetration without being assailed by a considerable number of newspapers and by a number of allegedly non-Communist organizations. (The effects of the uproar created by the Communists are discussed by David Lawrence in *United States News and World Report*, July 17, 1953, in an editorial entitled "After Six Months.")

The issue of "book burning" was so successfully distorted by the Communists and their friends that the books of certain Communists or pro-Communist authors are still to be placed in our information libraries overseas, in a project which ironically is dedicated to opposing Communism. The issue was falsely stated from the beginning, and was poorly interpreted by the executive branch of the government. This was due to the hullabaloo which the Reds succeeded in creating through non-Communist groups, just as they influenced the State Department in the Forties through the Institute of Pacific Relations.

The information libraries which the United States government establishes abroad are for the purpose of describing

American life, and to combat Communist propaganda. Only a limited amount of money can be used for this purpose. It would be the height of folly, and not conducive to the interests of the United States, to employ any amount of these funds in subsidizing Communist authors and in getting pro-Communist literature into the hands of other peoples. That is precisely what occurred, and that is precisely what has not yet been checked.

So far as the local libraries of America go, again the question of selection is involved. These libraries cannot buy every book that is published. It is therefore incumbent on them not to purchase pro-Communist books or authors and to put on their shelves a number of of books which intelligently criticize Communism. For twenty years, the Communists have had the advantage of penetrating our libraries, with cells in many of the important ones, and with influence in the library world and the book review world. As a consequence, pro-Communist books appear on the shelves in numbers out of all proportion to those of books which critically analyze the Communist movement. The examination of a normal local library will show that the readers are being deprived of accurate and intelligent accounts of what the Communist conspiracy is and how it operates. The real "book burning," in the sense of improper selection of books, has been favorable to the Soviet fifth column.

Program for Protecting Government

If the United States is to survive as a nation, much more will have to be done to combat Red penetration. Only a small beginning has been made in this direction.

Our dependence, in the first place, must be on the security agencies of the government, and specifically on the able and alert Federal Bureau of Investigation. A step forward was taken in 1953 when President Eisenhower issued an executive order making "security" the test for government employees rather than "loyalty," as was largely the case in the past. That will be of help, because it will no longer be necessary to prove conclusively that a government employee is a member of the Communist Party, which is almost impossible under the methods adopted by the Communists. A man is as dangerous to the government whether he is known to be a Communist or has a Communist record, or is indiscreet, or has Communist associates, or is guilty of certain abnormal habits which make him an easy victim of political blackmail. The "security" test will aid greatly to rid the government of all such persons.

Even at that, however, we must realize the limitations of the Federal Bureau of Investigation imposed upon it by law, and which are thought essential to keep a "bureau of investigation" and not a form of political police. The FBI cannot pass upon policy, and therefore must stand mute while pro-Communist pressures are exerted on the government. It cannot halt fully the personal conniving of concealed Communists with certain politicians. In New York, the Communists have learned that "the tail can wag the dog," and have made wide use of the American Labor Party to intimidate politicians in both the Republican and Democratic parties in that state. Strong forces of appeasement exist in both those parties in New York, which can be attributed in no small measure to alliances or influences brought about by the ALP. Thus, the Communists as a small group penetrate and control completely a larger group (the ALP)— though still small in the general political sense—and from that base bring pressure and influence to bear on national political leaders.

The FBI, within its limitations, cannot deal adequately with these activities of the ALP, even though it is established that this alleged political party is as much under Communist control as is the International Workers Order, which was ordered dissolved by the courts of New York. (See *Report* of House Committee on Un-American Activities, 1944; *Guide to Subversive Organizations and Publications*, same committee, 1951, p. 19; *Report*, California Committee on Un-American Activities, 1948, pp. 40, 41.) Nor can the FBI proceed effectively, at least at the present moment, against the Communist fronts, which are the biggest guns of the conspiracy in blasting our government and forcing it to make disastrous concessions. The present proceedings against these fronts before the Subversive Activities Control Board may eventually lead to their being outlawed, but the procedure will take several years. In the meantime, the fronts and those whom they influence in other organizations will be doing serious damage to American security.

Role of the Community Leader

What is urgently required, in addition to the work of the government security agencies, is intelligent and continuous action against the Communist line by American community leaders. Red penetration of government has always occurred on a larger scale when the Soviet fifth column in this country has created an unguarded attitude on the part of American public opinion. Pressure on government through the "reserves" has won the most decided concessions when there has been an inability to respond quickly for the defeat of a Communist line.

In order that community leaders who are patriotic may be able to function effectively for the protection of our government, the following is essential:

1. The Communist line at any given period must be definitely known. It is the tragedy of our times that so many American leaders have no conception of what the Communists are driving at at any particular period. This they could easily learn —for Moscow is compelled to give public directives to its followers throughout the world—by the examination of the Cominform organs, *New Times, Political Affairs,* and the *Daily Worker.* (See Chapter VII, above.)

There are a number of excellent journals which give valuable information on the Communists and their current activities, and in addition there is always at hand the indispensable *Counterattack* for reference to specific cases. The line as it should be pursued, if we are to be forewarned of what the Reds will do, is as yet examined continuously only in my column in the Catholic press and in *Counterattack*. (With a week-to-week study of these should go a reading of the current information appearing in the columns of David Lawrence, Fulton Lewis, Jr., and George Sokolsky.)

2. A revitalization of citizenship is required, through letters to the press and to Representatives and Senators, exposing the Communist line and how it is being followed, wittingly or unwittingly, by certain vocal forces.

3. Organizations are required as a patriotic duty to speak out for the protection of the United States against the machinations of the Soviet fifth column. Too much of American security is being lost by a sort of default. The voices of patriotic groups are not heard strongly or consistently enough in intelligent opposition to the connivings of the Communists.

4. Such positive measures as the Congressional inquiries and other government action against the conspiracy must receive continuous and vigorous support.

In other words, today more than at any other time, there can be no abdication of citizenship. A number of leading individuals, who are also rather conspicuous in bailing out the Communists when the conspiracy is in difficulties, have sought to bring about that abdication. They have done this through the advice, "Let the FBI Do It." This is either ignorant or dishonest advice, because as we have seen, the FBI can not supplant the duties of the ordinary citizen and particularly of the community leader. Moreover, it was established in the hearings in August 1953 before the Senate Sub-Committee on Permanent Investigations, headed by Senator Joseph R. McCarthy, that a Communist cell existed in the Government Printing Office for years, that the FBI reported repeatedly on certain Communists there, but that these reports had been ignored until the Senate Sub-Committee threw light upon them. The Senate Sub-Committee on Internal Security, under the chairmanship of Senator William Jenner, testifies to the same state of affairs.

This committee declares: "Despite the fact that the Federal Bureau of Investigation and other security agencies had reported extensive information about this Communist penetration [in government] little was done by the executive branch to interrupt the Soviet operatives in their ascent in Government until congressional committees brought forth to public light the facts of the conspiracy." (*Interlocking Subversion in Government Departments*, report of Sub-Committee on Internal Security, July 30, 1953, p. 49.)

The FBI's work in ridding the government of bad security risks is strengthened by strong public opinion combating and offsetting the Communist line. The obligation on the part of the citizen to act—and to act intelligently—for the protection of the government is intensified today by the fact that the fate of the United States hangs in the balance. That obligation is further emphasized by the first of the twelve conclusions of the Senate Sub-Committee on Internal Security, now known as the Jenner Committee: "The Soviet international organization has carried on a successful and important penetration of the United States Government and this penetration has not been fully exposed."

PART FOUR

How to Fight Communism

CHAPTER XIII

KNOWLEDGE AND FACTS AS WEAPONS

In a real sense, the conclusion to a study of the techniques of Communism is only a beginning. What has been told in these pages concerning the strategy and tactics of the Communists is worthless unless it is used to meet this enemy wherever he appears. While his world outlook remains unchanged, the "flexibility" in its operations which Stalin emphasizes, makes his "line" always in some process of change.

The reader is therefore urged to continue his study after completing this book. There is a need to become more familiar with the Communist philosophy, in order to be aware of how it affects Red tactics at any particular period. The realization of this has led several outstanding journalists, notably George Sokolsky, to return to the very basis and to show that Communism's fundamental objective is to prove that God does not exist.

To such studies must be added a constant acquaintance with the variations in the Communist line, as suits the purposes of Moscow. "Study, study, study," the Red directive for parrot-like instruction, must be turned to sound anti-Communist purposes.

Fortunately, there is now available a wealth of critical material. We have a whole library of such literature at our disposal. In addition to the works on the nature of Communism, to which reference has been made in Chapter I, there are so many volumes critical and analytical of Communism in its practices that special bibliographies have been prepared. The first additional readings I would recommend are my books, *Men Without Faces* and *The Cry Is Peace*, because they cover the operations of the conspiracy as a whole, on a national scope. Many others should follow, such as Whittaker Chambers' excellent work, *Witness*, Benjamin Gitlow's *The Whole of Their Lives*, Elizabeth Bentley's *Out of Bondage*, and Angela Calomiris' *Red Masquerade*. Three bibliographies deserve consideration, both for selections in personal readings, and for the placement on library shelves. One of these has been issued by Representative Charles E. Kersten of Wisconsin and can be obtained by writing to him at the House of Representatives, Washington, D.C. Another was prepared by Vice-President (then Senator) Richard Nixon and has been distributed by the National Americanization Committee of the American Legion, Indianapolis, Indiana. A third has been recommended by E. F. Tompkins, columnist for the Hearst chain of newspapers.

Keeping up-to-date also means an acquaintance with the hearings and reports of Congressional inquiries, and every student of these matters should get himself placed on the mailing list of the House Committee on Un-American Activities, and of the Senate committees investigating subversion. The actual developments in these hearings are often quite different from the manner in which they are reported in the general press, and the reports which follow the hearings furnish an excellent summary of information which can be of great value.

The handling of this material, which may at first seem formidable, is not so difficult if certain keys or guides are employed. To follow the Communist line, it is essential to read my weekly column and that is why I reiterate that recommendation. For detailed information on the concealed Communists and their friends, the weekly report *Counterattack* is indispensable. What each reader should do is to make a special effort to get these valuable sources of information on the shelves of local public and college libraries where he and others can consult them freely.

Bankruptcy of Red Promises

Another important measure to be considered in every community is the exposure of the bankruptcy of Communist promises, taken from the record. There may be an opportunity to bring to the attention of local organizations or the local press that Red propaganda, in regard to Soviet Russia for instance, is basically false and that a marked feature of the Soviet dictatorship is its violation of promises. We have dealt with the Soviet enslavement of labor, which can be called to the attention of the free trade unions, and with the Soviet misuse of "colonial liberation." By taking advantage of the large amount of source material before us today, from David Dallin's *Forced Labor in Soviet Russia* to the report of the American Federation of Labor on the same subject, we can make a real beginning in exposing the Communist lie that "the Soviet Union is the citadel of peace and democracy," and that in the Land of Socialism "exploitation of man by man had ceased." Our purpose can always be to explain the inherent perfidy of Soviet pledges, and to show that concealed Communist and pro-Communist activities in the community are conducted solely for the benefit of the Stalinite dictatorship.

Quite a bit is said and written today about the bad conditions behind the iron curtain, but very seldom is it brought out that the same dictatorship which betrays its promises is at work in this country through its agents and "peace partisans." If the Soviet union, the argument can run, has proved to be such a monstrous fraud where it has obtained control, the same fraudulent character will mark the practices of its fifth columns. Let us take as an example the contention of Soviet propagandists that Socialism has been established in Soviet Russia, and that it has placed the working class in power. We need not deny that this is Socialism, for our contention is that Socialism is a fraud, and we recognize that Stalin and Malenkov are the logical heirs of Marx and Engels. But we can show by the facts that the working people are being exploited, and that a new bureaucracy has arisen to sit heavily on the backs of the Soviet-dominated people. We could use to good effect a quotation from M. Yvon's book, which appears in the discussion of "A New Class Society" by Peter Meyer. That quotation runs in part as follows: "The position of the new masters is incomparably superior to that of the other strata of the population. They receive ten to twenty times as much income as the workers, they get the best apartments and the right to larger dwelling space; furnishings are often free; watering places and first class beaches are at their disposal . . . they travel in 'soft' or 'international' trains (the Soviet terms for first class and parlor cars); official business is a frequent pretext for free tickets. And then they have first call on 'secret funds,' the use of which is permitted to help important people out of difficulties. In case of sickness, they receive the best care in first class hospitals, naturally at no expense to themselves."

Mr. Meyer builds up much more evidence to the same effect, including the following pointed item: "According to the *New Republic*, Mr. H. F. Sinclair of Consolidated Oil in 1935 received eighty-two times the average wage in his company. Yet salaries are paid in the Soviet Union which are one hundred times higher than the average wage, and three hundred times higher than the minimal wage." (For the full story, see *Verdict of Three Decades*, edited by Julien Steinberg, New York, 1950, pp. 475-500.)

Armed with these facts, and with the analysis of the composition of this bureaucracy given us by Dallin, which indicates that it does not come from the working class, we could proceed to show that this privileged group subsists on slave labor, a regimented press, the terror system, and the repression of all opposition. This sort of exploitation of the mass of the people is represented as "the end of exploitation." The same Leninist morality of deceit exists in the "crusades" inaugurated by the dictatorship through its faithful followers in other lands.

Another instance that can be cited to advantage is that of the

Soviet constitution, the so-called Stalinist constitution adopted in 1936. We will observe that date, for it tells us at once that this constitution was "put into effect" only to deceive the United States into the belief that there was something "democratic" about the Soviet dictatorship. It was in 1936 that that dictatorship was engaged in courting the democratic countries, so that they would pull its chestnuts out of the fire against the Hitler whom the Communists had built up. In Article 135 of that constitution, "freedom of speech" and "freedom of the press" are guaranteed. Those words are mockeries. The complete monopoly of the Soviet press is well-known and has strikingly been proved again by the July, 1953, issue of *News From Behind the Iron Curtain*, the magazine published by the National Committee for a Free Europe. As that issue shows, this control of the press by Moscow goes into every country under a satellite regime, sometimes to the extent of imposing practically the same format for the Red-controlled papers in all of these countries.

But Article 125 carries its irony even further. It also guarantees "freedom of assembly" and "freedom of street processions and demonstrations." In 1953, in East Germany where the eyes of the West can penetrate to some degree, Soviet troops have shot down demonstrators in city after city. The "freedom of street processions and demonstrations" was a farce there, and it can readily be understood how much more complete is the suppression of any such display of the people's desires in Soviet Russia itself. Among the many sources of information on this point, the chapter "Super-Purge" in Victor Kravchenko's *I Chose Freedom* is enlightening. Scores of men were arrested arbitrarily on the mere allegation of having signed an opposition paper many years before. Thousands were sent to slave labor, so that at the end of the purge, "the whisperings" around the Kremlin declared that from 15 to 20 million human beings were in slave labor camps. No individual protests, much less anything resembling a demonstration, was possible under the iron rule of the Soviet secret police. In Louis Fischer's *Thirteen Who Fled*, a vivid account of one attempted demonstration is given from the mouth of a refugee from Soviet rule. It took place in a far northern lumber camp and consisted merely of a parade to ask for wages which had long been withheld. The whole business was squelched thoroughly when armed secret police came in the night and took into custody all the leaders of the "demonstration." They left permanently for parts unknown. These personal accounts are proved to be true by the Soviet labor laws and regulations themselves. The most cursory research will reveal that these laws provide for the labor passport system, whereby the "free" worker may not leave his job without the consent of the government bureaucracy, under severe penalties up to imprisonment for tardiness or absenteeism, and the forced "voluntary" giving of certain hours of labor without remuneration. No group of people who have any concept of freedom, if they actually had the right of demonstration, would accede to these decrees without protest that would be heard even through the iron curtain.

It is advisable to check constantly on such data for community use, since they bring out two important conclusions: First, that Soviet Communism of its very nature perpetrates a colossal fraud, and second, as we have said, that the same world outlook which dictates these broken pledges and deceits also controls the activities of the concealed Communists and the Communist fronts. It is now possible in America to tell some of the truths about what is happening behind the iron curtain without being vilified and smeared as was the case a few years ago. (We have only to remember the treatment received from so-called competent reviewers and journals by William L. White for his *Report on the Russians* and by General W. G. Krivitsky whose work, *In Stalin's Secret Service,* is still of great value. The statements of these men were widely assailed and their integrity held up to question. For information on how the assault on White's book was a Red softening up of the United States for the Potsdam betrayal, consult William Henry Chamberlin, *America's Second Crusade,* Henry Regnery Company, Chicago, 1950, pp. 242-43.)

The Little Iron Curtain Again

Today, such overwhelming information on Soviet tyranny and perfidy has become available, and so much has been said about the wretched conditions under the satellite regimes, that the Communists cannot muster as many non-Communists to assault the presentation of these facts as they could in the past. The fifth column's great successes now lie in persuading certain non-Communist sources to imply that the Kremlin is becoming benevolent "since Stalin's death," and also to snuff out all sane discussion of Communist infiltration in this country. During 1953, the Communists and their friends established "a little iron curtain" over all accurate and intelligent discussion of Red penetration within America. They have gone so far in this direction that it is now notorious that a person cannot tell the truth fully about the actual operations of the fifth column here without being punished by certain newspapers and assailed by other interests.

This should not deter us from seeking to break through this "little iron curtain." One way it might be done is by linking up Soviet practices with those of its fifth column and allies here.

This is only the beginning. Coincident with any such efforts, there becomes necessary the uncovering of Communist fronts and evidences of concealed Communists' work and influence, both in local communities and on a larger scale wherever possible. The greater our knowledge of Communism as a whole, the better will we be prepared to carry out this more specific function. For in local organizations our presentation of the problems will be more assured, our letters to the press will be more definite, and what we ask others to do will be more positive and effective.

Cautions in Anti-Red Work

In taking up the fight against Communist fronts and Red influences on a local community basis, several cautions are timely and will make this work more effective. First of all, a local expression of a front organization cannot always be detected by a knowledge of the national fronts. Very frequently, of late, the Communists have given purely local names to divisions of Red-created organizations functioning on a national basis. But the character of the propaganda made, the type of literature distributed, and frequently the methods employed, will readily reveal the character of pro-Communist organizations traveling under local names. In both Long Island and Westchester County, New York, a knowledge of the techniques of the fifth column, and an acquaintance with the propaganda of certain national fronts, has led to the exposure of local organizations which follow the same pattern.

Another item that is worth remembering is this: Speakers with long records of participating on Communist fronts, many of which have been declared subversive by the Attorney General, are brought into various communities under the auspices of non-Communist organizations. That is what happened in 1953 in New Brunswick, New Jersey, when Dr. Frederick L. Schuman lectured to a non-Communist organization, receiving a laudatory editorial in the *New Brunswick Home News* as an authority on international affairs. Knowledge of Schuman's membership on and sponsorship of numerous fronts, and his long pro-Soviet record, would have helped alert Americans in that New Jersey city to advise the local paper of his position. In many places, the engagements of such speakers have been cancelled when their records have been revealed to the organization sponsoring them and to the local press. This occurred in 1953 in the Far Rockaways, where Morris Carnovsky's appearance was cancelled when his record was made known.

And that is the whole nub of this matter: that the actual record of these people be obtained, so that the move against them will not be based on general charges but on factual data.

The third caution follows from the second. It is this: Do not call concealed Communists or their allies by the name "Communist." This is of the utmost importance, and for several good reasons. Today it is practically impossible for a citizen or group of citizens to prove that anyone is a Communist, all vestiges of membership now having been done away with by the conspiracy. With a court or Congressional committee, the case is entirely different, since such a body has access to information which the ordinary citizen does not have and can also in specific cases subpoena ex-Communists to testify.

The law of libel must also be taken into consideration. Even though proof could be established that a certain concealed Red is a Communist, the expense involved might be colossal. That was demonstrated once and for all in the libel action by Paul Draper and Larry Adler, erstwhile Hollywood celebrities, against Mrs. Hester McCullough of Greenwich, Connecticut. Although Mrs. McCullough did not call them Communists, but merely intimated that they were, her successful defense cost her a very large sum of money.

The chief factor here, however, is being certain of having factual information at one's fingertips before making charges. The sources of information on this matter, as we now know, are extensive enough to obtain the record of those helping the conspiracy. At the risk of repetition, it must be said again that it makes little difference whether a specific person is a Communist, a fellow-traveler, or merely a dupe—if he consistently stands for those movements and proposals which undermine the United States. This has been recognized for government employees in a Presidential order making "security" the test for such employment instead of "loyalty." The same rule applies, in a slightly different way but with the same force, to those who are playing a part in public life, whether nationally or locally.

Knowing the Line

When it comes to offsetting Communist influences locally, the possibility of showing affiliation with fronts will not always be as readily available as with lecturers coming from outside. Here we have, above all, the necessity of knowing the Communist line. If we are familiar, for instance, with the fact that the Communists officially declared "McCarthyism" to be the main danger to the conspiracy in the United States, we can be prepared to point out in our communities that campaigns "against McCarthyism" are echoes of the conspiracy, whether engaged in consciously or unconsciously as such. In the June, 1953, *Political Affairs* we are advised that the fight against McCarthyism means for the Communist "the fight against Joe McCarthy the individual" and also against "each and every McCarthyite." We can take a stand for Congressional inquiries, for the Federal Bureau of Investigation, and for strong action by the Federal Government against the conspiracy as an antidote to local drives "against McCarthyism."

When resolutions are put forward in women's clubs or local men's organizations representing that Mao Tse-tung may become another Tito, we can be on guard against such ideas and oppose them as aiding the chief item in the Communist current aim to win recognition for Red China. And so it is with all items in the line at any particular period. With practice, it will be recognized after a while that the same individuals who propose one feature of the line very frequently are the proponents of other of its features. In a number of communities, it is by this method that the champions of the conspiracy have been detected, their moves observed, and their efforts stalemated or defeated. With knowledge of the line, it will be possible to dissect and expose the false peace crusades and their by-products, to unearth Red activities in "teachers' workshops," and to deal with subversive influences in local school systems.

The mere presentation of factual material on the records of individuals or groups, important as it is, will not necessarily prove to be a magic formula in and of itself. Scarsdale, New York, "the richest suburban area in the world," is exhibit A. No more careful work of documentation has been done than that of the Scarsdale Citizens Committee, which opposed subversive lecturers and books in the schools. And yet, the report of the Town Hall Committee, composed of a number of executives of large corporations, "whitewashed" the whole situation. This should not cause discouragement, since pro-Communist influences have on the whole had a free hand to work in this country for the past twenty years. With some honorable exceptions— and they must never be forgotten—there has not been during those two decades any protracted intelligent opposition to the development of these influences. It will take time and patience, particularly in some communities (and among these, we would number the richest in our country), to overcome the "poisoning of the wells" of opinion which has gone on. In most instances, calling attention to what the Communist line actually is, and what it will do to injure America, will help in the concrete fight. It will give the background and rationale of subversive events within a community, whose full evil can not be readily appreciated otherwise.

When Howard Fast's books appear as recommended or required reading in our high schools, the notoriously seditious record of this Communist author should cause their removal from library shelves. But if a prominent section of the community is so obtuse or so pro-Communist that it successfully opposes this move, it might help to show that Soviet Russia has declared that "the peace partisans" are its main hope in defeating the United States. (These are the words given officially in November, 1951, at the celebration of the Bolshevik revolution and repeated by G. M. Malenkov in the "four tasks" set down in his October, 1952, report.)

Then, if we show to the community that Howard Fast is among the chief of the "peace partisans" in the United States, that he was chosen in that capacity to write up the notorious Waldorf-Astoria conference for *Political Affairs* in 1949, he will be seen more clearly in his true light. It can be brought home to the community that he is committed continuously to destroying the government of the United States of America and to impairing the morale of our armed forces. With Dashiell Hammett, the detective story writer, it is the same. And thus, an alertness to the Communist line helps to give substance to the fight against subversion in every community. (Howard Fast, member of ten Communist fronts, is an open Communist, for which see my *The Cry Is Peace*, pp. 99, 160; also that he is a leading Communist is attested to by his writing in *Political Affairs*, official theoretical organ of the Communist Party, May 1949, pp. 29-38. Before the Senate Sub-Committee on Permanent Investigations in April 1953, Fast refused to state whether or not he would fight the Chinese Communists on behalf of the United States. Dashiell Hammett, a member of fifty Communist fronts, demonstrated his adherence to the Communist cause by undergoing a prison sentence for contempt of Congress rather than divulge the records of the Joint Anti-Fascist Refugee Committee, cited as subversive and Communist by the Attorney General on December 4, 1947.)

Foresight a Necessity

Patience and foresight, as well as persistence, are necessary to those opposing the concealed Communists and their friends. Many persons are moved emotionally against Communism, and in a meeting or other discussion of this subject, will leap up and exclaim: "Why isn't something being done?" But in almost every case of this kind, the person involved has no idea of what can be done, has not examined the local scene, and does not know the people with whom he will have to deal. This business has to be worked out like the plan for a battle. The Communists are proceeding in that fashion. Enough foresight must be put into it. Not merely the first move needs to be worked out, but also the second and sometimes the third. There is a courageous school teacher in Long Island who has great difficulty in getting books critical and analytical of Communism on the shelves of the high school library, because of the obstacles put in the way by the librarian. Determined that a study of Communism, which would show it in its true light, was a necessity, this teacher proposed that the students learn all about certain categories in man's knowledge and experience. The first of these was to be about the stars, and the second about the mountains—each project including any book related to this subject, including scientific works, adventure accounts, and poetry. To further this work, certain shelves had to be arranged in the library. To this the librarian enthusiastically agreed. After these studies had been completed, the teacher proposed an examination of Communism on the same scale, with books exposing the true nature of Communism collected in the same manner. The librarian demurred again, but as she had cooperated in the other projects, she could not now refuse. It may be added, incidentally, that this course, revealing the bankruptcy of Communism and the character of its operations, was the most popular given to the students by this teacher. It was also favorably commented on by the parents, who were surprised at what their children had learned on this subject.

Another case is that of a woman who had been a leader in civic and social work in her community and who had become aware of pro-Communist activities in her field of endeavor. Before doing anything openly against these Red tendencies, she made it a point to attend the meetings of all local organizations, including those which she suspected to be under pro-Communist leadership. She took careful notes of the various moves in that direction, the resolutions suggested, and came to observe that there was always the same group serving as a nucleus for pro-Communist proposals. Armed with this information, she was enabled to become the leader of a group which offset these moves and operated successfully against the Communist line. Included in their achievements was the shake-up in the local school board, with those members who had favored pro-Communist ideas being defeated for re-election. She continued to work for community betterment including better housing, specifically for the Negro people in that vicinity. She became impressed with the need for a rounded knowledge of how the Communists and their friends operate, and instituted a class in the techniques of Communism. The studies which this class of fifty active men and women in the community undertook has led to a strengthening of the work against Red influences in that community. Follow-up work, in the form of group meetings which kept in touch with the development of the Communist line, nationally as well as locally, has added immeasurably to the effectiveness of this work.

Such preparation need not always be so detailed or prolonged, although some of it is essential. It is not so difficult as it may seem at first blush. There are interesting features to it, also, such as figuring out how certain persons will act under certain circumstances. With the Communists and their friends, despite their claim of "flexibility," set patterns of conduct will develop which make it comparatively easy to know what they will do next.

Of course, these patterns of conduct are modified in part by the "period" in which the Communists are operating. The general line of the international conspiracy always has some effect on the tactics employed down in the grass roots. Sometimes the dominant *motif* will be one of Trojan Horse blandishments, as was the case between 1936 and 1939 and again during World War II. Sometimes it will be extreme belligerency, as during the first period of the "cold war." Sometimes it will be a combination of the two—as in 1953. But in all "periods" the pattern remains substantially the same, always based in general upon the strategy and tactics laid down by Stalin.

Thus, in 1953, the Communists planned to penetrate the two major political parties or, as they put it, "the Democratic party and areas of the Republican party," but continued to hang on to the American Labor Party, to attempt penetration of the Political Action Committee of the CIO, and to influence the American Federation of Labor's political actions—building up "independent labor" entities through which they can blackmail or bludgeon certain politicians into line. They are also planning extended infiltration into the CIO and AFL, holding on at the same time to their own Red-ruled unions as means of finally getting back into the general labor movement to capture it. This tactic was applied with great success in France and Italy during

KNOWLEDGE AND FACTS AS WEAPONS

the "people's front period." So, too, in 1953 the Reds had as their objectives the infiltration and capture of "Negro bourgeois organizations," and specifically the National Association for the Advancement of Colored People. But this does not preclude them, when routed in local branches of the NAACP, from going out and forming "independent" Negro groups under their complete control. With these groups, they hope to harass the local divisions of the NAACP, and finally to rejoin that body, with the aid of certain sympathetic individuals near the top, either through the "united front" tactic or as individuals. Through the "united front" device, they would propose "merger" of the two groups, hoping in that way to re-capture control.

All such moves can be anticipated, and if anticipated can be nipped in the bud.

Letters to the Press

Every local group that opposes Communism must be informed as to the great weight the Communists place on letters to the press and to our public officials. Even the most cursory glance at a few copies of the *Daily Worker* will bring that home. Letters written to newspapers in all parts of the country and supporting the Communist line, are featured, in order that they will be copied by others. Resolutions or individual expressions which bring pressure on the government are played up, with the like intent. Those opposing Communism must remember that the average American is much more conscious of the danger of the Communist line than many public officials, editors, or so-called "intellectuals." But this average American normally does not have those ready means to express himself which self-appointed committees, which the Communists can more or less easily penetrate, have at their command. The writing of letters to newspapers becomes of the highest importance.

Here again it is essential to introduce the facts into every such attempt. The Communists and their friends can engage in misrepresentations and distortions and still will be given full credence by too many newspapers. We see this in the 1953 attack on Dr. J. B. Matthews which caused his resignation as an investigator for the Senate Sub-Committee under the chairmanship of Senator Joseph R. McCarthy. The occasion of the attack was an article by Dr. Matthews in the *American Mercury* magazine which showed the Communist front membership of many Protestant clergymen, supported by names and other factual data. This article was widely misrepresented as an assault "upon religious beliefs," whereas it was in reality an attempt to alert and protect the churches against Communist penetration. Many prominent persons who criticized this article clearly had never read it, but merely joined in the cry stimulated by the Communists.

The same rule applies with regard to letters to the newspapers. The Reds and their allies can write the most fantastic and non-factual communications, and they will frequently be published. But the critic of Communism and particularly of the Communist line must be certain to have the facts, well presented, if he wishes publication. Even then, he must expect difficulties and not be disappointed if his communications do not always appear.

Fortunately, we now know that there are many sources of information at our disposal. In some instances, local groups have resorted to a pooling of information in connection with letter writing. That is, two or three persons who are in positions to get hold of the facts more readily than others are assigned to find out what should go into certain letters. Sometimes these persons write the letters and they are signed by others. In that way, each member of a group can express himself and be certain that what he writes is accurate and effective.

If letter-writing is persisted in, the results will often be surprising. Sometimes such letters will affect a newspaper's policy, if only for a time. That is what occurred in early 1953 in New York City, when a deluge of spontaneous communications favorable to Senator Joseph R. McCarthy momentarily impressed the dailies there. So many of our local newspapers today enjoy a monopoly position that if a local daily is given to appeasement, it is very difficult to effect any change in its attitude. But even if it prints only a limited number of letters expressing the patriotic American opinion, these are bound to arouse support in the community.

The news columns of the papers should not be neglected. Whenever it is feasible, items should be released to the newspapers, either publicizing resolutions adopted by local organizations or expressing the views of an individual who can command attention. These resolutions and views will not have their maximum effectiveness if merely issued for private consumption. For this reason, someone who is conversant with newspaper work will prove to be a valuable ally.

When it is impossible to get adequate coverage in the local papers, either because of their peculiar view of what is news or because of their appeasement tendencies, special bulletins can be prepared and distributed through the community. This method has proved to be of value in many situations. Such a bulletin must be carefully prepared, not only to assure accuracy of the facts but also to give the authorities for the statements made. The voluminous hearings and reports of Congressional committees can be drawn on for this purpose.

To bring this work to head from time to time, it is almost imperative that lecturers be scheduled to speak publicly. While it is taken for granted that the speakers will be conversant with the subject, special pains should be taken to have them direct their remarks toward the main issues which are then being raised in regard to Communist infiltration. There has been too much of a tendency to generalize about Communism, and this has frequently overshot the mark. In arranging any lecture program, the plan will be largely valueless unless the lecturer comes to grips with apparent manifestations of the Communist line. Sometimes this will arouse the bitter opposition of the appeasement forces, but that is a sign that the work is hitting home. If no opposition arises to what a local group is doing, then a thorough examination should be made of its procedure;

frequently it will be found that its efforts are too general to interfere with the Communists and their friends in any way.

Setting Up Community Classes

From a rounded out understanding of the Communist problem, it will readily be recognized that community work against Red influences will be greatly aided by an intelligent study by community leaders of the philosophy and techniques of Communism. This is underscored today by the Report of the Senate Sub-Committee on Internal Security of July 17, 1953, entitled, *Subversive Influence in the Educational Process*. Among its few but emphatic recommendations was this one: "That school authorities, colleges, and local boards of education institute positive programs, under qualified experts in the field of combating Communism, to teach both teachers and school pupils the nature of the Communist conspiracy that is attacking the whole structure of our society."

This recommendation applies with equal force to community leaders, representing various organizations in a locality, town, or city. These courses, which can follow the outline of this book, have a great advantage in that they can also bring in current documents to enlighten the students on the subjects covered. On the question of the nature of Communism and its objectives, for instance, good use can be made of the Report of the Subversive Activities Control Board on the Communist Party and its role as an agent of Moscow.

When reports of this character are used to supplement such material as appears in these pages, it is well to direct attention to the authorities and documents cited. The Report of the Subversive Activities Control Board contains references to Communist official writings on Marxism-Leninism, to the Leninist theory of imperialism, and to an analysis of "democratic centralism" which are valuable supplements to the present book. (Report of Subversive Activities Control Board, April 23, 1953, Senate Document number 41, 83rd Congress, first session.)

Beyond the Local Field

Local groups opposing Communism cannot confine what they do solely to their respective communities. If that is their practice, the national battle for public opinion will go by default to the Communist camp. To give one example: Television and radio programs have been fairly heavily overloaded with pro-Communist commentators and participants in "forum" discussions. There is some obligation on the part of every American to protest against these pro-Communists, both to the radio stations and to the sponsors of the respective programs. It is an added obligation to insist that commentators and participants who have some critical and analytical knowledge of Communism can be given a voice over the air. Since television and radio, with a number of honorable exceptions, have contributed to the vacillations in enough areas of American opinion to affect even the government, this business of bringing pressure on these agencies is no second-rate undertaking. The Communists know that very well. A considerable part of the prestige of Norman Corwin, which built him up as a radio program expert until he was put in charge of such work for the United Nations, arose from the "audience support" mustered for him by the *Daily Worker*.

Anyone who examines a few copies of the *Daily Worker* will be struck by the constant directives given its readers to let Congress and the President know what they think. Most representatives and senators are not acquainted with the latest phase of the Communist line and do not know that these Red-stimulated communications have their source in the headquarters of the Stalinite conspiracy. Although American patriots are learning more and more to bring issues to the attention of their representatives and senators, much more has yet to be done. Organized local groups, even though not large, can accomplish a great deal in this direction. In 1953, these groups as well as all genuine Americans were called upon to advise their representatives and senators that congressional inquiries must be continued, since not one-half the information that exists on Communist infiltration has yet been exposed. They also had an obligation to emphasize the urgency for the United States to insist that Great Britain, if it is our "ally," withdraw its recognition of Red China. Although the average American thinks overwhelmingly in these terms, there was not enough expression of his thoughts to beat back fully the uproar created in the appeasement press favorable to the Communists.

Letters to representatives and senators need not be long; indeed, it is better if they are as brief as possible. They should, however, be clear-cut and to the point, and evade all vagueness in expression which will weaken their force and effect.

Beyond Mere Defense

In taking such measures on public affairs, individuals and groups cannot content themselves with merely offsetting the Communist line; they must beat it back. In defending Congressional inquiries into subversion in education, it is well to go beyond mere defense and to urge that the investigations be expanded. It is also advisable to accompany this insistence with a demand on the local school and college authorities to clean their own houses when necessary. The Reds, since they are on the offensive, appreciate that if they can win a stalemate, either internally or internationally, they can use that stalemate to disintegrate their enemies and eventually move forward again. That is their precise plan in the Korean "truce." It is their tactic in many local situations, and of course flows from Stalin's instructions in the *Foundations of Leninism.* A stalemate, whether on the domestic or on the international scene, is therefore a great disadvantage to those opposing Communism.

It is almost trite to say that every error contains a half-truth. Otherwise, the error would not be accepted at all by the mind of man. Communism is no exception to this rule. It has built up its successes on the imposition of an iron dictatorship, ruled by a small bureaucracy and maintained by deceit and force. But it has given a semblance of reasonableness to its proposals by taking advantage of the weaknesses in the world about us. Hence it is that Communists make such a display of their "devotion" to the cause of the workers, the Negro people, and "colonial liberation," although they betray their pledges once the Soviet dictatorship comes into power.

This Red tactic does serve to remind us, however, that positive measures for the strengthening of the American Republic are not to be forgotten. To the contrary, they are a proper facet of the battle against Communism. To defend the rights of free labor unions and to oppose discrimination against the Negro people are *must* actions. These measures are not taken primarily to combat Communism. They are carried forward so that the political health of our Republic will be assured and the demand for social justice satisfied.

An understanding of our American form of government will help us in all this work. It will reveal, for one thing, that our form of government has the means to defend itself against a conspiracy to overthrow it and also the means to deal with the internal subversion so prevalent at the present moment within our own borders. To bring about such a defense, an atmosphere has to be created which will give the leaders of the nation the will and alertness to proceed. How far the Communists have been able to go in distorting our processes can be seen in the constant plea of the fifth amendment as a protection against testifying. This plea is made successfully, even though being a Communist is not a crime in the United States, as it should be, and even though the chief purpose of the refusal is not to have to act as a witness in matters concerning the security of the United States. Even the proposal of Senator Pat McCarran of Nevada, that immunity be granted certain witnesses in order to compel them to testify, has met with the strenuous opposition of the Communists and their friends. This opposition throws light on the real reasons for the appeal to the fifth amendment. If anyone looks back across the history of our Republic and notes, among other things, President Lincoln's suspension of the writ of habeas corpus in a moment of national crisis, he will be impressed with the possibilities that exist for internal as well as external defense by the United States.

We can devote ourselves to exposing the fallacies of Communist economics, to which this book has not been able to pay detailed attention. In the name of opposing monopoly capital the Communists build up the most tyrannical monopoly of all, that of the dictatorship. In the name of opposing the lack of proper rewards to the workers, they deprive the working people of all ownership. Our attitude has to be, however, a positive one, as Bishop Fulton J. Sheen stresses in his valuable work, *Communism and the Conscience of the West*, in which he brings forward the importance of profit sharing as a necessary feature.

The fundamental philosophy of Communism can be answered only by a firm and enlightened belief in God. Nothing will give more strength to the hand-to-hand combat against the conspiracy, made possible by a knowledge of its techniques, than a great Credo from the hearts and minds of the American people. Those who are educated and among whom the ravages of unbelief have particularly paved the way for an acceptance of the doctrines of Red slavery, have a peculiar obligation to assert: "I believe in God, the Father Almighty, Creator of Heaven and earth." That humble expression of faith is the beginning of wisdom in the battle against Communism.

INDEX

INDEX

Abbot, Edith, 231
Aberdeen Training Center, 295
Abt, John, 163, 178
Academic freedom, 97, 138, 148, 159, 222, 246
Academy of Social Sciences, 103
Acheson, Dean, 136, 264, 287
Adams, James Luther, 231
Adler, Larry, 317
Adler, Solomon, 281
Aesopian language, 42-44, 58, 97
African Aid Committee, 170, 175
agrarian reformers, 42
Allen, James S., 228, 256, 257
Allis-Chalmers, 191
Amalgamated Clothing Workers, 178
Amerasia, 228
American Assocation of School Administrators, 201
American Association of Scientific Workers, 242
American Committee for Democracy and Intellectual Freedom, 170
American Committee for the Protection of the Foreign Born, 170, 175
American Communications Association, 193, 196
American Federation of Labor, 134, 185, 189, 204, 322
American Jewish League Against Communism, 276
American Labor Party, 161, 170, 178, 302
American League Against War

and Fascism, 35, 92, 175, 214, 220
American League for Peace and Democracy, 93, 170, 175
American Legion, 310
American Library Association, 227
American Newspaper Guild, 163
American Peace Crusade, 92, 176
American Peace Mobilization, 93, 241
American Russian Institute, 170
American Women for Peace, 92
Americans for Democratic Action, 128
Amherst College, 211
anarchists, 183, 184
anti-Semitism, 273
Apertheker, Herbert, 228
Aquinas, St. Thomas, 15, 16, 69
Asia for the Asiatics, 42, 87

Baltisky, N., 53-56, 58
Barr, Stringfellow, 174
Bedacht, Max, 281
Bentley, Elizabeth, 174, 234, 236, 280, 286, 290, 310
Benton, William, 287
Beria, Lavrenti P., 130
Berle, Adolf A., 136
Berman, Lionel, 33, 34
Bernal, John Desmond, 242
Bernocici, Leonard (Berkowitz), 285
Bernstein, Eduard, 72
Bible College, 232
Biddle, Attorney General Francis, 128

333

big lie, the, 58
Bill of Rights Committee, 170
Bisson, T. A., 235
Bittelman, Alexander, 24, 25, 49, 50, 52, 74, 76, 94
Board of Economic Warfare, 164
Board of Regents, N. Y., 312
Bodde, Dirk, 232
Bogolepov, Igor, 89, 173
Bolshevik, The, 133
Bolshevization, 110-15
book-burning, 128, 136, 249, 299-301
Book Union, 170
Boston University, 227, 232, 234
Boyer, Richard, 222, 243
Bradley, Lyman K., 118
Brameld, Theodore, 220-23, 247
Bretton Woods Conference, 235
Brewster, Dorothy, 231
Bridges, Harry, 31, 193, 200
Brooklyn College, 229
Brooklyn Polytechnic Institute, 212, 227
Brotherhood of Railway Car Men, 185
Browder, Earl, 23, 35, 61, 62, 107, 108, 165, 176, 197, 261, 293
Browderism, 52, 60
Brunauer, Esther, 286
Brunauer, Stephen, 286
Bryn Mawr College, 227, 237
Bryson, Hugh, 193
Burgum, Edwin Barry, 168
Butler, Alben, 231

cadres, 27, 80, 102, 103, 108
Cahiers du Communisme, 133
California Committee on Un-American Activities, 36
Calomiris, Angela, 310
Camp Beacon, 116
Camp Nitgedaiget, 116
Cannery and Agricultural Workers Industrial Union, 187
captive organization, 35

Carey, James B., 161, 190, 192, 201, 202, 203
Carlson, Anton J., 231, 240, 241, 242
Carlson, Oliver, 247
Carnap, Rudolf, 231
cell (Communist), 38, 39, 153, 179, 190, 224, 229, 281, 296, 305
Chamberlin, William Henry, 282, 314
Chambers, Whittaker, 174, 236, 279, 280, 281, 290, 294, 310
Charney, George Blake, 212, 289
Chi, Dr., 28
Chiang Kai-shek, 161
"China lobby," 145
Chinese Communist Party, 85, 101
Chicago Federation of Labor, 185
Churchill, Sir Winston, 107
C. I. Rep. (Communist International Representative), 23, 26, 28
City College of New York, 232
civil liberties, 55, 97, 127, 148, 201
Civil Rights Congress, 32, 33, 170, 176
class struggle, 14, 16, 20, 65, 83, 116
classless society, 10, 11, 12, 15, 57, 68, 73, 75, 80
class war, 27, 37, 83, 101
Clausewitz, General, 20
Clubb, Oliver E., 287
coalition government, 160, 251
cold war, 21, 53, 54, 108, 267, 275, 322
Coe, Virginius Frank, 235, 236, 288
Columbia University, 166, 169, 211, 212, 215, 227, 229, 230, 231
Commissions (of C. P.), 29
Cominform, 23, 25
Cominform organ, 26
Comintern (Communist International), 22, 23, 25, 26, 121, 236

Committee for a Democratic Far Eastern Policy, 170
Committee for Peaceful Alternatives to the Atlantic Pact, 92
Committee on Un-American Activities (House), 33, 119, 165
Communism, philosophy of, 6, 13, 126, 182, 229, 326
Communism, Soviet, 3
Communist apparatus, 20, 21, 26, 38
Communist front, 32, 92, 100, 164, 208, 290
Communist International, 20, 25, 65
Communist line, 34, 36, 38, 41, 85, 88-97, 109, 129, 130, 133, 139, 140, 206, 248, 303, 309, 310
Communist Manifesto, 8, 70, 72, 184
Communist Party (USSR), 25
Comrade Juniper, 190
concentration policy, 196-99
Congress of Industrial Organizations, 134, 147, 163, 181, 188, 189, 322
containment, 141
contradictions, 60
control commission, 225, 226
Coplon, Judith, 291
Cornell University, 227
Corwin, Norman, 327
cosmopolitanism, 274
Council on African Affairs, 267
Counterattack, 310
Counts, George S., 217, 222
Cranfield, Harold, 179
criticism, 106, 108, 109, 110
Cross, Ephraim, 232
cultural commission, 29, 33
Cultural and Scientific Conference for World Peace, 171, 175
Curran, Joseph, 194
Currie, Lauchlin, 285
Czolgosz, Leon, 183

Daily Worker, 26, 29, 90, 99, 127, 135, 136, 137
Dallin, David, 9, 73, 311
Davis, Benjamin J., 257
Davis, Elmer, 285
deceit, 13, 93
DeBoer, John J., 285
DeJaegher, Rev. Raymond, 277
DeLacey, Hugh, 296
democratic centralism, 22, 23
Democratic Party, 322
Dennis, Eugene, 111-14
Department of Agriculture, 281
Department of Commerce, 287
Department of Defense, 233
Department of Justice, 128, 179
Department of Labor, 288
Dewey, John, 214, 215, 217, 218, 223
dialectical materialism, 7, 8, 15, 18, 65, 67, 78
dictatorship (of proletariat), 3, 6, 8-11, 15, 21, 25, 40, 46, 48, 65, 67, 71, 85, 100, 182, 186
Dimitrov, George, 160
Dimock, Edward, 262
Dimock, Marshall, 233, 234
directives, v, vi, 20, 80, 114, 129, 137, 148, 160
discipline, Bolshevik, 27, 29, 37, 40, 41, 97, 123
Dodd, Bella, 213, 216, 225, 226
Dohrenwend, Otto E., 228, 229
Dolivet, Louis, 229
Douglas, Dorothy, 231, 233
Douglas, William O., 254
Draper, Paul, 229, 317
Du Bois, W. E. B., 177, 228
Duclos, Jacques, 282
Duggan, Lawrence, 282
Dulles, John Foster, 145, 146

East-West trade, 131, 139, 140, 141
Eby, Kermit, 231
economic determinism, 14
Einstein, Albert, 232

Eisler, Gerhart, 26, 123, 163, 173, 236
Emergency Civil Liberties Committee, 230
Emerson, Thomas I., 231, 235
Emspak, Julius, 190, 191, 192
Engels, Frederick, 8, 15, 66
Epstein, Israel, 228, 235, 284
espionage, 123, 154, 169, 211, 229, 278, 279, 284, 290, 297
espionage rings, 122, 123, 234, 286

Fairbank, John K., 87
Fairchild, Henry Pratt, 211
Fair Employment Practices Act, 269
Fascism, 20, 61, 94, 138, 225
Fast, Howard, 218, 227, 228, 234, 319, 320
Federal Bureau of Investigation, 122, 128, 179, 241, 286, 299, 301, 302, 304, 305
Federated Farmer Labor Party, 186
Federation of Architects, Engineers, Chemists, and Technicians, 169, 245
Feuerbach, Ludwig, 14, 66
Field, Frederick Vanderbilt, 33, 72, 118, 235, 287
fifth amendment, 236-39
fifth column, 40, 73, 91, 102, 126, 143, 158, 170, 173, 183, 195, 208, 213, 224, 233, 251, 299, 315
Finley, Moses, 212
Fischer, Louis, 313
Fitzgerald, Albert E., 192
Fitzgerald, Edward, 293, 294
Fitzpatrick, John, 185
Flaxer, Abram, 295
Flynn, Elizabeth Gurley, 32
Fogg, Kathleen, 296
Food, Tobacco, Agricultural and Allied Workers, 193

Food Workers Industrial Union, 187
For a Lasting Peace, for a People's Democracy, 4, 26, 127, 132
Ford, James W., 256, 257
Foreman, Clark H., 231, 266
Forman, Harrison, 228
Foster, William Z., 5, 11, 23, 59, 60, 125, 185, 188, 189, 239, 255, 293
Four Freedoms, 155
Freiheit, 274
Friends of Soviet Russia, 231

General Electric Corporation, 200, 205
genocide, 32, 264, 265
Gideonse, Harry, 247
Gitlow, Benjamin, 310
Glaser, Eda, 294
Glasser, Harold, 289, 290
Gold, Ben, 188, 193, 195, 292
Goldman, Irving, 229
Golos, Jacob, 123
Goslin, Willard, 246, 247
Gouzenko, Igor, 243
Government Printing Office, 305
Graham, Frank P., 266
Granger, Lester V., 270
Grauman, Jacob, 288, 293, 294
Green, P., 162
Greenberg, Michael, 284
Gretzinger, Marguerite, 215
Gussev, Sergei Ivanovitch, 162, 163

Haas, Bishop Francis J., 204
Hall, Gus, 102
Halperin, Maurice, 232, 234, 235, 285, 286
Hammett, Dashiell, 33, 319, 320
Harburg, E. Y., 34
Harding College, 206
Harlow, S. Ralph, 231
Harper, Fowler V., 231

Harvard University, 165, 222, 227, 231
Haverford College, 227, 230
Haywood, Harry, 259, 261
Hegel, Georg W. F., 14
Heller, A. A., 119, 214
Hellman, Lillian, 34, 228
Henderson, Donald, 193
Hicks, Granville, 219
Hillman, Sidney, 178
Hiskey, Clarence A., 212
Hiss, Alger, 72, 123, 163, 236, 254, 280, 281
Hitler-Stalin alliance, 30, 93, 111, 164, 212, 242, 274
Hood, William, 36, 267
Hook, Sidney, 219, 222
Hotel and Restaurant Workers Union, 169
Hughes, Langston, 228
Hunter College, 212, 229, 232
Hunter, Edward, 247

illegal activities, 96, 116, 122, 123
Independent Citizens Committee of the Arts, Sciences, and Professions, 34
Industrial Workers of the World, 185
infiltration, 24, 28, 30, 32, 35, 36, 89, 93, 115, 122, 123, 128, 153, 154, 156, 157, 208, 210, 213, 278, 279, 280, 281, 290, 293,
Information Bureau of Communist and Workers' Parties (Cominform), 21
Institute of Pacific Relations, 38, 118, 158, 178, 254, 283, 284
International Association of Machinists, 189
International Bank of Reconstruction and Development, 288
International Brotherhood of Painters, Paperhangers, and Decorators, 189
International Fur and Leather Workers Union, 161, 188, 193, 206
International Harvester Company, 203
International Labor Defense, 32, 265
International Longshore and Warehousemen's Union, 193, 200
International Monetary Fund, 235, 282
International Union of Electrical Workers (CIO), 205
International Union of Mine, Mill, and Smelter Workers, 193
International Workers Order, 177, 302
Isaacs, Stanley, 297

Jacoby, Annalee, 228
Jaffe, Philip, 281, 286
Jefferson School of Social Science, 118-22, 168, 171, 175, 221, 244
Jenner, Senator William, 128, 148
Jerome, V. J., 29, 225
Johns Hopkins University, 235
Johnson, Manning, 259, 269, 277
Joint Anti-Fascist Refugee Committee, 169, 175, 241, 320
Joliot-Curie, Frederick, 242
Jules, Mervin, 231

Kautsky, Karl, 62
Kersten, Charles E., 190, 310
Kilpatrick, William H., 217
Kleinberg, Otto, 228
Knowland, William, 144
Korea, 30, 56, 60, 94, 126, 140, 141, 284
Kravchenko, Victor, 313
Kremlin, 28, 54, 125
Krivitsky, W. G., 314
Kropotkin, Prince Peter, 183
Kuhn, Irene, 218, 277

Lamont, Corliss, 228, 231
language groups (of C. P.), 276

Lansberg, Hans, 287
Lardner, Ring, Jr., 34
Larkin, Oliver, 231
Lattimore, Owen, 87, 145, 228, 235, 284, 285, 287
Lauterbach, Richard, 228
Lautner, John, 212
Lawrence, David, 128, 300, 304
Lawson, John Howard, 34
League of American Writers, 171, 241
League of Struggle for Negro Rights, 265
Lehman, Herbert H., 128, 295
Lenin, V. I., 3, 5, 69-71, 73, 76, 77, 98, 99
Lewis, Fulton, Jr., 304
Lezevsky, Solomon, 186
liberalism, 108
Liberal Party, 161
liberation, 58, 85, 97
Liu Shao-chi, 104
Loewenberg, Bert, 229
Louisville Courier-Journal, 142
Lovett, Robert Morss, 210
Loyalty Review Board, 286
Luccock, Halford E., 231
Lynd, Robert S., 211, 231
Lyons, Eugene, 66, 218

Macalester College, 232
Mackay, John A., 231
Magdoff, Harry, 293, 294
Malenkov, Georgi M., 5, 6, 9, 11, 17, 37, 60, 70, 73, 124, 130, 319
Manuilsky, D. Z., 4, 43, 44, 47, 48
Mao Tse-tung, 42, 101, 140, 161, 318
Marine Transport Industrial Union, 187
Marcantonio, Vito, 273
Marx, Karl, 8, 10, 14, 66, 184
Marxism-Leninism, viii, 5, 8, 13, 16-19, 26, 41, 44-53, 58, 66, 75-78, 98, 103, 105, 112-14, 117, 119, 124, 171, 209, 210, 214, 253

Marzani, Carl, 285
Massachusetts Institute of Technology, 168, 227, 230
Masses and Mainstream, 148, 168
mass organization, 35, 36, 42, 117, 153, 157, 163, 298
Massing, Hede, 123
materialism, 15, 229
Matles, James, 190-94
Mather, Kirtley, 165, 231, 240, 242
Matthews, Dr. J. B., 211, 232, 247, 328
McCarran, Senator Pat, 329
McCarran Act, 94
McCarran Sub-Committee on Internal Security, 55, 89
McCarthy, Senator Joseph R., 128, 131, 140, 148, 228, 239, 286
"McCarthyism," 94, 127, 128, 134, 135, 143, 147, 148, 225, 299, 318, 324
McCullough, Hester, 317
McKinley, William, 183
McMillen, Wayne, 231
McWilliams, Carey, 228
Medina, Judge Harold R., 45, 261
Meigs, Peveril, 286
Melby, Ernest O., 248
Merrill, Lewis, 119
Mexican Americans, 269, 271, 272
Meyer, Agnes E., 201
Meyer, Frank, 120
Meyer, Peter, 312
Mid-Century Conference for Peace, 92, 232, 273
Mikolajczyk, Stanislaw, 161
Mikoyan, A. I., 18
Miller, Arthur, 298
Mindel, Jacob "Pop," 116
minority groups, 250, 276, 277
Mitchell, Kate, 228
Mitchener, Lou, 31
Montague, Montague Francis Ashley, 232
Moore, Harriet Lucy, 235, 239
morality, Communist, 13, 116

Morgenthau, Harry, 281
Morgenthau plan, 281
Morris, Robert, 288
Morrison, Philip D., 239, 240, 241
Mt. Holyoke College, 232
Murray, Philip, 191, 192

National Association for the Advancement of Colored People, 265, 267, 268-71, 323
National Committee (CPUSA), 23, 27, 107, 196
National Council for American Soviet Friendship, 172, 231
National Council of the Arts, Sciences, and Professions, 33, 34, 92, 171, 175
National Education Association, vi, 219
National Federation for Constitutional Liberties, 32, 171, 241
National Labor Conference for Peace, 92
National Labor Relations Board, 203, 205, 235
National Lawyers Guild, 165-79, 180
National Maritime Union, 194
National Miners Union, 187
National Negro Congress, 265, 266
National Negro Labor Council, 26, 265, 267
National Research Project, 288
National Textile Workers Union, 187
National Union of Marine Cooks and Stewards, 193
National Urban League, 270
Needle Trades Industrial Union, 187, 188
Negro Soviet Republic, 256-59
Nelson, Eleanor, 193, 295
Nelson, Steve, 245
Newlon, Jesse H., 217-19, 222
New Masses, 168
New Times, 26, 133, 137

New York Joint Council, 169, 188
New York University, 211, 219, 229, 230, 232
Nineteenth Party Congress, USSR, 6, 11, 18, 73, 106, 126, 129
Nixon, Richard M., 234, 290, 310
Noel, William, 277
Nolan, William A., 261, 263, 268
North American Aircraft, 31, 191
North American Cyanimid Company, 203

Oberlin College, 232
Odets, Clifford, 228
Office of Strategic Services, 123, 164, 234, 285
Office of War Information, 164, 285
Old Age Pension Union, 297
Olgin, M., 22
Open Letter, 161-63, 173, 196, 209, 218, 219, 265
open schools (CP), 103
opportunism, 61
Osman, Arthur, 194
Overstreet, Harry A., 247
Owen, Robert, 14

Pact of Peace, 86, 90, 93, 94, 142
Palmer, Ben W., 230
Panofsky, Dr. Erwin, 232
Panuch, J. Anthony, 254, 287, 288
Parent-Teachers Association, 38, 229
Parker, Dorothy, 228
Patterson, William L., 32, 33, 264
Pauker, Anna, 101
Pauling, Linus C., 239, 240
peace crusades, 86, 87, 92
Peace Information Center, 92
peace partisans, 319
people's front, 209, 265
People's World, 145, 149
Pepper, John (Pogany), 26, 256
Perry, Ralph Barton, 231
Peters, J., 21, 22, 103, 121, 236, 237, 281

Peters, John, 231
Pius XI, Pope, 11, 77, 78, 79
Politburo (Political Bureau of CPUSA), 22, 28, 29, 30, 38, 112, 113, 159, 197
Political Affairs, 26, 90, 127, 133, 136, 137
political strike, 182
Posniac, Edward, 286
Potsdam agreement, 60, 126, 282
pragmatism, 214, 215
Pressman, Lee, 163
Primus, Pearl, 229
Princeton Institute for Advanced Study, 232
Princeton Theological Seminary, 231
progressive education, 215, 216, 220
Progressive Education Association, 217, 219, 224
Progressive Citizens of America, 171, 241
Progressive Party, 175
proletariat, 9, 10
Proudhon, Joseph, 14
psychological warfare, 57, 109, 126, 153, 166, 255

Quill, Michael, 194

Rapp-Coudert Committee, 120
Rautenstrauch, Walter, 119, 211, 231
Red China, 56, 86, 87, 93, 125, 142, 143, 154, 248, 253, 254, 318
Red International of Labor Unions, 186
Red Poland, 86, 154
Reed College, 232
reformist, 3, 49, 62, 65, 69, 95, 96, 251, 265
religion, 66
Republican Party, 322
reserves, 90, 94, 210, 300

Reuther, Walter, 178, 190, 200, 201, 203
revisionism, 3, 42, 49, 61, 62, 107, 108, 261
Rhee, Syngman, 144, 145
Riess, Bernard F., 212, 229
Robeson, Paul, 218, 264, 267
Robinson, Jackie, 264
Roosevelt, Franklin D., 34, 89, 93, 107, 146, 206, 285, 287
Rosenberg, Julius and Ethel, 244-46, 290
Rubin, Jay, 189
Rugg, Harold, 218, 219
Rutgers University, 212, 230, 232

Sabath, Adolph, 298
sabotage, 111
Sacher, Harry, 119
Saint-Simon, 14
Salt, Waldo, 285
Sarah Lawrence College, 227, 229
Scarsdale Citizens Committee, 228, 318
Scherer, Marcel, 245
Schlauch, Margaret, 119
Schultz, Rabbi Benjamin, 274, 275
Schuman, Frederick L., 89, 172-75, 210, 211, 231, 316
Schwartz, Harry A., 73
Science and Society, 148, 214
science of society, 15, 19, 168
Scottsboro case, 262
secret police, 57, 130
secret schools (CP), 103, 115, 116, 117
Seldes, George, 228
self-criticism, 106-10, 115
self-determination in the Black Belt, 162, 255-60, 271
self-incrimination, 213, 234
Selly, Joseph, 193
Selsam, Howard, 120, 121
Sergio, Lisa, 229
Service, John Stewart, 286
Seventh World Congress, 3, 4, 160, 188

Shafer, Paul W., 220
Shapley, Harlow, 165, 222, 231, 239, 240, 244
Sheen, Bishop Fulton J., 330
Shoe and Leather Workers Industrial Union, 187
Sinclair, H. F., 312
Siskind, George, 116, 117
Sixth World Congress, 5, 64, 74, 187, 250, 256
Slansky, Rudolf, 101, 109
slave labor camps, 57
Smedley, Agnes, 228, 284
Smith, Louise Pettibone, 232
Smith Act, 94, 178, 261
Smith College, 227, 231, 233
Snow, Edgar, 228
social democrats, 184
Sokolsky, George, 304, 409
Southern Conference for Human Welfare, 266
Soviet Communism, nature of, 7, 11, 73
Snyder, Richard Carlton, 230
Spanish Rescue Ship Mission, 241, 242
Stachel, Jack, 120
Stalin, J. V., 4-6, 12, 17, 18, 35, 51, 52, 61, 70, 71, 73, 104, 107, 114, 117, 118, 134, 208, 260, 293, 299
State Department, vii, 32, 55, 123, 154, 161, 164, 167, 234, 280, 283, 284, 287, 300
Steel and Metal Workers Industrial Union, 187, 190
Stefansson, Vilhjalmur, 228
Stein, Guenther, 228, 235, 284
Steinberg, Julien, 108, 312
Stern, Bernhard J., 166-70, 212, 213, 231
Stern, Charlotte Todes, 168, 169
Stettinius, Edward R., Jr., 287
Stevens, Bennett (Stern), 168, 214
Stockholm Peace Appeal, 92, 242
Stone, William T., 287
strategy, Communist, vi, vii

strikes, 30, 31, 186, 191, 197
Struik, Dirk J., 119, 168, 240, 244, 245
Subversive Activities Control Board, 303, 326
Sub-Committee on Internal Security, vii, 120, 121, 123
Supreme Soviet, USSR, 5
Swarthmore College, 230
Syndicalist League of North America, 185
Syndicalists, 184, 185

tactics, Communist, vii, 9, 13, 84, 91, 93, 94, 101, 169, 246
tactic, smear, 248
tailism, 99
Taylor, George, 285
Teachers Union, 118, 226
Teheran, 60, 61, 107, 108
Tennien, Rev. Mark, 277
Thomas, Elbert, 298
Thompson, John B., 231
Thorez, Maurice, 61
Togliatti, Palmiro, 4
Tool and Die Makers Union, 189
Town Club (Scarsdale), 229, 318
Trachtenberg, Alexander, 29, 119
Trade Union Educational League, 185-88
Trade Union Unity League, 187-88
transmission belts, 35, 36, 127, 132, 133, 163, 165, 298, 299
Transport Workers Union of America, 194
Travis, Morris, 193
Treasury Department, 235, 289
Trojan Horse policy, 134, 147, 160, 209, 268
Turck, Charles J., 232
Tydings Committee, 287

Union Theological Seminary, 211
United Automobile, Aircraft, and Agricultural Implement Workers Union, CIO, 31, 36, 179, 200, 267

United Brotherhood of Carpenters
  and Joiners, 189, 190
United Electrical, Radio, and Ma-
  chine Workers Union, "UE,"
  36, 161, 178, 190, 193, 194, 203
United Federal Workers, 296
united front, 159, 160, 188
United Furniture Workers, 193
United Mine Workers, 189
United Nations, 32, 234, 281, 286,
  288
United Office and Professional
  Workers, 119, 193
United Public Workers, 193, 295,
  296
University of California, 235
University of Chicago, 211, 227,
  231
University of Kansas, 232
University of Kentucky, 232
University of Miami, 232
University of Nebraska, 232
University of Oregon, 232
University of Pennsylvania, 232
University of West Virginia, 232

vanguard, the, 10, 24, 27, 35, 48,
  67, 74, 75, 91, 99, 104, 253
Velde, Harold H., 128, 148
Veterans of Abraham Lincoln
  Brigade, 171, 176
Vincent, John Carter, 284
violence, 8, 9, 47, 52, 78, 96

Waldorf-Astoria Conference, 92,
  176, 221, 241
Wallace, Henry A., 163

Walton, Eda Lou, 232
Ward, Harry F., 119, 211
Ware cell, 179
Warne, Colston E., 211, 233, 234
War Production Board, 288, 293
Watson, Goodwin, 218-20
Webb, Sidney and Beatrice, 89,
  231
Weiner, Robert William, 233
Weintraub, David, 293, 294
Weir, Ernest T., 248
Wellesley College, 232
Weltfish, Gene, 212
White, Harry Dexter, 280, 281,
  282, 289
White, Theodore, 228
White, William L., 314
white chauvinism, 255, 263
Wholesale and Retail Workers,
  189, 194
Williams, Albert Rhys, 228
Williams, Boris, 26
Williams College, 172, 211
Williamson, John, 154, 155, 156,
  157, 159, 197, 209
Witt, Nathan, 235, 283
Wolfe, James H., 176
Workers School, 221
World War III, 53, 74, 263
Wu Ch'iang, 108

Yale University, 227, 231
Yalta, 60, 126, 280, 287
Yvon, M., 312

Zaslovsky, Z., 4
Zhdanov, A. A., 114
Zionism, 274